L6   s12.50

S0-AIX-371

POWER
ON
DISPLAY

LEONARD TENNENHOUSE

POWER ON DISPLAY

The politics of Shakespeare's genres

METHUEN NEW YORK & LONDON

First published in 1986 by
Methuen, Inc.
29 West 35th Street, New York
NY 10001

Published in Great Britain by
Methuen & Co. Ltd
11 New Fetter Lane
London EC4P 4EE

© 1986 Leonard Tennenhouse

Typeset in Monophoto Apollo by
Vision Typesetting, Manchester
Printed in Great Britain by
St Edmunsbury Press, Bury St Edmunds, Suffolk

All rights reserved. No part of this book may be
reprinted or reproduced or utilized in any form
or by any electronic, mechanical or other
means, now known or hereafter invented,
including photocopying and recording, or in any
information storage or retrieval system, without
permission in writing from the publishers.

Library of Congress Cataloging-in-Publication Data

Tennenhouse, Leonard, 1942–
Power on display.

Includes index.
1. Shakespeare, William, 1564–1616 – Political and social views.
2. Literary form. 3. Politics and literature – Great Britain.
4. Great Britain – History – Elizabeth, 1558–1603.
5. Great Britain – History – James I, 1603–1625.
I. Title.
PR3017.T46   1986   822.3′3   86–8670

ISBN 0-416-01271-X
ISBN 0-416-01281-7 (pbk.)

British Library Cataloguing in Publication Data

Tennenhouse, Leonard
Power on display: the politics of Shakespeare's genres.
1. Shakespeare, William – Criticism and interpretation
I. Title
822.3′3   PR2976

ISBN 0-416-01271-X
ISBN 0-416-01281-7

For Nancy Armstrong

CONTENTS

ACKNOWLEDGMENTS

I thank Stephen Orgel and Stephen J. Greenblatt for their sustaining encouragement. Each published essays of mine in which I began to think out the problems generating this book. Jonathan Goldberg was kind enough to read the completed manuscript.

With Leah Marcus and Peter Stallybrass I exchanged work in progress and carried on a dialogue that helped my work immeasurably. I also benefited from the intellectual generosity of A. R. Braunmuller, Jonathan Goldberg, Richard Helgerson, Ann R. Jones, Authur Marotti, Louis A. Montrose, Annabel Patterson, Maureen Quilligan, and Don E. Wayne. Alan Sinfield and Jonathan Dollimore published an earlier version of the chapter on the history plays. I thank them and Manchester University Press for permission to reprint sections of that essay; I also thank the editors of *Genre* for permission to reprint an earlier version of material that has gone into Chapter Four. Special gratitude goes to the Department of Literature at the University of California, San Diego, where I began assembling the final draft of this book. Finally, I want to thank Nancy Armstrong for questioning every literary assumption I ever took for granted.

A NOTE ON THE TEXT

Unless otherwise noted, I have used *The Riverside Shakespeare* edited by G. Blakemore Evans (Boston, Houghton Mifflin, 1972) throughout this book.

INTRODUCTION
Shakespeare and the scene of reading

There are several political Shakespeares, two of whom are certainly well-known to literary scholars. The most familiar of these is the canonized Shakespeare, a product of the tradition of reading, whose name is identified with culture itself but whose plays are often used to maintain a difference between literature and popular culture. The modern literary institution generally uses this Shakespeare to organize culture according to the thematics of a post-Enlightenment humanism which finds universal psychological truths in his characters and loves him best for writing poetry that transcends history. This ahistorical Shakespeare is, in other words, quite clearly a construct who speaks the politics of culture in the tradition of Arnold and Eliot. Another political Shakespeare familiar to the Anglo-American literary establishment is the Renaissance playwright. He is also a construct, albeit one who has been assembled to supplement and – on rare occasions – even to challenge the ahistorical Shakespeare. Where the literary figure is presumed to have written truths that obtain over time and across cultures, the man Shakespeare is situated in a Renaissance context. His writing is largely topical and allegorical as he comments on the figures and policies of his time in relation to which, then, one can fix his political identity. This historical personage is produced by scholars who set their work in opposition to the idealizing themes of literature. They use Shakespeare as the means of constructing culture-specific conditions for reading. In this other scene of reading, which grounds literature in history, Shakespeare becomes a means of turning the canonized Shakespeare into a window onto Renaissance social relations, a mirror of his times, a text that presupposes a context "outside" of itself. While opposed, these Shakespeares are in large part the product of the same modern literary institution and speak its politics. Indeed, one reason

Shakespeare remains so central to our work is because he had been used to constitute a field of argumentation which appears to be composed of contradictory and competing positions. By so doing, we have also performed an act of containment. Rarely do we feel compelled to entertain the possibility of any other Shakespeares, so intrinsically coherent is the logic of this outside/inside, popular/literary, historical/universal Shakespeare.

The tenacity of both ways of reading Shakespeare bears witness to the fact that the Shakespeare who is a man of his historical moment dwells quite comfortably with the imaginative genius who belongs to the ages. All the same, another political Shakespeare can be identified, one radically incompatible with the more familiar two, precisely because he reveals the political compatibility of the historical Shakespeare with his transcendent double. In pursuing the assumption that Shakespeare was constantly in tune with his time, one discovers an author who at all times seemed to know the rhetorical strategies for making sense, as well as what it was politic to say. We also find it necessary to imagine a situation where literature and political discourse had not yet been differentiated in the manner of a modern critical discourse. To the degree his work was in keeping with that of other writers in that same situation – authors of political prose as well as other successful playwrights – Shakespeare exists for us as several different rhetorical strategies. It is the purpose of this book to demonstrate how these constituted the Renaissance debates concerning the nature and origins of political power.

Shakespeare's chronicle history plays offer a particularly clear demonstration that such a political Shakespeare existed. For one thing, these plays were successful in entertaining an Elizabethan theater-going audience even though they were obviously political – the audience apparently saw no conflict in an aesthetic performance that was also a political one. In this respect, the tradition of reading Shakespeare provides us with inadequate options, inadequate precisely when it comes to understanding the politics of his use of chronicle history. For over fifty years these plays have generally been read in one of three ways: as overtly political texts which one can interpret by reference to the historical source material; as dramatic entertainments to be classed as an aesthetic genre comparable with comedy, tragedy or romance; or as part of a process of Shakespeare's personal development which accompanied his youthful comedies and preceded the grand metaphysical tragedies and the mature vision of his lyrical romances.[1] Each of these positions testifies to the distinction between literature and politics and so serves the interests of modern society by imposing this belief on the past. Yet none of these can begin to explain the peculiarities of *Henry VIII*. Shakespeare – whether alone or in collaboration – could not write a chronicle history play at the close of his career that meets the standard, according to readers, set by *Richard II, I Henry IV,* or *Henry V.* Some scholars have classified this later play with the romances, but their doing so is simply more testimony to suggest this play departs in some fundamental way from Shakespeare's other work in the genre. Rather than pursue the argument whether there is something wrong with *Henry VIII,* however, I want to consider if there is not something wrong with the categories we use to read the chronicle histories, since this designation of genre does not seem to come to terms with the way Shakespeare uses the materials of chronicle history when he sets them forth upon the stage. No amount of thematizing will make "chronicle history plays" a coherent category for describing dramatic art.

But chronicle history is not the only genre that reveals something amiss with conventional literary categories. We seldom read the romantic comedies as if they were political texts on the order of the histories. Yet after 1601/2 Shakespeare seems to have been unwilling or unable to write a romantic comedy. We classify the comedies he did write after *Twelfth Night* in a manner that suggests the inadequacy of the genre in another way. By designating a play such as *Measure for Measure* a "problem" comedy – a modern term to be sure – we may not agree on what problem the play poses, but we do agree that in some basic way the play problematizes an Elizabethan notion of comedy. Nor can *Measure for Measure* be called *sui generis* in this respect, for it bears striking resemblance to other absent monarch plays which came into vogue after 1603. It also bears certain affinities to the city comedies that became popular during the reign of James I. Shakespeare was not alone in abandoning romantic comedy after 1602, furthermore, for none of his fellow dramatists took up the form again either. The tradition of reading romantic comedy, like that of chronicle history, breaks along predictable lines. The overwhelmingly popular tradition of reading looks at comedy as an utterly apolitical form. Simply because it is about love and courtship, it cannot by definition be political, so the argument goes. Critical interest turns to these plays for evidence of the artist's growth and development or for signs of his preoccupation with specifically literary themes, Shakespeare's version of love in the western world, for example, or his celebration of art. A minority of Shakespeare scholars look for political import in the manner of his topical allusion and allegory. But seldom has criticism asked what political interests romantic comedy and chronicle history share that bound them together in a common fate.

Tragedy appears to be the one dramatic genre in which Shakespeare worked throughout his career. Yet here, too, history appears to have made its mark upon Shakespeare's genre. With the obvious exception of

Hamlet, tragedies written during the 1590s cannot be understood in the same terms as the grand metaphysical tragedies of the Jacobean Shakespeare. In that it concludes with the transfer of dynastic power from one family to another, furthermore, *Hamlet* bears strong resemblances to *Julius Caesar* and to *Titus Andronicus*, both of which disrupt genealogy and heap bodies upon the stage to display the destruction incurred when the state goes to war against itself. In open contrast with Elizabethan tragedy, such plays as *Antony and Cleopatra*, *Macbeth*, *King Lear*, and *Coriolanus* focus on the restoration and the consolidation of political power. These later tragedies display different political strategies, strategies – I will argue – explicitly aimed at revising those found in earlier dramatic genres, including even his own earlier tragedies. In their representation of the aristocratic community, in the prevalence of scenes of punishment, and in the radically altered powers attached to the female body, the later drama reshapes Shakespeare's dramatic materials to observe the same rules of production as Webster, Chapman, and Tourneur. To account for the rhetorical conflicts and discontinuities within the generic categories of modern criticism, then, it appears we would have to posit a Shakespeare changing, turning against himself, and declining. But such a logic intrinsic to his career will not explain why his contemporaries followed a similar pattern during the same historical period or why audience taste also changed over the course of Shakespeare's career. So long as discussion of the plays remains within the conventional literary genres, I am suggesting, the questions which motivate this book cannot find an answer. One cannot explain why certain forms were abandoned, why others were taken up, or why a genre might turn against itself and openly renounce a logic that was one and the same as its form during an earlier period of time. That is to say, traditional literary categories will not allow us to discuss the politics of Shakespeare's genres.

The problem of classifying Shakespeare's work according to dramatic genres is certainly not a modern one, but rather one which began with the earliest attempts to organize his plays. Indeed, the "Catalogue" printed in the First Folio divides plays into the comedies, histories, and tragedies. *Cymbeline* is listed as a tragedy, *The Tempest* and *The Winter's Tale* are placed under the comedies, and missing altogether from the "Catalogue" is *Troilus and Cressida* which does in fact appear sandwiched between the histories and the tragedies. That such obvious conflict within and among genres should arise in 1623 bodes further confusion for subsequent attempts at internal organization of the canon. It is as if once these plays are collected and put into print, they necessarily become texts of a different order than the dramatic performances they both replicate and displace. We might say they take on a life independent of their origins in the theater as they are made into an internally coherent relational text. At this point, the process of dehistoricizing the texts has clearly begun. The arrangement of plays according to generic categories automatically detaches the work from history and presumes the internal organization of its meaning. To understand the process by which Shakespeare's plays are so organized according to generic categories, we would have to trace a course of some three hundred years from the First Folio to the appearance of Northrop Frye's *Anatomy of Criticism*. The history of this great game of suppressing the political operations of writing – an act Frye is keenly aware he is performing – would require a wholly different study from the one I have undertaken in this book. I can imagine such another project where each attempt to fix the generic identity of Shakespeare's texts would be understood as a stage in a complex political process. It would be necessary, among other things, to understand the important movement to include Shakespeare within an educational curriculum for women at the end of the eighteenth and the beginning of the nineteenth century. This movement culminated with Joanna Baillie's theory of dramatic genres in which each genre was informed by one of the passions, a notion that Hazlitt, among others, excoriated in an effort to save Shakespeare from middle-class sentimentality.[2]

My own study began with a set of questions quite different from those governing most generic criticism. These aim at discovering the historical principle which divides literary genres internally or makes them overlap in certain respects, not at developing criteria which bind them together. I have asked myself, for instance, what if it could be shown that a play such as *Henry VIII* represents power in much the same way as in dramatic romance and tragicomedy? And what if *Henry V* understood political conflict in terms resembling those of romantic comedy as well as contemporary political debate? Suppose one could show that *Hamlet* shares certain rhetorical strategies with the chronicle histories and that these oppose the strategies governing *King Lear* or *Macbeth*. Under such circumstances, would we not have to rethink the whole notion of artistic genres – what constitutes a history play as opposed to a tragedy, or a romantic comedy or a dramatic romance if these dramatic forms had more to do with the vicissitudes of political conflict than with any cultural logic intrinsic to a particular dramatic form? And this, even though the texts in question were written by the same author over the length of his career? Were such a relationship among various forms of Renaissance writing to be demonstrated, it would suggest, among other things, that the opposition between a literary use and a political use of similar cultural materials is largely an invention of the critical process. We might have to conclude that Renaissance drama displayed its politics in its manner of idealizing or demystifying specific forms of power. It is my contention that such display and not a work's transcendence or referentiality made it aesthetically successful.

My goal, then, is to argue for a Shakespeare whose dramatic forms participated in the political life of Renaissance England. This is not to say, I must insist, that his drama held up a constant mirror to political events as if it stood somewhere outside of the field of activity, any more than to say the theater could adhere to a literary logic or take its shape from the development of an author's personality. I argue this in the face of a critical tradition which has insisted art and politics are essentially opposed in their strategies and objectives. Because my effort is directed at showing the basic political aims of Shakespeare's plays, I focus on those strategies I imagine his audience understood almost as we know common sense itself. Indeed, I have not even attempted to show — as well one might in describing the political Shakespeare — how the writer immersed in this milieu sought to question political authority. By examining how he includes recalcitrant cultural materials and dramatizes their suppression under the pressure of official strategies of idealization, some scholars have begun to identify such a subversive Shakespeare.[3] My point is more simple than that: to show that, during the Renaissance, political imperatives were also aesthetic imperatives.

It is one thing to call for such a study that avoids the pitfalls of the literary institution; it is another to adhere to the general criteria for the political Shakespeare that my questions invoke. With an explanation of this difficulty is perhaps the best place to begin my effort. Whenever I teach Shakespeare, I become acutely aware of the place he occupies in modern culture, just as writing about his plays and poetry has sensitized me to the importance of his role in modern literary criticism. Most of all, I am impressed by the difficulty one has in describing a political Shakespeare, a difficulty — or prohibition, rather — which I can only attribute to my academic role and to literary criticism. Indeed, our most characteristic procedures for reading appear capable of converting almost any historical text into an object of modern culture. When I claim to describe a Shakespeare who is neither the aestheticized nor the historicized figure of traditional criticism, then, it is only my way of arguing against certain colonizing strategies of that criticism even as I participate in it. This is certainly not to claim I am in touch with the ''real'' Shakespeare. It is rather to use the body of writing we call Shakespeare as a means of unthinking some of the strategies of appropriation that may be common critical practice for someone in my position as an academic critic and literary scholar at this historical moment. Most of my procedures are in this sense antiprocedural. I have developed them over the past four or five years as I found it necessary not to do to Shakespeare what my education – from the earliest years on – has virtually compelled me to do. With the purpose in mind of making this approach less strange by explaining the antiprocedures I have developed, let me now provide a sense of the genesis of this project.

For a number of years I have worked collaboratively with someone who writes on nineteenth-century British literature and history. In discussions of our respective domains of literary history, I have had frequent occasion to draw examples from Shakespeare. With remarkable frequency, the plot I summarized, the character I described, or the reading I offered struck my colleague as something that could have been written in post-Enlightenment England. If I argued for the historical specificity of some feature of Shakespearean drama, my collaborator could often procduce counterexamples to demonstrate that almost anything I inferred from a Shakespearean drama about Renaissance culture could also – and more appropriately – be said of a novel.

In the name of historical criticism, I had to conclude, I had been performing an anthropological gesture which translates any and all cultures into the categories of modern culture. I had done this to mark a distinction between "us" and "them" – in this case between the modern and Renaissance milieux for writing and producing drama – in order to create historical difference. In reflecting upon this behavior, however, it seemed rather obvious how it served quite another objective. My reading of Shakespeare tried to distinguish my writing from the products of an earlier epoch, all the while transforming Shakespeare into the product of my own culture, namely, literary criticism. This is to say, by making Shakespeare other than myself in terms of his "context," in effect I authorized the production of criticism. To constitute Shakespeare elsewhere in time was to create a reference outside of writing to which my critical strategies provided special access. In a word, contextualizing Shakespeare gave me a certain kind of power – resembling the Olympian perspective of most anthropology – over Renaissance culture. At the same time – and this is the extraordinary thing, the real legerdemain – even while I situated him in another "context," I could make Shakespeare testify to the timelessness of the modern individual, my own ambitions, fears and desires. In one crucial respect, however, I always stopped short of carrying out the sort of work nineteenth-century novelists typically performed on Shakespeare.

For them, this critical move was admittedly political. By way of demonstration, I borrow a passage from an author whom literary criticism has succeeded in depoliticizing more than most. In *Shirley*, her most openly political novel, Charlotte Brontë includes a scene of reading near the beginning of a narrative set at the time of the Luddite rebellions. In this scene *Coriolanus* is read aloud and commented upon, as if to instruct the reader in the procedures for reading not only such an openly political text as Shakespeare's but the narrative to follow as well. It demonstrates both what procedures should be used to appropriate Shakespeare for middle-class culture and the very real political interests the reading of literature served. My own point in using this example from a novel is to show the novelist was utterly conscious of depoliticizing Shakespeare. That she understood the political functions of reading Shakespeare as a work of literature is apparent in this breakdown of the scene in question:

Mediating.   Brontë represents the reading of a Shakespeare play as a way of regulating relationships between individuals. Caroline Helstone, Robert Moore, and his sister Hortense debate how they shall spend their evening. When they reject such activities as chess, draughts, backgammon, and even gossip as frivolous or boring, Caroline proposes that Robert read Shakespeare aloud to the women. In contrast with other forms of play, the reading of Shakespeare provides a beneficial way of occupying leisure time, or as Caroline says, ". . . it would be pleasant to go back to the past; to hear people ... speak to us and tell us their thought, and impart their ideas."[4] Shakespeare thus displaces other symbolic practices onto words and, further, allows writing to mediate all human relationships.

Socializing.   Robert Moore is half Belgian, half English. Caroline tells him that by reading, "Tonight you shall be entirely English" (p. 114). It is by acquiring the language of Shakespeare, then, that one benefits from the work of literature; it socializes the individual. As Caroline explains, "Your French forefathers don't speak so sweetly, nor so solemnly, nor so impressively as your English ancestors, Robert" (p. 114). Even as it constitutes Shakespearean drama as written text, then, this scene of reading turns writing into the record of and basis for speech. More than that, speech is made the direct expression of emotion which exists prior to the speech act and arises, then, from within the individual. Thus Shakespeare's mediation brings one individual in direct contact with the other. As Caroline explains, she has tried to select a passage for Robert to read aloud which "is toned with something in you. It shall waken your nature, fill your mind with music, it shall pass like a skillful hand over your heart. . . . Let glorious William come near and touch it; you will see how he will draw the English power and melody out of its chords" (p. 114).

Psychologizing.   At the same time, one can see what happens to history. Rather than estranged and culturally other, Renaissance man becomes the voice of Robert's ancestor (even though Robert was born and reared in Belgium!) who speaks to him across time and cultural boundaries. Brought to life as it is read aloud in this setting, the written Shakespeare encloses the poles of human experience within the subjectivity of the reader: "It is to stir you," Caroline explains, "to give you new sensations. It is to make you feel your life strongly, not only your virtues, but your vicious ... perverse points . . . discover by the feelings the reading will give you at once how low and high you are" (p. 115). Robert's extremely controversial political position as a factory owner intent on mechanization has in a stroke been translated into psychological terms which locate one within a hierarchy of emotion that all men presumably are capable of feeling. And "the English power" which Shakespeare brings to the fore in the individual is simply the power of knowing human nature in this way. This is how Brontë describes the transformation Robert experiences as he reads Shakespeare under the loving tutelage of Caroline Helstone: " . . . stepping out of the narrow line of private prejudices, [he] began to revel in the large picture of human nature, to feel the reality stamped upon the characters who were speaking from that page before him" (p. 116).

Moralizing the text.   In saying this, she is asking Robert to renounce one mode of power — that which she associates with the imperiously patriarchal nature of Coriolanus — and adopt another one — that which she identifies as a benevolent form of paternalism. She is, in other words, depoliticizing Shakespeare in order to make him represent a new kind of political authority, if only by virtue of negation. This is a form of political authority that appears *not* to be a form of authority as such, because it models itself upon family relationships and operates in and through subjectivity. As it is taken up by modern culture, then, Shakespeare finally becomes the means by which this historical change is brought about, the means, that is, by which authority is internalized and subjectivity becomes a self-regulating mechanism. Caroline explains the moral Robert should "tack to the play" of *Coriolanus*: "you must not be proud to your workpeople; you must not neglect chances of soothing them, and you must not be of an inflexible nature, uttering a request as austerely as if it were a command" (p. 114).

Brontë was not being the least bit ironic here in saying this. She understood better than we do the power of reading. Indeed the point of this entire episode is to show that Caroline is well trained as a reader and will therefore make Robert a wonderful wife, in which capacity she will carry on the primary work of acculturation. Nor was Brontë alone in understanding Shakespeare as such an instrument of social control. Her epoch saw him introduced into the standard curriculum with the formation of a national system of education. Shakespeare became part of a reading program designed to produce individuals that would inhabit and perpetuate a modern institutional culture, as opposed to the classical education that had once initiated gentlemen into the language of power. Robert Moore is a factory owner badly in need of such domestication to prepare him for managing the mechanized workplace. This is the same kind of education he needs to make him a good husband and father. If nothing else, it should be clear from this example how reading Shakespeare translates a language at once political and historical into one that appears to be neither because it is pure ideology – or, more accurately, because it is so like our own ideology.

To tell the truth, my own experience with Shakespeare has not been all that different from Robert Moore's, although I hope I have proved to be a more recalcitrant subject than he. Along with the work of acculturating individuals, the scene of reading in which one encounters Shakespeare may have shifted from the parlor to secondary schools and universities, but the strategies of reading do not differ substantially from those Brontë dramatizes in *Shirley*. We still enclose Renaissance culture within our own discourse and thus make it speak our notion of sexuality, the family, and the individual. And acquiring such literary competence still performs the work of socialization. Not only does it teach us how to moralize symbolic practices other than written literature, it also compels us to understand those practices as expressions of a truth that exists to them – within individuals. In this sense, it is perhaps more accurate to say that Shakespeare has written us than for us to say that, as literary critics and scholars, we have done so to him, for we do not acknowledge the political objectives working themselves out through the procedures I have described above. A novel such as *Shirley* openly acknowledges what it is doing to Shakespeare and why. We, more thoroughly than Brontë no doubt, are products of the hegemony we perpetuate, of the forgetting which occurs when literary criticism sophisticates the reading procedures once used chiefly to educate women in the home. I catch embarrassing glimpses of my own complicity in this ongoing project of modern educational institutions. As literary criticism makes Shakespeare's texts speak a sophisticated psychological theory or articulate ever more carefully researched political conflicts, one tends to forget that Renaissance drama is nevertheless caught up and contained in our writing. Writing that induces such forgetting cannot help but use Shakespeare to produce a political unconscious even as we are discussing the politics of

Renaissance drama.[5] It is in this respect that Shakespeare criticism resembles a novel.

This encounter with *Shirley* represents a moment in my ongoing relationship with Shakespeare, the moment of self-questioning which hatched this project. But let me hasten to add that it was not with the least bit of dejection I experienced such alienation from my education and work then in progress, even though, because of it, I gave up all possibility of being the one to corner "truth." The Shakespeare toward which criticism ordinarily aspires would obviously have to be a pristine figure, Shakespeare as he might have existed before he was written by the last three hundred years of criticism, and I am not after that Shakespeare. I never was. Just as I have been acculturated by the Shakespeare of the literary institution, I have also been well-trained to develop ever more sophisticated techniques for acculturating him. I understand my scholarly and critical task in this book, then, as something akin to wriggling out of my cultural skin, much as someone might wriggle out of a particularly close-fitting turtleneck shirt.

Behind this seemingly frivolous comparison lies a theory that hangs on from a period when I was intensely interested in psychoanalytic criticism. In his notion of cultural countertransference, the anthropologist George Devereux notes how often the procedures which social science has devised to protect against the contamination of data actually operate as elaborate defenses for just this – the appropriation of data by the observer's culture.[6] Devereux is certainly not the only one to claim that under the illusion one has screened out any such bias, the social scientist invariably reclassifies cultural material, selects his data, and interprets symbolic behavior accordingly. Such distortion certainly occurs when areas of culture are turned into noise or primitivized, on the one hand, or when, on the other, another culture appears to offer no resistance to the observer's characteristic strategies for encountering reality. Devereux draws on Freud's notion of countertransference not to protect against such distortions so much as to use them to his own advantage. Using his countertransference, the analyst is supposed to turn himself into an object of knowledge, according to this later development in Freud's theory, so that he may enter into the communication situation fully capable of recognizing the difference between self and other.[7] As Devereux notes, among even those psychoanalysts who write of this phenomenon, this tends to be an ideal rather than a real possibility to be achieved. In extrapolating this concept for anthropology, Devereux contends there can be no analysis of another culture that does not at some point include or – better – presuppose an analysis of our own. I would add but one qualification to his contention: that it is not so necessary to analyze one's personal feelings of the primitive desires in which such feelings are supposed to be rooted. What strikes me as far more important to factor into any reading of Shakespeare is the reclassifying activity, the procedures for selecting and suppressing certain kinds of data, and the interpretive behavior that comes with occupying an academic position within the humanities.

Where a critical strategy something like countertransference necessarily figures into the comparison between my work and a tight shirt will soon become clear if we recall the scene of reading offered by Charlotte Brontë. If there is any truth to my contention that this scene reveals how Shakespeare is appropriated by and used to perpetuate a modern humanist discourse, then certain implications for a historical reading of Shakespeare can be derived from this scene in terms of cultural countertransference. The student/reader in this configuration, namely Robert, is asked to offer up his reading of Shakespeare as a kind of transference where, in his identification with the "haughty" Coriolanus, he exposes everything that is Belgian rather than English in a light which subjects it to remediation and Robert himself to assimilation. Brontë is less than subtle in dramatizing this process; she knows exactly what kind of political objective reading Shakespeare accomplishes as it inscribes Robert's desire within the ethos of the new middle classes. But the teacher's investment in this relationship is never interrogated. Retiring, feminine, and thoroughly benevolent, Caroline's power is never even acknowledged. Yet it is she who declares that reading "is to stir you; to give you new sensations. It is to make you feel your life strongly, not only your virtues, but your vicious, perverse points" (p. 115). And when Robert finishes, she is the one to catechize him, "Now, have you felt Shakespeare?" (p. 117) She deliberately suppresses all that is political in *Coriolanus* as so much noise in her effort to foreground the grand human emotions. She also establishes the framework for reading the text in oppositional terms, as the difference between French and English. This framework turns everything "French" into a lack, a lack of the English language which is also a lack of humane emotions. In considering how little the procedures for reading change when that scene is translated into an academic setting, one is obliged to examine the countertransference which comes along with the teacher/critic's role in an academic position. In that position, one is never obliged to acknowledge the political power he or she exercises, much less to validate the students' resistance to the traditional procedures for reading. That would be quite as absurd as requiring Caroline to consider French as if it were complex and different rather than the absence of English. I draw on Brontë's association of "glorious William" with everything English in comparing her scene of reading to my own because it strikes me as one that has not passed into obsolescence. Teaching Shakespeare remains a means of disseminating a specialized language, a set of psychologizing procedures for turning all manner of cultural materials into works of high culture, and a testament, therefore, to the universality of the modern self.

By examining those strategies which have suppressed political literacy, I had hopes of encountering a Shakespeare who is in certain respects culturally "other." Specifically, I have tried to picture his drama as an instrument of political literacy that openly acknowledged its relationship to the power of the state. This is to say my reading of Shakespeare will be an oppositional one; rather than opposing the political element in Shakespeare by strategies for producing high culture, I read him against that tradition of reading. I regard the plays as a series of semiotic events, the staging of cultural materials, the mobilization of political representations. My goal is to represent such events as part of the political thinking of the culture. To this end, I have borrowed a strategy from Foucault. His historical work does not, I think, lend itself to illuminating Renaissance practices nearly so well as it does to understanding the symbolic behavior of Enlightenment and post-Enlightenment culture. Nevertheless I have borrowed heavily from the beginning of *Discipline and Punish* where Foucault imagines a time before writing was the primary means of social control. He uses a figure – the scene on the scaffold – to represent a culture where power worked more effectively through theatrical display than through writing. In such a culture, with neither police force nor standing army to enforce the law, the representation of punishment was itself an important form of power. Performed in public places, often on raised platforms for all to see, the criminal's torture was carefully designed to be spectacularly horrible, out of all proportion to the crime. Such a scene was supposed to create a visible emblem of the king's absolute authority over the body of the condemned. The individual criminal hardly mattered at all. To stress this point, Foucault includes Bruneau's account of an execution where the criminal died before most of the elaborate procedures of dismemberment had been completed:

The condemned man was blindfolded and tied to a stake; all around, on the scaffold, were stakes with iron hooks. 'The confessor whispered in the patient's ear and, after he had given him the blessing, the executioner, who had an iron bludgeon of the kind used in slaughter houses, delivered a blow with all his might on the temple of the wretch, who fell dead: the *mortis exactor*, who had a large knife, then cut his throat, which spattered him with blood; it was a horrible sight to see; he severed the sinews near the two heels, and then opened up the belly from which he drew the heart, liver, spleen and lungs, which he stuck on an iron hook, and cut and dissected into pieces, which he then stuck on the other hooks as he cut them, as one does with an animal. Look who can at such a sight.'[8]

Foucault notes that the "infinitesimal destruction of the body is linked here with spectacle" to show the crowds who gathered for such occasions the radical dissymmetry of power relations. It was not the punishment so much as the *spectacle* of punishment that enforced the power of the state.

For Foucault, then, the scene on the scaffold provides an historically different way of thinking power. The scene has been constructed in opposition to modern thinking where punishment does not sweep down arbitrarily upon the body of the criminal in a demonstration of its absolute political power over that body, but rather works invisibly through disciplinary strategies which constitute subjectivity. Early modern culture could not have been constructed in this oppositional fashion — backwards — as a way of unthinking the power characterizing our age; to figure it out in these terms is just that — to figure it out. My own way of proceeding departs from Foucault's in that he uses the scaffold as a platform from which to launch an account of the development of modern institutions, from which to write in his words, "the history of the present." My effort shares his desire to avoid discovering the past as the present, but I am interested in figuring out further the operations of a form of political authority that was other than our own. Of necessity my account of Renaissance drama as a way of thinking power also operates backwards, historically speaking, to construct this authority in opposition to that maintaining modern institutional culture. My project also draws upon Foucault's scene on the scaffold for the whole notion that display is a form of power.[9] I simply insist that such displays were not already produced to the degree Foucault suggests. I see them as providing a site where the iconography of state power was formulated in tension with various forms of representation that contested the ideology of the Renaissance court. The stage was in this sense a place where political events occurred and where history was being produced.

In thus representing an earlier moment in cultural history, I have settled upon no single kind of text to offer as a context or grounding for historical truth. At least I have tried not to hierarchize symbolic practices in this way. I have resorted to other kinds of writing mainly to prevent my reading Shakespeare as a novel. Whenever I felt myself caught within a developmental narrative from which a lesson might be extracted, when, further, that narrative seemed to take on the logic of personal motivation, I have interrupted my reading and sought reference to another kind of Renaissance text. Amidst the roughly historical arrangement of plays I have selected from the canon for reading, on these occasions I have interposed a royal speech or a proclamation, information concerning a ledger report or parliamentary debate, as well as descriptions of plays or poems by Renaissance authors other than Shakespeare. Thus the reader will encounter a sequence of modules, designed to disrupt our conventional logic of explanation and to identify some important differences between it and the cultural logic which organized Shakespeare's plays. Such paradigmatic procedures as I am proposing have their own limitations, however. It is my hope that these strategies of defamiliarization will provide some sense of the larger debate which rippled across the entire field we call Renaissance culture to produce certain changes within it. To avoid the hypostatic tendencies of paradigmatic thinking, I have also cast the sections of this book into narratives representing some of the conflicts and oppositions that enabled changes to occur.

In conclusion, let me briefly describe the kind of narrative I have produced in my attempt to overturn some of the depoliticizing tendencies of my discipline. In refusing to discriminate between literary and non-literary practices, this narrative regards all the texts under examination both as agents and as documents of history. In such a narrative, political conflict does not exist somewhere outside of these texts, for it concerns itself with the struggle among competing ways of representing power. Mine is, in other words, an account of a hegemonic process which differs in certain crucial respects from the one in which the modern Shakespeare is implicated. To the degree that the Renaissance theater performed a political function utterly different from the scene of reading, we may assume Shakespeare's plays, unlike the written Shakespeare, were not enclosed within an aesthetic framework. They opened onto a larger arena of events and observed a transgeneric logic. In my account of Shakespeare's drama, then, stagecraft collaborates with statecraft in producing spectacles of power. The strategies of theater resembled those of the scaffold, as well as court performance, I am suggesting, in observing a common logic of figuration that both sustained and testified to the monarch's power, a logic which by definition contradicts that inhering in a generic study such as Frye's.

Rather than any traditional notion of literary genre, then, I fixed upon certain figures of power as my own strategy for describing the politics of Shakespeare's genre, and the narrative organizing my study is the history of their political formation and behavior upon the stage. Some of these I have borrowed, most notably the figure of the grotesque body from Bakhtin, and both the "theater of punishment" and the "city under plague" from Foucault. Others are attempts of my own devising to represent the logic of theatrical representation in terms at once aesthetic and political, always with the object in mind of isolating a semiotic event which occurs outside as well as inside the theater, always, too, with the aim of situating that event within a larger political struggle.

Although I discuss a number of these "figures" as instances of such a political narrative, I must confess – finally – there is only one. I have in this sense created an opposition that organizes my observations of Renaissance culture. All the figures of the theater I describe are either versions of the one I call the aristocratic body, or else – like the grotesque body – they acquire meaning by virtue of the relation of the "other" to it. The logic inhering in this figure works in a number of ways depending upon which features of the aristocratic body dominate. It is my argument that these variations in the behavior of power – whether the inclusive and generous nature of the aristocratic body is stressed as it is in feast and comedic weddings, or whether it is divided against itself, or appears harshly punitive as in rituals of punishment – determine the differences by which we distinguish literary genres. I argue further that the possibilities for representing the aristocratic body changed along with the emergence of new discursive strategies to oppose it, as well as with the vicissitudes of the monarch's body itself. In a very real way, I believe, this body authorized other symbolic forms of power, so that they in turn might authorize that body.

1
STAGING CARNIVAL
Comedy and the politics of the aristocratic body

Beginning in the 1570s and continuing for almost thirty years, the literate classes in England developed what seems to have been an insatiable appetite for writing concerned with the vicissitudes of erotic desire. There was the Petrarchan poetry for which the epoch is known. Collections of love poems, as well as the sonnet sequences, circulated in manuscript and at times even found their way into print. There were also poetic games played out through conceits of love, answer poems, courtier disquisitions on love, and a wide variety of love poetry and prose translated from classical and continental sources. Narratives of tragic desire appeared in print, as did Ovidian elegies, anacreontics, epyllia, along with the many pastorals devoted to the trials of courtship.[1] The drama, too, made love its obsessive concern. Court entertainments – masques and plays – along with comedies and tragedies, staged at the Inns of Court or in the great halls of prominent Elizabethans, seemed bent on figuring out the permissible and forbidden forms of sexual relations. But from a literary historical viewpoint, perhaps the most important manifestation of the new *ars erotica*, was the rise of a public theater which worked variations within the same problematic of desire. This is all to suggest that England had never before experienced such intense interest in the permutations of love and the pursuit of desire. Although this chapter will attend primarily to Shakespeare's romantic comedies, it is important to remind ourselves at the outset that his comedies appeared in the wake of nearly twenty years of intense literary activity of this kind, much of it produced and consumed by members of the same audience who attended his plays. Available to him was an elaborate language of desire out of which sophisticated comedies could be made and presented to an audience already familiar with these materials.

While Shakespeare was clearly the master at realizing these tropes in dramatic form, it was to Sir Philip Sidney's writing Shakespeare and his contemporaries regularly turned for their model and inspiration. Although not the first work of its kind in England, the *Arcadia* was one of the most influential, and its appearance in print in the 1590s coincided with the vogue for romantic comedies such as Shakespeare's.[2] No single writer was as fully conversant with this language of desire as Sidney, and no writer produced more important literary texts for his generation than Sidney. After his death in 1586, manuscript circulation of his work apparently intensified. Celebrated in handbooks by Fraunce and Puttenham before it appeared in print, his romance was quickly received as exemplary. Obviously, popular interest in his work was due in part to his claims to high rank and associations with the court. But such fame alone can not explain why Sidney's writing was so closely followed, his figures so widely imitated, his plots so regularly repeated, or his language quoted so frequently. We have to assume the amorous adventures comprising the Arcadian text must have represented sexual relations in a way that was particularly meaningful to Shakespeare's audiences, just as they were particularly useful to young men like Sidney at Elizabeth's court. In this respect, Sidney's *Arcadia* makes a particularly appropriate background against which to read Shakespeare's romantic comedies.

In his first version of the *Arcadia*, as in his later obsessive rewriting of that work during the 1580s, Sidney gathered together the elements of earlier romance plots, reordered them, and made them available in such a way that his work anticipated most of the plots that would comprise Elizabethan drama. Sidney's great accomplishment consisted of dismantling plots from Montmeyer, from the *Amadis de Gaulle*, from the *Aethiopian History*, from *The Morte D'Arthur* and various other medieval and classical sources and then reassembling these materials into countless permutations which introduce the language of desire into English romance.[3] By so doing, he not only eroticized the form of romance itself but also domesticated it. For the first time in literary history, erotic desire provided the agency of the romance plot. No one before him – neither Sannazaro, nor Boiardo, nor Malory, nor Ariosto – had seen fit to use this language so single-mindedly to produce a series of plots all generated by erotic desire. In this sense, Sidney's romance remains something of a watershed in literary history. I want to stress, however, that the initial writing and the extensive rewriting of the *Arcadia* was itself more than a matter of producing a collection of tale types or an encyclopedia of narratives on the order of *The Arabian Nights*, *The Decameron*, or in Sidney's own day, Painter's *Palace of Pleasure* or Pettie's *Petite Palace of Pettie his Pleasures*. Rather I will argue that to write about erotic desire or courtship and marriage in Elizabethan England was to take up a political argument.

Position, place, and power were almost exclusively a matter of kinship and courtship. This fact of Elizabethan culture governs the design of the *Arcadia* and every narrative of its author's life. To illustrate this point we need only consider the plot which Sidney carries over from the first *Arcadia* to the later *New Arcadia*. In both versions the king takes measures to avoid the fate foretold by an oracle:

> Thy elder care shall from thy careful face
>> By princely mean be stolen, and yet not lost.
> Thy younger shall with Nature's bliss embrace
>> An uncouth love, which Nature hateth most.
> Both they themselves unto such two shall wed,
>> Who at thy bier, as at a bar, shall plead
>> Why thee (a living man) they had made dead.
> In thine own seat a foreign state shall sit.
> And ere that all these blows thy head do hit,
> Thou, with thy wife adultery shall commit.[4]

By so describing the situation which will generate the narrative of his romance, Sidney has presented us with a political crisis that must be understood and resolved in sexual terms. Faced with the possibility of marriages below rank and the possibility of adultery within the royal household, Basilius abandons the court and renounces the political responsibilities of a monarch. In withdrawing the royal family from the political world, he seeks a resolution to the problem posed by the oracle. Sidney explains Basilius's solution in this way, "The point of his daughter's marriage, because it threatened his death withal, he determined to prevent with keeping them, while he lived, unmarried" (p. 396). He withdraws from the political world in order to withhold his daughters from the rituals of sexual exchange. But if allowing his daughters to marry will lead to regicide, then it is also true that not allowing his daughters to marry will eventually produce a political crisis of similar proportions. In one way or another, the kingdom will find itself without a monarch.

This problem is a peculiarly English dilemma. That is to say, the fact of the king's having only daughters for heirs represents a clear threat to the continuity of power: the oracle hints at the possibility that one daughter will be stolen and the other will make an unsuitable match. Both these possibilities call the patrilineal distribution of power into question. This suggests that once embodied in the female, power can be transferred to an outsider, a foreign line perhaps, or a family not of aristocratic lineage at all. In a strictly patrilineal system, the marriage of a daughter automatically removes her from the father's family. Should she be the sole heir of her father when she goes to a rival family through marriage, there is the danger that she might take her father's property with her or, barring this, that his property will descend to the next male kin, namely a brother's family or a nephew's. In both cases the father's power passes out of his family. In a purely patrilineal system of inheritance, then, daughters are not allowed to inherit. The English system modified strict patrilineage. Aside from the obvious cases of Mary and Elizabeth, we know of other instances of female inheritance.[5] Sir Thomas Smith's remarks about English rules of inheritance allow for this variation on patrilineage: women are not permitted to

> medle with matters abroad, nor to beare office in a citie or common wealth ... *except it be in such cases as the authoritie is annexed to the bloud and progenie*, as the crowne, a dutchie, or an erledom for there the bloud is respected, not the age nor the sexe.[6] (italics mine)

Any woman who acquired the economic and political prerogatives of a man was overturning the social order of things, according to Smith. But, as Smith makes quite clear, aristocratic blood always authorized the exercise of these powers no matter the sex in which blood might be embodied. We might say, then, that when Sidney opened the possibility of having the power of blood descend through the female, he worked a distinctly English variation on his sources almost all of which prohibit female inheritance. Thus I would like to consider why Sidney should construct a whole narrative problematic around the question of female inheritance and, further, why his work should have been so closely followed for doing so.

II

Late in 1578, Queen Elizabeth opened discussions of a possible match with the Duke of Anjou. Unlike earlier marriage negotiations, this one was initiated by the queen herself. Through marriage she hoped to create a more secure alliance with France. The exchange, Wallace T. MacCaffrey suggests, was to protect French Protestants while guaranteeing their loyalty to Henri III, as well as to end French Catholic interference in England and Scotland.[7] In addition, such an alliance between England and France would force Philip of Spain to moderate his harsh treatment of the Dutch. For my purposes, however, it is important to note the argument voiced by those of Elizabeth's subjects who were opposed to her proposed match. It was assumed by many including the queen herself, that the popular opposition to her plans for marriage to the Catholic Anjou was based on religious grounds. To quell this opposition, Elizabeth stepped up the persecution of Catholic dissidents at home. Camden, for instance, tells us that when the Duke of Anjou came to England, Elizabeth "permitted Edmund Campian . . . Ralph Sherwin, Luke Kirby and Alexander Briant, Priests, shoud be arraigned" indicted, condemned to die and executed. She did this, in Camden's account, because it would "take away the Fear which had possessed many mens minds, that Religion would be altered, and Popery tolerated. . . ."[8] But the voices rising in opposition to her marriage seem to have objected to the duke on other than simply religious grounds. A greater fear had to do with the integrity of the English nation, as if the very concept of nationality were jeopardized by the marriage of an English queen to a member of the French royal family.

Of those who opposed her policy, one of the most famous was John Stubbs. Although Camden and subsequent historians treat his as the argument of a Puritan zealot, Stubbs's is a closely reasoned case against the marriage from the position of a nationalist for whom England and its Reformation were inextricably bound. The title of his pamphlet – *The discovery of a gaping Gulf wherein England is to be swallowed by another french marriage . . .* – announces this nationalist theme. The great danger, he says, is that having rescued England from the threat of a Spanish ruler, Elizabeth will now subject her people to another foreign ruler: "It is natural to all men to abhor foreign rule as a burden of Egypt."[9] Elizabeth punished Stubbs for this political pamphlet by having his right hand cut off. On the scaffold he is reported to have received his punishment with a patriotic testimony that his fate would not undermine his loyalty to the queen:

> I praie you all to praie with me, that God will strengthen me to endure and abide the paine that I ame to suffre, and graunt me this grace, that the losse of my haunde do not withdrawe any part of my dewtie and affection toward her Maiestie. . . . Praye for me, nowe my calamity is at hande.[10]

To question the queen on the matter of her marriage was obviously regarded as a challenge to her authority. We may believe that Stubbs's patriotism made it perfectly consistent for him to oppose Elizabeth's marriage and to accept the punishment which was his due for challenging the policy of an English monarch. Stubbs was not alone in acting as if the definition of English nationalism was at stake in the enactment of such a policy which questioned the symbolic bond between the land and the blood.

Another famous statement opposing the marriage was Sidney's letter detailing objections to the Anjou match. Possibly put up to this by his uncle the Earl of Leicester, if not simply acting out of the presumption for which he was notorious, Sidney was quite aware of what had happened to Stubbs. Unlike Stubbs's pamphlet, Sidney's letter was intended to be received as a private correspondence. But Sidney was not an advisor to the queen, nor had she asked his opinion. As a result, or so the story goes, Elizabeth so strongly resented Sidney's letter that he was forced to absent himself from court and retire to his sister's estate where he drafted the first version of the *Arcadia*.[11] We should note how closely Sidney's letter follows the argument of Stubbs's pamphlet. He, too, advises against the match for fear it will allow England to be ruled by this foreigner. Echoing Stubbs, Sidney warns Elizabeth that these consequences will follow from her marriage to Anjou:

> . . . if he come hither, he must live here in far meaner reputation than his will well brook, having no other royalty to countenance himself with; or else you must deliver him the keys of your kingdom and live at his discretion. . . .[12]

He predicts that, like her sister, Elizabeth will find it necessary to turn over "the keys of your kingdom" to the foreign prince. He assumes, in other words, that the patriarchal principle will subordinate England's power embodied in a female to the male heir of the French line should they marry, and English power thus would lose its sovereignty as such.

Sidney and Stubbs were not the only two to express anxiety lest marriage would obscure the line between English power and that of another kingdom. Camden summarizes the dilemma about the queen's deliberations concerning her prospective marriage. "Some were of the opinion," he says,

> that she was fully resolved in her Mind, that she might better provide both for the Commonwealth and her own Glory by an Unmarried life than by Marriage; as foreseeing that if she married a Subject, she should disparage herself by the Inequality of the Match, and give occasion to domestical Heart-burnings, private Grudges and Commotions; if a Stranger, she then should subject both herself and her People to a foreign Yoke, and endanger Religion: Having not forgotten how unhappy the Marriage of her Sister Queen Mary with King Philip a Foreigner had been. . . . Her Glory also, which whilst she continued unmarried she retained intire to herself and uneclipsed, she feared would by Marriage be transferred to her Husband.[13]

The same fear that marriage to a female monarch would provide access to the power inhering in the Tudor blood prompted others during Mary's reign to join in the Wyatt rebellion upon the announcement she intended to marry Philip of Spain. But since the rule of England did not in fact pass into foreign hands with Mary's marriage to Philip, the question remains as to why there should be such fear at the prospect of Elizabeth's marriage to Anjou? Nor can the anxiety inspired by her marriage be explained away simply as a frenzied outburst of anti-Catholic sentiment.

I would like to suggest an alternative explanation: that with the accession of Mary a significant gap developed between the distribution of power according to law and the way people imagined that power to have been distributed. Within the population's memory, there had been no cause to see power in other than strictly patrilineal terms until the last year of Edward's reign. According to the English version of patrilineage as it was then understood, political power passed from first son to first son or to the nearest male equivalent. When a daughter married, then, it was as if she and any property she might inherit would be understood as passing out of her father's family and into that of her husband. On this basis, she could be used as a medium of exchange for making alliances between powerful families. But the queen provided a form of currency in a system of communication as well as in the power structure of agrarian England. Over and against a system which allowed only males to possess patriarchal power, Henry VIII's will followed a particular form of primogeniture according to which the daughter of the first son would inherit before the son of the second son. Since Henry had only one son and two daughters and no brothers survived him, this peculiar version of patrilineal descent seemed to assure the continuity of the Tudor line. The inheritance was to pass to Edward and, should he die without issue, then to Mary. Should she in turn die without issue, Elizabeth would inherit. The continuity of the family line was thus assured even if the power was to descend through females in doing so. Once having been opened with the ascension of Mary, this seeming contradiction within the English system of inheritance could breed the peculiar form of anxiety we have been noting. That is, it could well have engendered the fantasy of England passing into foreign hands with the marriage of its queen, for such a fantasy embodies certain elements of the English kinship system and plays them out in the form of a contradiction: a patrilineal system which privileges sex (the first son) and a bilateral system which distributes power through the female (the daughter of the king).

As a fact of law, no contradiction existed within the English system of distributing power. When the female was of the "greater nobility," the family title and patriarchal prerogative passed through her to her male heirs, not into the hands of her husband and his father's family. Yet the fantasy persisted which linked power to sex rather than to the father's bloodline and made the marriage of Queen Elizabeth, in particular, appear to threaten the integrity of the English state. In response to this fear that sexual domination of the English queen by the French duke would impugn the integrity of English political power, the articles of agreement drawn up by Burghley, Leicester, Walsingham and Hatton emphasize the limits on the duke's power after the marriage: "After the Marriage consummated [sic], he shall enjoy the Title and Honour of King, but shall leave the management of Affairs wholly and solely to the Queen."[14] And there was more to be worried out in these articles than simply the relations of power between the French duke and the English queen under the conditions of their marriage. For it was not only necessary to take exception to the usual hierarchical subordination of female to male in the case of the English that worried the authors of these articles. The separation of English power from that of French had to be worked out as the genealogy of power that future generations would realize, the whole emphasis of which was to maintain the separateness of the two nations even if the right to wear their respective crowns should be embodied in a single monarch:

> What shall be concluded concerning their Children in the Parliament of England, shall be verified and confirmed in the Parliaments of France, to this effect. The Males or Females shall succeed their Mother in the Inheritance of England. If there be two Males, the eldest shall succeed in the Kingdom of France, and the second in his Mother's Right in England. If there be but one Male, and he come to enjoy both Crowns, he shall reside in England eight Months in every two years. . . . If the Queen die without Children, the Duke shall claim no Propriety in the Kingdom of England.[15]

The need for such a statement, we should note, arises from the peculiarly English problem that daughters were in line to inherit all the power that came with the title of a peer after the sons of the first-born male. Such a female solved a problem of succession by carrying on the blood of the eldest son, but she also created a problem in that her subordinate role as wife to a husband appeared to compromise the sovereign power of England if a female monarch should marry. The French imagination had no such dilemma to deal with. If the royal offspring were a male, he could inherit the French throne, but if female, then she could only inherit property that came through the mother's line.

The *Arcadia* rehearses this very dilemma. By making this observation, however, I do not want to read Sidney's prose romance as an allegory of topical events but rather to suggest that the problems of courtship and kinship which organize his texts organized the political thinking of many other people as well. I want to see the *Arcadia* as one of a number of texts which sought to figure out solutions to political problems in sexual terms. The complications in Sidney's romance arise out of a situation where the daughters of the first born male displace the son of the second born. Intending never to marry, Basilius originally promised the kingdom to his younger brother. This promise was jeopardized when Basilius broke his own intention not to marry, for the marriage produced two daughters. Such a distinction − between a strictly patrilineal system of inheritance where power is always embodied in a male, and a bilateral system where power descends through the daughters of the first son − situates the *Arcadia* in an historical environment where this was to be the conceptual problem. What is more, the *Arcadia* takes up the continental and classical romance tradition and makes it a form in which the English political dilemma could be figured out. When patriarchal power descended through the female, what would happen to that power with a marriage which brought the priorities of sexual relations into conflict with those of rank or patronage? To put it another way, under what conditions could a female monarch marry without compromising the power inhering in the Crown?

The resolution Sidney offers his reader is just as instructive historically. It again dramatizes a way of thinking through a distinctively English problematic of power. The narrative is set in motion by the fear that the father's patrimony would pass out of the father's family with the daughter's marriage and into the possession of a foreigner. This situation generates all the plots and subplots and it is not resolved until the final paragraph of *The Countess of Pembroke's Arcadia*. The princesses marry, one of them to receive her father's patrimony, the other to receive that of her husband's father. These marriages create two competing families each of which observes the rules of patrilineage in a manner resembling the marriage articles drawn up in preparation for Elizabeth's marriage to Anjou. It is not difficult to construe the point: the patrimonies of each family have been preserved, one through the eldest son, the other through the second daughter, the rules of English primogeniture holding fast in both, yet violating the integrity of family and nation in neither. Descent of the father's power through the male and through the female thus acquires equivalence in Sidney's narrative.

III

I would like to turn now from the problem that had to be thought through when the English throne passed to Henry VIII's daughters and consider how this problem shaped symbolic practices at Elizabeth's court. One understood his place in Elizabethan society in terms of his relation to the monarch and, short of that, in relation to a member of the aristocracy who enjoyed some relationship to her. Membership in the empowered class was determined almost exclusively by marriage and birth. As Lawrence Stone notes:

> Looked at as a power elite, [the aristocracy] consistently filled high political office, they occupied at least half the seats on the privy council, formed one of the two great legislative bodies in Parliament, had a near monopoly of the Lord Lieutenancies, and were in a position to exercise great influence in county politics and administration.[16]

We should recall that it was only within Sidney's lifetime that the legal definition of the peer was finally and firmly established. Elizabeth sought means to delimit membership in the aristocracy and, I will argue, to make membership in that group more important than membership in any particular family.

Beginning in 1570, it is fair to say the importance of one's membership in the peerage increased sharply as the number of peers for all practical purposes became fixed. Stone writes of Elizabeth's policy, "If she was frugal in her distribution of knighthoods, she was even more conservative in the creation of new peerages." On this point he quotes Sir Thomas Fuller's rather wry observation that Elizabeth "honoured her honours by bestowing them sparingly."[17] Her parsimony in granting promotions as well as renewing lines was such that there were a total of 57 peers when Elizabeth became queen and no more than 55 when she died. If their number was limited, however, their privileges were considerable. Only peers had access through birth to land, office and privilege, powers that were akin to the monarch's. Thus they were the first who stood to benefit from being as cautious as she about limiting access to the empowered community. What happened to the number of peers consequently happened, with one exception, to membership in the other classes of the nobility. Strict regulation of marriage provided an obvious means for marking the boundaries between aristocracy and gentry as well as for governing the distribution of land and wealth. Strict regulation of marriage insured the power of those inside the empowered community, which in turn enhanced the value of their bloodline and the desirability of marrying into it. In short, strict regulation of marriage insured the value of aristocratic women. Roy Strong puts the matter this way, "Elizabethan marriages were politic alliances of wealth and connection. They represented accumulations of money and of land, cementing relationships between old and new families."[18] From this it follows that marriage was considered an overtly political activity, certainly not something to be left to the whim of the children – often barely in their early teens – by means of whom alliances were made and the value of blood perpetuated.

For over forty years the most eligible aristocratic woman on the Elizabethan marriage market was Elizabeth herself. The fact that after the Anjou negotiations collapsed she never seriously put herself in the market again in no way contradicts the fact that she remained the single most valuable female in a carefully regulated system of exchange where value was calculated in terms of one's bloodline. In addition to the power inherent in her value as the most desirable – according to this standard, the very embodiment of desirability itself – of all unmarried women in England, she jealously guarded the patriarchal prerogative to oversee the exchange of women. Closely regulating the sexual relations of women at her court and balancing alliances among the adult members of the aristocracy, she also claimed the power of the monarch to oversee the finances and marriage arrangements of any ward who came under the jurisdiction of the Court of Wards.[19] Since an orphan came under the jurisdiction of the Court of Wards if the inherited estate included any land held of the Crown, it meant – given the short life expectancy of the average Elizabethan – that many children from propertied families would become wards of Elizabeth through her Court of Wards. Indeed the wealthier and the more prominent the family, the more likely it would hold some land from the Crown. In this manner at any given moment Elizabeth indirectly controlled the marriage possibilities of a significant number of people of the blood and of property. Even when she gave or sold the wardship in question to clients who sought to profit from managing the land holdings of the estate or from arranging the marriage of the ward before he or she came of age, Elizabeth could intercede. To keep property within a family, rich heirs and heiresses in their minority sometimes found themselves married off by their uncles within days of their parent's death. This was done to avoid the Court of Wards. Such was the case with the marriage of Barbara Gamage. Within two weeks after the death of her father, this rich and very young heiress was married to Robert Sidney, a man she had never seen before the day of her wedding.[20] The marriage had been quickly arranged between her uncle and Sir Henry Sidney to prevent the girl's wardship from going to one of Elizabeth's courtiers. Ralegh was particularly anxious to gain control of the wardship and notified Elizabeth as soon as he heard of the death of John Gamage. Elizabeth sent a messenger to prohibit the match and to claim the monarch's right to wardship. The messenger arrived just hours after the wedding. Knowing full well that the speedy marriage was intended to circumvent her authority, Elizabeth made Robert Sidney pay for this haste by denying most of his requests for favor over the next twenty years.[21] His fortunes did not improve until James came to the throne.

Elizabeth pursued a policy which increased her value as an aristocratic female. In a letter to Robert Markham, Sir John Harrington tells a story that reveals something of Elizabeth's cunning in filling this role:

> She did oft aske the Ladies around hir chamber, If they lovede to thinke of marriage? And the wise ones did conceal well their liking hereto, as knowing the Queenes judgment in this matter. Sir Matthew Arundels fair cosin, not knowing so deeply as hir fellowes, was asked one day hereof, and simply said she had thought muche about marriage, if her father did consent to the man she lovede. You seem honeste, I'faithe, said the Queen; I will sue for you to your father. – The damsel was not displeased hereat; and, when Sir Roberte came to Cowrte, the Queene askede him hereon, and pressede his consentinge, if the match was discreet. Sir Roberte, much astonied at this news, said he never heard his daughter had liking to any man, and wantede to gain knowledge of hir affection; but woude give free consente to what was most pleasinge to hir Highness wyll and advise. Then I will do the reste, saith the Queen. The Ladie was called in, and . . . tould her father had given his free consente. Then, replied the Ladie, I shall be happie, and please your Grace. So thou shalte, but not to be a foole and marrye. I haue his consente given to me, and I vow thou shalte never get it into thy possession. So go to thy busynesse. "I see thou art a bolde one to owne thy foolishnesse so readilye." I coude relate manye pleasant tales of hir Majesties outwittinge the wittiest ones, for few knew how to aim their shaft against hir cunninge. We did all love hir, for she said she loved us, and muche wysdome she shewed in thys matter.[22]

The story is pure gossip. It bears the signs of a folk narrative which has been told and retold many times over. Its plot recalls the opening to romantic comedies where some patriarchal figure harshly constrains the eligible young women under his charge, who spend their time dreaming about marriage. For dreaming that her father would consent to the man she loved in Harrington's story, this woman loses her father's consent and the ability to marry according to the dictates of her desire. This is to endanger his political power in that it questions his ability to use his wealth for political alliances. If modern readers expect Harrington to pity the girl in this unhappy romance, it is because we accept a notion of sexual relations which denies their inherently political nature. On the other hand, Harrington admires Elizabeth's cleverness and approves of her behavior, noting the loving reciprocity of love she maintained with her subjects. Far from criticizing the queen's uncompromising regulation of marriage among the nobility, he understands it as a crucial feature of her domestic statecraft, a sovereign right, and thus as a source of state power.

It is from this perspective rather than through the lens of modern psychology – which tends to show Queen Elizabeth a neurotically jealous woman – that one must understand the way Elizabeth dealt with unauthorized sexual mergers among members of the great families and those who kept company at her court. The marriage of the Earl of Hertford and Lady Catherine Grey occasioned one of the most famous instances of Elizabeth's wrath, but besides that of Robert Sidney and Barbara Gamage, other such cases come easily to mind: Leicester's marriage to Lettice Knollys, Ralegh's to Elizabeth Throckmorton, or Essex's marriage to the widow of Philip Sidney. Each of these cases challenged the queen's authority, and each consequently caused her to display a different strategy for maintaining that power. Consider, for one, the Hertford situation. Having married without the queen's permission, his marriage threatened to establish a line in contention for the throne: according to Henry VIII's will, Catherine Grey could be next in line after Elizabeth. With this Seymore-Dudley alliance, two of the most powerful aristocratic families in England had merged, and the birth of their son established a line of succession. When Elizabeth learned of their secret marriage, she immediately incarcerated both husband and wife and annulled their marriage, thus rendering any of their offspring illegitimate. But there was always the possibility of overturning that annulment and thereby legitimizing the children born to the couple, which would make the boys contenders to the throne. Although Lady Catherine Grey died in 1567, as late as 1595 Hertford was trying to set legal maneuvers into motion which he hoped would overturn the annulment. For seeking to determine her successor, Elizabeth sent him back to the tower. She evidently found the task politically necessary and carried it out without personal animosity, for she sent a consoling letter to his second wife to say that in her eyes Hertford's crime was "not more pernicious and malicious than as an act of lewd and prowd contempt against our own direct prohibition."[23] She promises to use no more severity "than is requisite for other's caution in like cases." The other cases which have helped to make Elizabeth notorious for her anger at unauthorized marriages were all sexual infractions which posed a challenge to the monarch's authority. She was as concerned with marriages that might in some way impugn the purity of the aristocratic community as well as increase its size. She strongly disapproved of such marriages as the union of the Earl of Essex and Sidney's widow that seemed to undervalue aristocratic blood. That marriage, writes Thomas Birch, "gave offense to the queen as it was contracted without her consent and considered by her majesty *as below the dignity of his family"* (italics mine).[24]

In this respect, too, Sidney perfectly exemplified the political dilemma informing sexual relations among the nobility during Elizabeth's reign. If any man in England not born into a direct line of inheritance had reason for great expectations, that man was Sidney. His grandfather was the Duke of Northumberland and four uncles were earls, to two of whom – the Earl of Leicester and the Earl of Warwick – Sidney was heir presumptive. Should either of his mother's brothers die childless, Sidney would have inherited lands, riches, and title. But heir presumptive was not the same as being in the direct line of descent, and Sidney was treated accordingly, as someone of promise but not yet of the blood. His failure to contract a marriage with a daughter of some noble family indicates how rigidly this distinction was actually maintained. Beginning in 1568, Sir William Cecil negotiated for three years with Sir Henry Sidney to arrange a marriage between Philip and Cecil's daughter.[25] Both men were of comparable rank and both reasonably expected to be given a barony, the lowest rank of hereditary title. Cecil was made Baron Burghley in 1571. Sir Henry was offered a barony but declined it in May 1572 because the queen did not include any property to support the honor. When Cecil became Baron Burghley, however, he broke off negotiations with the Sidneys and arranged the marriage of his fifteen-year-old daughter to his ward Edward de Vere, the Earl of Oxford. The queen's permission was sought and readily granted for that marriage. Given the disparity, then, between Burghley's title and Sidney's lack of one, Burghley found it convenient to end his dealings with Sir Henry. The course of Philip Sidney's subsequent career dramatizes perfectly the social consequences of the exclusionary marriage rules organizing alliances among the nobility of his day and the form desire takes in such a central Elizabethan document as the *Arcadia*.

IV

The powers inhering in her blood – not the least of which was the power to regulate marriage in a way which enhanced the power of blood – made Elizabeth politically the most desirable woman in England whatever the limitations in physical charm or temperament she might have displayed. But to understand why she was the inspiration if not the object of so much love poetry and many other court practices in which she was wooed, one must consider the fact she was also the single most important patron in England. As Wallace T. MacCaffrey demonstrates, the Tudors in particular used patronage as a means of maintaining loyalty to the central government.[26] The strict regulation of marriage made attendance at court necessary for those eager to rise. Due in part to the century-long practice initiated by Henry VII to centralize power in the monarch and to limit the regional powers of the peers, and owing as well to the decline of the Church as a source for personnel to staff the government, the court displaced many of the more traditional means of advancement that ambitious men could formerly pursue. During Elizabeth's reign, the court therefore seemed to promise an increasingly important means of compensating for the disadvantages of birth. This was particularly true for those who, like second sons, lacked other prospects for advancement.

Patronage could come in many forms such as the rights to monopolies, leases, grants, the management and sale of wardships, the right to work certain lands, and the opportunity to purchase land seized by the Crown. Or one might acquire a position in the Church, at one of the universities, or even in government. Finally, there were titles and honors that men coveted. But the real power of patronage derived from the belief that a successful client had somehow earned the love of his patron. The rights, positions, or titles he acquired were signs both of his value and of the patron's power to endow his client with value. Regardless of rank, whoever could acquire the privileges of patronage enjoyed – if only to a limited degree – the privileges of the blood. Since in concept at least Elizabeth was the ultimate source of all patronage as well as the power of the blood, her client or a client of her client could enjoy in some small measure the privileges inhering in her blood, much as the men of her court feared that Anjou would were he ever to marry Elizabeth. The fear of a foreign claimant to English power arose from the same understanding of the queen's body. Since the monarch was female, one could acquire some of her power with the successful negotiation of sexual relations. To seek patronage therefore came to be understood as an act of wooing the queen. This was the form such political negotiations assumed from the early years of her reign to her very last years. Thus when William Herbert, the future Earl of Pembroke, came to London to seek opportunities at court, it was said he "very discretely follows the course of making love to the Queen."[27] To describe Herbert's quest for patronage in such terms conveyed a meaning that was neither ironic nor allegorical in nature. "Making love to the Queen" was a public and political act, and if carried out successfully, it brought one position and power, signs that the suitor was favored by the queen. More often than not, however, the queen did not find the suitor's behavior indicative of merit. In such terms, Rowland White explains Pembroke's failure to Robert Sidney:

> he is much blamed for his cold and weake Maner of pursuing her Majesties Fauor, hauing had soe good steps to leade him vnto it. There is want of Spirit and Courage laid to his Charge, and that he is a melancholy young man.[28]

Herbert's manner of wooing Elizabeth extended well beyond the personal in that it had serious political consequences not only for the young man himself but also for members of his immediate family, including Pembroke's uncle and White's patron, Sir Robert Sidney.

The passing of the old guard, together with the earlier disgrace of Ralegh and Essex's troubled position after his Irish expedition, thinned the ranks of the queen's favorites. This promising economic environment insured the presence of many young men at court pursuing favor. Each wished to be the queen's favorite, and each competed for specific opportunities. In fact many who wooed could in theory win some favor. There were men whose careers testified to the possibility that services brought powerful positions (Hatton enjoyed one), wealth (Ralegh by the mid 1580s could bear witness to this), and promotion to a hereditary title such as Burghley earned. Indeed, one of the most frequent complaints from her most successful suitors was that Elizabeth distributed her favors to members of different court factions. White knew Herbert's success as a suitor depended on his presence at court. In contrast with Herbert's standoffishness, White describes another potential client of the queen in this manner: "Young Carey followes it [the queen's favor] with more care and boldness." The court scene made it amply clear there could be any number of competitors. White had advised his charge, "that this yong Competitor might purposely start up, to try what he would doe . . . Yt is not yet to late, if he [Herbert] stay not to long in the Cowntry." Finally, White wishes Sir Robert were at court to advise young Herbert "in a Matter of such Greatness; for surely it wold be to your good to see him a Favorit."[29] It is important to recognize that this is what the politically knowledgeable men of some prominence understood the patronage system to be: a courtship situation where several competitors had to pursue the hand of the same woman.

Thus it is reasonable to think of the language of courtship and love as a highly specialized political language which served a very different purpose in the Elizabethan court world than such language would serve in negotiating historically later, "companionate" relationships. It did not indicate the subject's erotic attraction to the queen nor even his affection in any personalized sense of the term. Rather it represented relations in a manner that acknowledged the queen's supreme power to determine those who should receive economic and political benefits. It also allowed those who pursued such favor to strive to attract her attention which – in extreme cases – might even entail membership in the aristocracy. The very powerful Dudley family was one who gained entry into the aristocracy through marriage. The grandfather of the Earl of Leicester and the Earl of Warwick was never granted a title. His service to Henry VII alone enabled him to wed the coheiress of Edward Grey, Viscount L'Isle, without the attribute of high rank with the result that his son became Viscount L'Isle, Duke of Northumberland and Earl of Warwick. Even though few were actually taken into the privileged group which linked them – however indirectly – by blood with the queen, the availability of favors and a few notable examples, coupled with the tight restrictions on marriage among the nobility, not to mention the queen's own cunning style of statecraft, encouraged young men to believe the surest way to economic and political advancement was through courting the queen. Given her supreme authority as the source of such power, furthermore, such a means of pursuing advancement should not be considered indirect or conniving but an accurate representation as to how they imagined political relationships to be. When we find such terms as "fortune," "suitor," "hope," "envy," "favor," "despair" and "love" in both letters of clientage and in the poetry coined for the queen as well as that circulated among members of a court coterie, then, it can be nothing else but a language for negotiating with a patron for the client's position.[30] Neither allegorical nor secretly encoded, this is quite simply a political language. It is from such a political perspective, I would argue, that we should understand Shakespeare's sonnets.

If the vocabulary of Petrarchan love was adapted to represent the relations between the unavailable aristocratic female and her suitors, then its sexual terms could be extrapolated to represent power relations between any patron and his client. In the most general way, it could also represent the relationship of the queen to her subjects. When Ralegh was sent to the Tower for marrying Elizabeth Throckmorton, he accordingly wrote Robert Cecil lamenting the fact that his imprisonment prevented him from enjoying the queen's company on one of her progresses: "My heart was never broken till this day, that I hear the Queen goes away so far off – whom I have followed so many years with so great love and desire. . . ."[31] This description of the privations of imprisonment reads like a string of Petrarchan clichés, and much the same can be said for the way in which Ralegh recommends himself to the queen for her mercy: "All those times past, – the loves, the sythes [sighs], the sorrows, the desires, can they not way down one frail misfortune?"[32] This may strike us as markedly disingenuous, but in fact such language was used to negotiate dozens of relationships with the queen, as well as hundreds of others at some remove from the Crown. Letters and poems in the Petrarchan mode were just one of the symbolic practices at court for wooing the queen. She was often the guest at an entertainment or a pageant which celebrated her virtue, or she might be the recipient of a gift in an elaborate gift-giving system operating at court.[33] These practices did not serve the needs of female vanity, we may argue, but comprised an effective system for negotiating political relationships which acknowledged Elizabeth's supreme power, held her at a remove from her courtiers by emphasizing differences of rank and blood, and yet offered them some access to her power should a courtier play the game exactly right. Ralegh and Cecil knew well the lesson young William Herbert would have to learn: that not to flatter the queen was to deny her power as their patron.

To complete the background against which I will read Shakespeare's romantic comedies, I would like to return once more to the figure of Sidney, and I would emphasize the word "figure." Sidney provided a cite where various political features combined in a way which proved particularly meaningful to the aspiring young men who produced much of the literature for which the Elizabethan period is known. His career brought together the political contradictions which organized Elizabeth's court, and it embodied those contradictions without resolving them, embodied them – even so – in a manner that testified to Elizabeth's sovereign power. Sidney exemplified both the promising possibilities of patronage and the dominion of blood, the power that came with good connections and the utter helplessness of one who was dependent on favors from those of higher rank. Perhaps no one possessed so many of the features desirable in an Elizabethan courtier and yet was so undervalued that he enjoyed neither patronage nor the opportunity even to serve.

The English political situation uniquely required strategies for wooing an unavailable woman as the means to government posts, titles, honors, and all sorts of patronage opportunities. Such political use of this language differentiates English Petrarchanism from that of Italy and France. Thus we find that his efforts at domesticating literary materials – particularly his efforts at love poetry – became part of Sidney's political career. His example was followed by hundreds of young men – they may have numbered 2500 – who waited on the fringes of the court or at the Inns of Court, waited to be noticed and, while they waited, practiced the social graces that would woo and win a patron's love. They practiced various forms of self display in language and dress. Some of these men waited for more than ten years for patronage opportunities; others were fortunate to have an older brother die; others still sought adventures to provide capital or to win a knighthood. The raid on Cadiz provided one such opportunity. With the hope of raising capital, some signed on to such privateering "ventures" as the one which led to the capture of the *Madre de Dios* with all its gold, silks, and perfumes. These young men also pursued their fortunes through the verses which fill hundreds of surviving manuscript miscellanies or the handful that found their way into print despite the Elizabethan stigma against publication. In their letters, especially, we can see them wooing some patron or other.

Throughout the period from 1572 to 1581, Sidney sought opportunities to earn a respected position in the government. By his own standards and those of any courtier, however, he was, as F.J. Levy puts it, "a failure."[34] Until 1581 at least, he was always within sight of either place, position, or marriage to a prominent woman, but this proximity to power depended largely upon his eligibility to inherit. In the words of one of Sidney's recent biographers, Sidney's "status as a desirable match changed utterly when Lettice, Lady Leicester gave birth to a son"; this child displaced Sidney as the heir to both Leicester and Warwick.[35] Sidney, it is said, immediately drew a line through the motto – "*speravi*" – on his tilting shield. Without income from a marriage or inheritance, and without office, he suffered crushing debts. When he finally married in 1583, fifteen years after his father and Burghley first started negotiating an alliance, it was to the daughter of Sir Francis Walsingham, Elizabeth's secretary of state. It is interesting to note that despite the fact that neither Walsingham nor Sidney held hereditary titles, the queen still raised an objection to the marriage because she had not been consulted before the arrangements were announced. Walsingham apologized for this oversight on grounds that he did not consider the marriage of his daughter to a mere "free gentleman" to be of sufficient rank "worthy of asking the Queen's permission."[36] When Sidney was finally knighted in 1583, it was only because Count Casimer was unable to attend his own induction into the Order of the Garter and asked Sidney to stand as his proxy. Since a proxy had to be of a rank no lower than knight, Sidney was duly promoted. It was in writing the *Arcadia*, then, that he commanded a certain kind of cultural authority which he lacked in the political world.

Arcadian desire does not come from God, law, providence, history or even some literary text outside the romance. Rather it is an agency empowered by the artist himself. Because the power of this specialized literary language did not derive from the power of political institutions, it could do nothing to change the rules for distributing such power. Disruptive though it may seem, Arcadian desire did not translate into another form of authority. This is the very paradox manifested in Sidney's life and in those of the other young men who wrote poetry, filled their commonplace books with poetry, prose and letters of famous men, and attended the theater. Their productivity invariably increased when they were out of favor with the queen or otherwise lacked economic opportunities. Accordingly, they represented their situation as one of frustrated desire and imagined possibilities for wooing an unavailable object of desire. Thus the very situation that inspired such writing also identified the author as someone excluded from the institutions of power. Even though Sidney could produce a master text like the *Arcadia* or *Astrophel and Stella* and thus bring about what appears now as a major change in literary history, he was unable to modify the social reality that brought about his exclusion from the privileges of blood. As a writer, Sidney defined himself not as the aristocrat he wanted to become but as the perfect representative of the desiring courtier he turned out to be. The theater such men attended, like the literature they produced and read, displayed the same paradoxical figure organizing their political life: that of a perfect world to which an unavailable aristocratic woman alone could provide access. The Petrarchan mode thus allowed the ambitious a means of imagining some other relations to the political reality – some softening of boundaries between the empowered community and the people, some levelling of hierarchy. But it never challenged the status quo. It authorized the desirability of the community of blood and confirmed its distance from the suitor's condition by understanding the love relationship not as one of self and self but as one of self and other. Only by flattering representations of her as remote and unobtainable could the aristocratic woman be sought.

V

When Sidney wrote the *Arcadia*, he as much as announced to family and friends that he was not in the service of the queen. By the same token, Ralegh's *Ocean to Cynthia* announces itself as a poem written by an exile from court. For these men as well as for numerous other courtiers who used the language of love and courtship to negotiate their relations with Elizabeth, writing of this sort was often conducted when one was out of favor at court and without active employment in the service of the state. A dramatist whose livelihood came from the public stage, however, was considerably lower on the social scale than those who waited for privilege at court, lower indeed than even the scholar. For a mere gentleman was, as Sir Thomas Smith noted, still presumably someone whom "blood and race doth make noble."[37] With considerable condescension Smith observes, however, that whoever studies the law "professes liberall sciences, and to be shorte, who can live idly and without manual labour, and will beare the port, charge and countenance" could now qualify as a gentleman.[38] As common as gentlemen had become in Smith's opinion, they still occupied a position superior to Shakespeare's. An actor or a playwright simply "had no rank or function in the recognized scheme of things," Leo Salingar observes.[39]

Though his social position was very different from that of the young men who waited for patronage opportunities at court, however, Shakespeare was no less ambitious than they. He sought membership in the gentry class to which they belonged and which they sought to transcend by promotion or title or by marrying exceptionally well. We know that in 1596 Shakespeare applied for the grant of arms his father had pursued thirty years earlier, and in 1599 the playwright wanted to add the coat of arms of his mother's family. The mere fact of Shakespeare's desire to sign his name "gent." indicates how far below Sidney the playwright stood on the Elizabethan social scale. We might compare their positions in Elizabethan society in this fashion: while Sidney was as close to membership in the aristocratic community as one could be without bearing the hereditary title, Shakespeare was as close to his yeoman's roots as one could remain and still acquire a gentleman's status. After he did acquire such status, furthermore, Shakespeare's title did not go altogether without comment. In a dispute among heraldic purists, E.K. Chambers recounts, Shakespeare's new social standing formed part of the evidence for a charge that grants of arms were being made to "base and ignoble persons. . . ."[40]

These familiar facts concerning Shakespeare's status should not be glossed over lightly. They were one reason why Shakespeare never wrote like Sidney, but they were also the reason why Shakespeare used courtier writing as he did. Shakespeare was always by definition someone who could at best be a social outsider to the aristocratic tradition of letters with which Sidney obviously felt very comfortable. His comedies invoke courtly tropes as a way to mock the communication situation of the court in which these tropes were used in all earnestness. One need only look at the excesses of the courtiers at Navarre's court to see the element of parody which enters into courtly discourse when Shakespeare reproduces it upon the public stage. But there are a host of characters who materialize the courtly lover just as absurdly: Lucentio from *The Taming of the Shrew*, the lovers in *A Midsummer Night's Dream*, Bassanio in *The Merchant of Venice*, as well as such figures as Orlando and Orsino. Too often we forget to consider the mockery of aristocratic culture as one feature which sharply distinguished Elizabethan romantic comedy both from preceding comic forms and from the Jacobean city comedy that was to follow. After 1601, neither Shakespeare nor any of his contemporaries wrote romantic comedies again. More to the point, the idea of treating the tropes of aristocratic culture so irreverently had clearly lost its appeal. The materials of romantic comedy began to be dismantled. By the time James came to the throne, aristocratic heroines with the ability to invert the social order had given way to comedies which featured as heroes and heroines the sons and daughters of lower gentry, merchants, and craftsmen. In place of a lighthearted look at aristocratic love were tragicomedies and dramatic romances which treated aristocratic love affairs with notable gravity.

Although Shakespeare found countless and wonderful ways to mock the aristocratic tradition of writing, we cannot, in my opinion, conclude that he and his company imagined another political reality – one where the community of blood was not separated by an immutable principle from the people, or even one in which the power relations of the two social bodies were inverted. The public theater was permitted to exist because it officially served the queen. The Privy Council certainly assumed public theaters existed for this purpose when it regularly requested the lord mayor to permit these theaters to reopen after a plague threat or civil disturbance. In the words of a typical request from 1598, the lord mayor was asked to allow players to "practise . . . stage playes, whereby they might be the better enhabled and prepared to shew such plaies before her Majestie as they shalbe required at tymes meete and accustomed, to which ende they have bin cheefelie licensed and tollerated. . . ."[41] Unlike Henry VIII or James I, Elizabeth did not maintain a company of actors. Powerful figures at court provided patronage for acting companies so that the queen might receive them when she chose. Leo Salingar offers a useful speculation as to why such patronage even existed:

> The patrons who ensured that there would be skilled men to present to her were, above all, the great lords of her Council and household – like Leicester, Sussex, Pembroke . . . Charles Howard (the Lord Admiral) and the two Hunsdons, father and son, both Lords Chamberlain and Shakespeare's masters in succession from 1594 until the end of the reign. It does not appear that these grandees planned their actors' repertory in any way, but their indirect provision of plays at court was a form of tribute to their sovereign, an extension of the principle of entertaining her when on progress, much cheaper no doubt but possibly for that very reason, more competitive.[42]

Ample evidence exists to show that members of these companies benefited from their service to such patrons. Not only did the importance of one's patron help considerably in gaining local permission to perform when touring the provinces, but more than one player also escaped prosecution for some minor offense by claiming to be one of "my lord chamberlain's men" or of "my lord admiral's men." This relationship to the empowered community privileged the companies only on their submission to certain conditions, however. Whenever the Master of the Revels or the Privy Council construed dramatic material as the least bit offensive, the government did not hesitate to seize the playbooks, imprison the author, and punish the players. Thus the companies enjoyed the titular support of some of the most powerful people in the country and, at the same time, felt the full force of an authoritarian government ready to descend upon them.

If indeed plays were understood to serve similar ends to those of entertainments on progress, and the audience was always implicitly the queen, then we have to consider the drama as a forum for staging symbolic shows of state power and as a vehicle for disseminating court ideology. Like other public entertainments sponsored by patrons for the queen, we have to assume these had to be presented without challenging her policies or demeaning her person. At the same time, public theater was not the same as other forms of court culture, nor was a playwright for the public theater in the same relationship to the court as a courtly writer. There was probably intense competition among patrons and their companies, as well as between dramatists and her authors who identified their interests with those of the court and queen.

In considering the particular conditions for a successful dramatic performance, then, the dramatist evidently saw himself in a competitive relationship with the courtly discourse of which Sidney's *Arcadia* was the most grandiose and perfectly developed performance. Such a relationship was evidently crucial in defining the role of dramatist during Elizabeth's reign. I must stress this point because, in considering Shakespeare's literary language alongside the writing of men with Sidney's class aspirations, it has been common practice to obscure the difference between a public theatrical performance and writing that circulated within court coteries. In actuality, Shakespearean drama identifies a markedly different relationship with the empowered community and with people who had no hope of access to aristocratic privileges and thus saw themselves strictly as subject to that authority. Like the courtier, the dramatist also aimed at ingratiating himself with those in power. An Elizabethan playwright's economic survival depended upon his winning favor through the medium of theatrical performance in a more literal way than did the courtier's. But it was also true that the dramatist had no hope of obtaining membership in the privileged class to which his patrons and censors belonged; he represented their class to them from the viewpoint of the outsider and subject.

One might speculate that these conditions for writing – conflict-ridden as they undoubtedly were – provided the perfect situation within Elizabethan culture from which the public theater could play an especially vital political role. The drama itself provides grounds for such speculation as it develops ingenious ways to parody courtly behavior. Against the figures of courtier writing which located value in the exclusionary nature of aristocratic power, the dramatist figured forth a political reality which allowed different segments of the audience to understand themselves in relation to the aristocratic community of blood. For many in Shakespeare's audience this meant that – though outside the immediate parameters of the empowered community – they were part of the same nation whose welfare was inextricably linked to that of the aristocracy. His special relationship to the court consequently situated the dramatist in a position to transform the materials of courtly discourse into forms which gave substance to a nationalist ideology. The transformation in question I am suggesting involved the entire Petrarchan configuration which defined and maintained power relations at court: the suitor, the unavailable woman, and the differences which keep them apart. The romantic comedies mock the aspiring young man who professes desire for an unavailable woman from a station above him, but this transformation also involved certain changes in the representation of aristocratic women.

Given the identification between Elizabeth and English power that had been established with her accession to the throne and reinforced by her lack of heirs, and given as well that the whole communication situation at court turned upon her gender, one can understand why the use to which gender was put on the stage could influence the way people understood the distribution of political power. Unlike any female character in Sidney's romance or, for that matter, any female in the entire tradition of letters from which Sidney drew the materials of the *Arcadia*, Shakespeare's comic heroines are capable of embodying sexual desire and still remaining chaste. In earlier as well as later literature, it is usually the common woman who can experience desire without losing value. She is the stock-in-trade of the fabliaux tradition, while the aristocratic woman almost always experiences desire at the expense of her virtue and the risk of incurring tragic ends. Turning to the *Arcadia*, one finds that desire – at least desire that is socially sanctioned – arises strictly from the male. Pyrocles and Musidorus, for instance, are drawn into their adventures when portraits of the Arcadian princesses arouse their desire. In those situations where Sidney allows an aristocratic female to act upon desire, she is either someone so evil as Andromana or one tragically doomed in the manner of Zelmane. Only his low-life figures go unpunished for experiencing desire. To remain pure, the aristocratic woman refuses desires, and when desiring, she never marries happily. By contrast, Shakespeare's romantic comic heroines are both pure and capable of desire.

Only for a brief time, during the 1590s, then, did the London stage see female characters go to great lengths to pursue their desires without incurring punishment. They could disguise themselves as men, hurl insults in the manner of fishwives, banter in bawdy terms, speak with the authority of the law, and even arrange their own marriages. They could invert the social order and enjoy the freedoms reserved for either the common woman or the male aristocrat, all without tainting aristocratic blood. Unlike the Petrarchan lady or the idealized heroine of romance, Shakespeare's romantic heroines act with energy and ambition to challenge political hierarchies in such places as Venice, Athens, and Padua. The male equivalent to these romantic comic heroines was, of course, the overreacher. This figure of ambition always sought to transcend his birth by possessing a woman of much higher status. So Faustus desires Helen of Troy, and Tamburlaine must have his Zenocrate. But unlike the ambitious male, the aristocratic heroine of romantic comedy has a Faustian capacity that is not finally incompatible with patriarchal principles. This female's ability to incorporate features of low life, invert order, and yet to remain pure does not endanger the patriarchal state but actually appears necessary to maintaining social order. Incorporating the features of aggression within the female enables drama to assume comic form. Shakespeare's comic heroines never threaten to seize control of the state or its icon – the body of the aristocratic female. They can therefore provide the means of interrogating certain features of aristocratic culture without challenging the hierarchy based on the purity of the aristocratic community.

By the same token, the features of these heroines would have made them culturally antagonistic to the idealized heroines of Sidney's romance and verse. Shakespeare adds features to his aristocratic women which cancel out those that create the value of the Petrarchan heroine. Pamela, Philoclea, or Stella could never be aggressive or bawdy in the manner of a Kate or a Beatrice, nor could Sidney's aristocratic heroines act with the freedom of commoners and the power of patriarchal institutions as Portia and Rosalind do. The very behavior that distinguishes the romantic heroine would destroy the signs of difference which make the unavailable lady of the sonnets and the romance so desirable. If Sidney's practice of restricting the language of his aristocratic heroines has everything to do with his political fantasies, then Shakespeare's practice of making his romantic heroines out of the mix of incompatible languages drawn from the aristocratic romance tradition and the topsy-turvy tradition of carnival and marketplace, tell us how public theater allowed one to imagine a different relation to political power.

Bakhtin's twin figures of the grotesque body and the mass body offer us a way of imagining an alternative social formation to our own that has all the features of this essentially anti-aristocratic discourse. As anti-literary in modern terms as it was anti-aristocratic in those of Elizabethen culture, this "other" universe of language referred to all those material practices of the body which would contest the symbolic regime of the blood, and contest that form of power in a manner joyful and fearless, as if in mockery of legitimate power. Bakhtin's figures have special appeal for people interested in researching political history from a viewpoint antagonistic to power, a viewpoint which privileges the history of the subject rather than that of the state. Bakhtin himself obviously wanted to discover in the past whatever forms he could find that resisted the joyless and fearful conditions of the totalitarian government under which he wrote. Thus he used Rabelais to construct a figure that would idealize all those symbolic practices which resisted the exclusionary political body authorized by courtly romance. Contrary to this closed, rigidly hierarchized and pure figure of the desirable woman which authorized the body of blood, the grotesque body is open and protruding, heterogeneous and undifferentiated, sensual, concrete and renewable all at once. Contrary to the tradition of letters in which the aristocratic body is inscribed and through which it speaks, the grotesque body is constituted out of the curses, obscenity, laughter, spittle and oaths of marketplace and carnival.

The behavior of festivity and marketplace, in particular, helps us translate the figure of the grotesque body into a form of political power radically different from that which exerted itself in and through the aristocratic body. Explaining how its form constitutes such political resistance, Bakhtin says of the "mass body":

> The carnivalesque crowd in the marketplace or in the streets is not merely a crowd. It is the people as a whole, organized *in their own way*, the way of the people. It is outside of and contrary to all existing forms of the coercive socioeconomic and political organization, which is suspended for the time of the festivity.
> This festive organization of the crowd must be first of all concrete and sensual. Even the pressing throng, the physical contact of bodies, acquires a certain meaning. The individual feels that he is an indissoluble part of the collectivity, a member of the people's mass body. In this whole the individual body ceases to a certain extent to be itself; it is possible, so to say, to exchange bodies, to be renewed (through change of costume and mask). At the same time the people become aware of their sensual, material bodily unity and community.[43]

When the state is thus split into two bodies — one, continuous and impermeable and the other, heteroglot — this double-bodied state tends to authorize the exclusionary ethos of courtly writing.

By way of contrast with Sidney, however, Shakespeare constitutes something on the order of a grotesque body and endows it with some of the same positive features Bakhtin does. Shakespeare constructs this figure, however, in a way that only makes the aristocratic community appear less rigidly exclusive, more flexible and inclusive. That is, he makes the aristocratic community contain within it a purified, ordered, and hierarchized people. His representation of the social body thus encompasses a much broader social range than that which Sidney was willing to countenance. Rather than splitting the social world into the community of blood and that of the people, Shakespeare uses the comic stage to represent a more coherent and compatible social reality. And his romantic heroines are of crucial importance in producing such a reality. Shakespeare endows these heroines with the power of inversion and the language of bawdy to assault the aristocratic constraints that make the welfare of the state one and the same as the welfare of the aristocratic community. Even so, Shakespeare stops short of blurring the distinctions between the two social bodies. They remain distinct and separate. His theater only makes space within a more expansive state where a purified populace can participate in rituals and processionals that celebrate hierarchical power.

No other scene makes this point quite so emphatically as that which has come to be known as Bottom's dream. Several times displaced by theatrical artifice, the mating of grotesque body and queen is one marked as simultaneously forbidden – a breakdown of all the boundaries which make sense of the play – and also impossible – a form of boundary dissolution requiring the combined forces of magic, dream and stagecraft. But in staging such phantasmagoria to allow one to imagine the body of power overpowered by the forces incorporated as the grotesque, Shakespeare does more than preempt the possibility of this inversion and the loss of boundaries which such inversion – by its very nature – threatens to effect. The scene in question is part of a process of transformations that ultimately authorizes the political hierarchy whose categories the dream also levels. This levelling begins as Bottom mangles the Pyramus and Thisbe story in a way that, first of all, mocks aristocratic culture and ridicules the seriousness with which lovers at court pursued impossible desires. These were desires, we should recall, whose gratification required nothing less than a transformation of the social body of which they were part; the aristocracy would no longer be the pure community of blood if the suitor were to marry into it. It is therefore doubly significant that Bottom should give voice to Petrarchan tropes which spell out a fantasy where a daughter unsuccessfully defies monarch and father to marry someone of her own choosing. Bottom's version of these courtly materials drains this subversive form of desire of its dangerous features. In accomplishing this, he becomes fit to participate in the celebration of the duke's marriage.

Rather than dissolving the boundaries which authorized aristocratic power, the inclusion of the parodic – the mechanicals play about aristocratic love – within the official festivities of the state offers perhaps the most perfect manifestation of the political fantasy driving romantic comedy and lending it its characteristic form. By this, I mean to suggest that comedy takes shape as it marshalls all manner of cultural materials to produce a specific social formation. As represented on the stage this society had all the hierarchal features inhering in the sexual relations comprising romance. But it was neither understood nor authorized in opposition to the mass body, even as it distinguished the pure aristocratic body of blood from that of the people. A romantic comedy is not a romantic comedy, in other words, without the banquet scene, marriage ceremony, processional, or dance which incorporates the whole range of social elements within a celebration of state power. *A Midsummer Night's Dream* is the most forthright of the romantic comedies in declaring the power of theater to create the illusion of a totalizing community out of the contradictory bodies of power. Certainly this is the one comedy which concludes with the literal staging of a play, produced by members of the mass body to celebrate aristocratic marriage. The grotesque body has been included within the social order without overthrowing it, indeed with the effect of invigorating that order, as the entire community appears on stage, reconciled and joyful, all its elements reinscribed within a traditional hierarchy.

Following Pierre Bourdieu's observation that ideologies are "doubly determined," Alan Sinfield explains that "writing, even when it is purposefully in the service of an ideology, will very often manifest a slant toward the interests of the writer *as writer*."[44] He adds that the category "writer" should be specified with regard to a structural position such as preacher, courtier, dramatist and so forth, but also the writer's class or origins along with his or her relationship to the state, the aristocracy and bourgeoisie, and the institutions of cultural production. The playwright in Elizabethan society was engaged in an act of self-advertisement, and in the public theater a writer such as Shakespeare would have made a case for himself as one having a significant role to play in the culture. No base and ignoble person he. While for Sidney the act of writing set him in a marginal position in relation to court, Shakespeare was in a very real sense serving the queen by writing to the public. He demonstrated that he was capable of making a world he called into being through wit and disguise. Though his world existed only on stage, it could announce itself as occupying a more potent political role in Elizabethan political life than the writing of courtiers. Shakespeare obviously recognized he was forging a more inclusive form of nationalism, one that both employed the signs and symbols of the state and revitalized them in the service of the queen. Thus he regularly displayed his own importance as a playwright within his plays in authorizing her power as monarch.

VI

Central to the special status Shakespeare claims for his drama is the manner in which the wellborn lady, and only the wellborn lady, becomes invested with certain powers to make a more flexible and inclusive political world. To that end, he modifies the subject of courtier poetry and romance and, in exposing the limits of its social fantasy, transforms the stage into a social space where the popular imagination can understand itself in relation to a centralized form of power. Of the comedies, *The Taming of the Shrew* would seem to be far from the tradition of aristocratic letters. Based on folk materials and possibly an earlier dramatic text, *The Taming of the Shrew* does not usually strike us as a play which lends itself to a light-hearted critique of aristocratic culture so easily as *Love's Labors Lost* obviously does. Yet the features of *Taming* which have proved most puzzling for literary criticism are the very elements with which Shakespeare took up the same political issue motivating Sidney's romance and revised that political fantasy.

The Induction to *The Taming of the Shrew* lays out the terms for a joke which runs through the play, organizing its symbolic material into a political statement. The Induction materializes the Petrarchan fantasy that presents an unavailable aristocratic lady as the means to status, power, and wealth if only she could be persuaded to love the devoted courtier. Implicit in this fantasy is the assumption that to possess her body is to have access to the aristocratic blood. That Stella, for instance, is both sexually and socially inaccessible to the lovesick Astrophel is precisely what drives his desire to see her, to be seen by her, and to write about her. Similarly, by withdrawing his daughters from the world, Basilius only increases the desire of Pyrocles and Musidorus to find these women and woo them.

The Induction literalizes the operative fiction of courtier poetry that a patronage relationship could be conducted as a sexual relationship. The drunken Sly can live like a lord so long as he agrees to accept the woman by his side as a lady. The jest rests on the illusion of a page passing for such a woman. Neither an afterthought nor a minor detail, the creation of this particular female mocks the most important of the Petrarchan tropes. A fiction transforms a male page of no particular importance into a woman of extraordinary value. As long as she retains this form, Sly can live out a fantasy of membership in the aristocratic community. Almost as obtuse as Bottom, the drunken tinker accepts the fantasy of his transformation into a powerful lord. Although they are supposedly married, this woman is as unavailable as if she were married to someone else. It is only his delusion and the illusion of her theatrical performance that maintains Sly's belief in his status, for the moment he tries to possess her in any material sense, the illusory nature of his power will of course be revealed. Shakespeare never allows us to believe that Sly could enter into the aristocratic body any more than he allows us to believe Bottom could be desired by the queen of the faeries. Sly incorporates certain features of the grotesque body openly hostile to the institutions of state. When first we see him, he refuses to leave the tavern, resisting the mandates of social life first by ignoring the call for the local constabulary and then by falling asleep. As the figure of recalcitrance itself, he becomes, for the Lord who stumbles upon him, the occasion of a "jest," "a flattering dream," or a "worthless fancy." The Lord's art – which displays the power of the theater more than it does anything else – is designed to make Sly "forget himself." So refashioned, the tinker believes he was originally a lord who dreamed he was a tinker but now awakens to his proper station. As in any quest for patronage, the desiring client fantasizes that he will be discovered, loved, and magically translated into the aristocratic community. Sly's promotion into the aristocracy is the result of this collective fiction. One of the Lord's huntsmen explains the paradox of power underlying the fiction: "He is no less than what we say he is" (i. 70). Sly in turn forgoes the desires of the grotesque body – drink and sex – in order to sustain the illusion of his power, declaring, "I am a lord indeed," (ii. 72).

In materializing the Petrarchan dream, however, Shakespeare does not mean to have the dream go unquestioned, allowing his audience to imagine the simple transgression of some boundary between the mass body and that of blood. To the contrary, Shakespeare materializes the fantasy of transgression as a joke where the tinker, believing himself a lord, does not possess the linguistic skills required to sustain such a belief by the audience. Sly must ask what, as a lord, he may call his wife, to which the Lord replies, "Madam." "Al'ce Madam or Joan Madam," Sly asks again, only to be told, "Madam, and nothing else, so lords call ladies." I cite this example as just one of the many instances in the play where Shakespeare calls attention to the role of the dramatist and his power to produce and shatter the illusions in terms of which one understands identity. The figure of desire held up and simultaneously withheld from Sly is a male disguised as a female. Besides making explicit the unnatural and illusory nature of this desire, the transvestite is also an emblem of the theater's power to create illusion, for Sly's wife – a boy costumed as an aristocratic woman – is also the figure of the actor on the Elizabethan stage.

The play performed for Sly uses the same strategy of materializing the Petrarchan fantasy. The unavailable woman, Bianca, the object of both erotic and mercantile desire, is wooed by Gremio and Hortensio. Joining the competitors is Lucentio who is more like one of the princes from an

Arcadian romance than the hero of *Supposes*, the source for this subplot. Lucentio falls in love with Bianca at first sight, abandons his studies, and disguises himself as one below his station to serve as her tutor. This, all because of her silent beauty. Overvalued as the Petrarchan lady when she is unavailable, Bianca turns shrew once she is married. But this inversion is only one part of the joke. If Shakespeare turns the Petrarchan lady shrewish, then he has the shrew become the most desirable wife according to the aristocratic model which she assaulted with such ardor. Quite inappropriate for a lady from the empowered class, her anger and abusive wit give Kate the features of Bakhtin's marketplace fishwife – a woman fit for Sly – in marked contrast with Sidney's soft-spoken aristocratic heroines. More to the point, her abusive behavior, when joined with the social features of the aristocratic lady, prevents marriages, produces chaos within the family, and threatens the social order itself.

Unlike many of the folktales about shrewish women, however, Shakespeare not only gives Kate the language to cause social chaos among aristocratic families, but he also makes her responsible for restoring patriarchal authority. The fault lies not in her, Kate argues, but in a system that overvalues the woman who is submissive and unavailable. It is in the courtier's inverted notion of what is desirable that her shrewishness itself originates. Such is the charge she levels at her father for his overvaluation of Bianca:

> She is your treasure, she must have a husband;
> I must dance barefoot on her wedding-day,
> And for your love to her lead apes in hell.
> Talk not to me, I will go sit and weep,
> Till I can find occasion of revenge. (II.i.32–6)

Having created a dilemma where the desirable woman is unavailable and the available woman is undesirable, Shakespeare brings on Petruchio to transform Kate into something other than a shrew, but not something that conforms exactly to the courtly notion of desirability.

This refashioning of Kate as an object of desire takes the form of linguistic reform. Gremio says of his master, that Petruchio "will throw a figure in her face, and so disfigure her with it" (I.ii.113–14). Petruchio in turn announces that his disfiguring of the shrew will be governed by various strategies of dissimulation. He announces first that his speech will be governed by strategies of inversion, allegory, and reversal:

> Say that she rail, why then I'll tell her plain
> She sings as sweetly as a nightingale;
> Say that she frown, I'll say she looks as clear

As morning roses newly wash'd with dew; . . .
If she do bid me pack, I'll give her thanks,
As though she bid me stay by her a week;
If she deny to wed, I'll crave the day
When I shall ask the banes, and when be married. (II.i.170–80)

These lines play on well-known figures of courtier love poetry. In turning to Puttenham's discussion of courtier writing, one finds them in the chapter entitled "Of sensable figures altering and affecting the mynde by alteration of sence in whole clauses or speeches." Petruchio proposes among other things to employ antiphrasis, which Puttenham describes as the figure one uses to speak "plaine and flat contradiction, as he that saw a dwarfe go in the street said to his companion . . . see yonder Gyant."[45] According to Puttenham, antiphrasis acts along with related figures of speech using conceit, metaphor, irony, or enigma as, "souldiers to the figure *allegoria*." Allegoria is the courtly figure one uses "when we speake one thing and thinke another, and that our wordes and our meanings meet not."[46] With it one may "fight vnder the banner of dissimulations." Despite the element of game inherent in the figures of dissimulation, such troping is used by courtier, counselor, and prince "in earnest as well as in sport."

Petruchio is a courtly figure, of a noble father, having come to Padua "to wive it wealthily." Neither sentimentalist nor mercenary, he is about the very serious business of marriage, and the mock combat he wages with Kate becomes more than a means of wooing. It is a struggle to define the aristocratic female herself in a way that makes her both valuable and accessible to him. As Petruchio begins to woo Kate, Shakespeare casts their exchange into a punning contest. Since the pun always sets two incompatible meanings of a word in a contestatory relationship, this use of puns thus recasts the battle between courtier and the object of his desire as a battle between two ways of defining that relationship. The outcome depends upon which has the stronger claim to referentiality. These memorable lines constitute a round of such verbal combat which goes to Petruchio:

Pet.   Come, come, you wasp, i' faith you are too angry.
Kath.   If I be waspish, best beware my sting.
Pet.   My remedy is then to pluck it out.
Kath.   Ay, if the fool could find it where it lies.
Pet.   Who knows not where a wasp does wear his sting?
In his tail.
Kath.   In his tongue.
Pet.   Whose tongue?
Kath.   Yours, if you talk of tales, and so farewell.

Pet.　　What, with my tongue in your tail? Nay, come again,
　　　　Good Kate; I am a gentleman –
Kath.　　That I'll try.　　　　　　*She strikes him.* (II.i.209–19)

It is particularly evident here that Kate's shrewishness provides a form of resistance in the face of a political structure where silent submission makes a woman desirable. Petruchio takes her on in verbal combat – her stinging critique of male authority against his language of the body. We watch her terms give way before puns which translate them into somatic images that assert her sexual subordination to him as "tongue" and "tale" cease to refer to her stinging language and instead constitute the grotesque figure of his penetration of her body. Punning takes the "tongue" from her mouth as well as the sting from her "tale" and bestows all the power of her coarse speech upon Petruchio, who uses this "tongue" to turn Kate into the object of a crude sexual joke. Simply put, the turns in their terms appropriate her "tongue" and insert it in her "tail," thus inverting the inversion of power relations Kate created by speaking in the tongue of a fishwife in the first place.

　　Having established Petruchio as the agent of such disfigurement, Shakespeare proceeds to define a form of resistance quite different from that of an unruly woman. He appears at their wedding in apparel which mocks the official ceremonies of state. Though not a member of the people by birth, he bears certain features of the other social body in his monstrously heterogeneous dress and, as such, makes the self-fashioning power of the courtier to debase rather than to exalt an aristocratic bearing:

> a new hat and an old jerkin; a pair of old breeches thrice turn'd; a pair of boots that have been candle-cases, one buckled, another lac'd; an old rusty sword ta'en out of the town armory, with a broken hilt and chapeless. . . . (III.ii.43–8)

His horse is lame, its gear is in disarray, and his servant is described as "a monster, a very monster in apparel, and not like a Christian footboy or a gentleman's lackey" (III.ii.69–71). By giving Petruchio those features of the grotesque body, Shakespeare puts Kate in a curious situation. Refusing to heed Petruchio's order that the couple depart for Verona, Kate again asserts herself in opposition to him, "I see a woman may be made a fool, / If she had not a spirit to resist" (III.ii.220–1). Resistance, in other words, now authorizes the very ceremonies of state it once obstructed, while Petruchio exercises his male prerogative, first, to infuse the solemn ceremony of marriage with the spirit of carnival:

> Go to the feast, revel and domineer,
> Carouse full measure to her maidenhead,
> Be mad and merry, or go hang yourselves. . . . (III.ii.224–6)

Again, what Shakespeare does by setting the dialogue of male and female in this contestatory relationship is to translate the official forms of power into the material practices of the body which those forms displace and debase. He has Petruchio carry the levelling process one step further and describe the body of the aristocratic female for what it really is in the system of exchange:

> I will be master of what is mine own.
> She is my goods, my chattels, she is my house,
> My household stuff, my field, my barn,
> My horse, my ox, my ass, my any thing. . . . (III.ii.229–32)

As such, Kate has value, but hers is not that of the Petrarchan mistress whose value lies in the metaphysics of blood.

This description of Kate in fact removes her from the Petrarchan ideal as far as she could be, according to Elizabethan thinking, and still mirror the form of desirability embodied by Bianca. To drive home this point, then, Shakespeare has Petruchio treat Kate as if she were the idealized figure celebrated in courtier verse and romance, that is, as if she existed in denial of the material practices of the body. She is kept hungry by a husband fearful lest she be served anything but food flawlessly prepared. Her solicitous husband prefers to read to her from moral and religious tracts rather than to consummate their marriage. By this means, he prevents her from sleeping as well as eating. He treats her, in short, as if she were indeed something other than that material body which is figured in terms of eating, procreating, drinking, and sleeping.

On first glance, the banquet scene with which Shakespeare concludes the play may appear a somewhat gratuitous gesture. Kate's role as the figure of resistance to aristocratic practices and patriarchal authority has been neutralized. With Kate tamed, the exchange of women can proceed: the wedding of mercantile interests is contracted between Hortensio and the widow and the sentimental liaison between Lucentio and Bianca is ratified. One might argue, however, if the goal of comedy is to marry off the next generation, then Shakespeare accomplishes his comic aims before the last scene begins. Indeed, it might strike us as heavy-handed, if not heartless, for him to stage a scene that displays once again Kate's utter domestication and the subservience of her tongue to her master's interests. To take her words at face value, we must assume Shakespeare approved of Petruchio's breaking her spirit. Alternatively, one might regard Shakespeare as a protomodernist and read Kate's as a wonderfully ironic statement. But to accept these as the poles within which we can understand Kate's behavior, is I think, to miss the point entirely. I would like to suggest – contrary to both traditional interpretations of this scene –

that this scene gives Kate real political power for the first time in the play. If she is no longer the Petrarchan ideal, neither is Kate the fishwife and bawd. In remaking her language, Petruchio appears to have invalidated the opposition that initiated the action of the play and prevented the inclusion of various women in the system of sexual exchange.

The banquet scene is no afterthought but a resolution to the problem which Shakespeare posed at the opening of the play. Shakespeare does not strip from Kate's speech the aggressive features which made her a vigorous figure throughout the play. He does, however, direct her aggression against the other – supposedly more desirable – women in the play. Bianca overthrew her father's rule, and married herself to Lucentio in defiance of the principle of patriarchal prerogative. Once married, then, she overthrew her husband's authority by refusing to heed his summons. Shakespeare gives Kate the power to reorder these unruly women. He makes her more obedient than they so that she may beat them into submission. Then he gives her nothing less than powers of speech which appear to authorize patriarchal power itself:

> Thy husband is thy lord, thy life, thy keeper,
> Thy head, thy sovereign; one that cares for thee,
> And for thy maintenance; commits his body
> To painful labor . . .
> Whilst thou li'st warm at home, secure and safe;
> And craves no other tribute at thy hands
> But love, fair looks and true obedience –
> Too little payment for so great a debt. (V.ii.146–54)

Neither cruelty nor irony must have prompted Shakespeare to put these words in the mouth of the reformed shrew, I believe, for he gives her the most important political lines in the play. These explain the politics of sexual exchange. As they express the sentiments of a grateful client, furthermore, these lines imply the power of theatrical display to authorize certain forms of desire. Thus Kate concludes, "Such duty as the subject owes the prince, / Even such a woman oweth to her husband." Shakespeare apparently identified his own performance with Kate's, understanding both as acts of service which empowered and legitimized power. Be the power of husband/monarch arbitrary, seemingly limitless, or humane, it is still the source of power, including even the power of resistance. Shakespeare offers an extravagant acknowledgment of this fact as Kate places her hand beneath Petruchio's foot.

This willful act of humiliation demonstrates the paradoxical relation of subjection to power which is the other side of Renaissance overreaching. It is worth recalling that the Renaissance state had little in the way of domestic police or even a standing army, let alone something as sophisticated as a secret police. Its totalitarian government depended largely on the subject's willingness to submit to the monarch. That the subject in such a situation had the power to authorize state power seems to be the point of the scene in which Kate and Petruchio encounter Lucentio's father on the road back to Padua. When Petruchio makes Kate address the old man as if he were a young girl or describe the sun as if it were the moon, he is demanding nothing less of her than to grant him the power to determine the identity of things and what words mean. Making her submit to his terms of speech is, in other words, Petruchio's primary method of taming the shrew. In the banquet scene, Kate demonstrates her own power to refashion him from a madman and a fool into a wise and enviable man — because he has married the most desirable of the three women. She uses her Rabelaisian energy along with her position as aristocratic female to reassert the hierarchy of husband to wife which invokes that of subject to sovereign. Even as he reinscribes her within a patriarchal hierarchy, however, Shakespeare has given this heroine a range of linguistic features that includes the many social voices of the play from Sly to Baptista. In dismantling the opposition between fabliaux heroine and Petrarchan lady, then, Shakespeare has produced a reformed speech which goes beyond the semiotic limits of that opposition to figure forth a society that is rigidly hierarchical and more inclusionary at once.

VII

I have no doubt Shakespeare knew perfectly well the degree to which desires arise from symbolic behavior. Because certain critical theories have allowed us to consider the possibility that political thinking is less sophisticated than Shakespeare's, we might mistakenly congratulate him for this prescience where the material power of language is concerned. It is of course we who for the past two hundred years or so have privileged language that disappears into the thing represented, even if the "thing" in question is artistic consciousness itself. Far from holding a modern view of language, Shakespeare and his peers evidently granted their audience acute awareness both of the cultural materials with which the dramatist worked, and of the consequences of his revisionary moves. This would mean that literary characters were valued to the degree they could be identified with recognizable rhetorical strategies. In another cultural arena, as I have argued, such strategies were used to negotiate relations between the queen, her counselors, and her courtiers. They informed rituals of state, gift-giving ceremonies, royal progresses, and even public executions. The public display of these strategies on the stage instigated bitter debate among churchmen and divided religious sects. In a society where all manner of cultural practices — dress and architecture, for instance — were read in terms of rhetorical conceits, the symbolic in general and writing in particular were recognized as instruments in the social construction of the individual. Rhetorical handbooks themselves explained figures of speech simply by anthropomorphizing them in the manner of Puttenham. Peachem, for one, demonstrated this point still more emphatically when, in *The Garden of Eloquence*, he called them "martiall instruments both of defence & invasion."

If there is one Shakespearean drama more than any other that declares the political importance of writing, it is *The Merchant of Venice*. For all their differences, the two arenas of dramatic action, Venice and Belmont, have this in common: writing determines what reality is and therefore the role an individual can play. Because contracts underwrite the economic life of Venice, that type of writing is so powerful not even the duke can modify it. In Belmont, similarly, her father's will constrains Portia's behavior, specifies the conditions for her marriage, and determines who shall control the father's patrimony. While these two places oppose one another in terms of where the authority of writing originates — in economic arrangements or in a father's will — they concur on the fundamental point that authority resides in and operates through writing.

Belmont is constituted of thoroughly familiar pieces of writing. The story of a beautiful maid withheld from the world by her dead father's wishes is the material of Arcadian romance. Desire for the woman intensifies under such conditions, and courtiers from around the world compete for the patriarchal power that comes with possession of the daughter. Thus Belmont affords another instance where Shakespeare materializes the political fantasy that shapes courtier writing. Those who fail to win admission to this world through the wooing of Portia are those who fail to understand this principle. Morocco is the case in point. Speaking in the manner of an overreacher, much like Tamburlaine he says:

> By this scimitar
> That slew the Sophy and a Persian prince
> That won three fields of Sultan Solyman,
> I would o'erstare the sternest eyes that look,
> Outbrave the heart most daring on the earth, . . .
> To win [thee], lady. (II.i.24–31)

Such language confuses the value inhering in the woman's body with that arising from sources within the individual. As Morocco says, "to be afeard of my deserving / Were but a weak disabling of myself" (II.vii.29–30).

From this position in relation to the economy of court he sees the woman's value as equivalent or even dependent on gold in the manner of the gemstone to its setting. His speech uses the aristocratic female to suggest another source of value beyond her blood but accruing to it: "never so rich a gem / Was set in worse than gold" (lines 54–5). Morocco chooses the golden casket because he views Portia as the fitting sign of his worth within a patronage system which offers money as the alternative to the privileges deriving from blood.

Arragon's speech is equally familiar. It is the language of the malcontent or failed overreacher. But this does not place Arragon in opposition to Morocco, for both misunderstand the economy of courtly discourse; Arragon's choice of the silver casket is not all that much different from Morocco's choice of the gold. Like the man who contests inherited title and territory on the basis of his own strength or cunning, Arragon assaults the metaphysics of blood when he voices the typical malcontent's complaint against a system that does not mete out reward on the basis of merit alone:

> Let none presume
> To wear an undeserved dignity.
> O that estates, degrees, and offices
> Were not deriv'd corruptly, and that clear honor
> Were purchas'd by the merit of the wearer! (II.ix.39–43)

This twist in the logic of patronage sees silver as more valuable than gold because "common spirits" and "the barbarous multitude" value gold. But to make this claim for silver is doubly doomed to fail, first, in terms of the market economy, but secondly and more fundamentally, in terms of a courtly economy that makes blood the source of all other value including that of gold itself.

Of the three competitors, Bassanio wins because he alone adheres to the metaphysics of blood that courtier writing professes. He understands that all of Portia's value derives not from her wealth or land but from what Portia calls her "gentle spirit." While other suitors sought to decipher the father's will by drawing some direct relationship between desire for Portia and desire for money, Bassanio alone aims desire at the woman and the power she embodies by virtue of being whose daughter she is. By winning Portia, of course, he wins her wealth, just as Lorenzo does when he steals Jessica from Shylock. In believing in the value of blood, we should note, Bassanio does not value the woman for "herself" any more than he does for her money; these are modern alternatives. Rather, he exalts the entire community of blood over the value of any particular member in a magical calculus that underlies Portia's profession of devotion to this particular suitor. She says,

> for you,
> I would be trebled twenty times myself,
> A thousand times more fair, ten thousand times more rich,
> That only to stand high in your account,
> I might in virtues, beauties, livings, friends,
> Exceed account. (III.ii.152–7)

Nor does Shakespeare mean to diminish such power by having it depend to such a degree on the successful troping of courtiers. To the contrary, in calling forth a particular solution, the riddle of the caskets acknowledges the reciprocal relationship between those who were entitled to power by blood and those who would woo and pursue such power by devising various rhetorical performances as testimony to the value of noble birth. Shakespeare demonstrates this reciprocity of patron and courtier by awarding Portia to Bassanio for observing the figure of *false semblant*, Puttenham's figure of the courtier himself. Unlike Arragon who quite arbitrarily claims silver more valuable than gold, or Morocco who considers gold the measure of value, Bassanio uses the principle of inversion to decode the caskets: ". . . the outward shows be least themselves – / The world is still deceiv'd with ornament" (III.ii.73–4).

In the game of selecting the caskets by means of which Bassanio courts Portia, wooing constitutes a political practice. It is in such terms that Bassanio pleads for the chance to enter into the game of courtship, and in pleading, displays his ability to perform the tropes of love. The courtier performance begins with a familiar conceit: "Let me choose, / For as I am, I live upon the rack" (III.ii.24–5). Its political component emerges as Portia asks him to explain the offence for which he has been subjected to such punishment. Investing all hope for gratification in the sexual relationship he desires, Bassanio explains that any other form of gratification constitutes treason, "There may as well be amity and life / 'Tween snow and fire, as treason and my love" (III.ii.31–2). Typically extravagant in drawing a comparison between patriotism and the elements of nature ("snow and fire") this conceit uses the figure of comparison to de-familiarize desire and political loyalty, as if this coupling of categories were not a strange one in the first place.

The political theme emerges still more clearly, then, when Bassanio correctly performs the courtier's role and selects the leaden casket. Shakespeare has Portia profess her subjection to Bassanio in terms of precisely the same homological relationship between sexual and political relations that organizes Kate's speech at the end of *The Taming of the Shrew*. In the earlier play this homology asserted that the relationship between sovereign and subject could be dramatized, confirmed, even constructed in and through the relationship of wife to husband. Much the same thing is at stake, then, in *Merchant*. Here, too, the dramatic action aims at producing a set of terms for totalizing the same form of subjection and making this form desirable. Thus we find Portia, like Kate, rewarding her suitor with tangible political power in return for his fidelity to the idea that power flows strictly from her. Her power, she says,

> Commits itself to yours to be directed,
> As from her lord, her governor, her king.
> Myself, and what is mine, to you and yours
> Is now converted. But now I was the lord
> Of this fair mansion, master of my servants,
> Queen o'er myself; and even now, but now,
> This house, these servants, and this same myself
> Are yours – my lord's! – I give them with this ring. . . . (III.ii.164–71)

Where such a statement could both effect and announce the construction of a comprehensive social order in *Taming*, however, the words of the aristocratic Portia conspicuously lack the power to constitute such a totalizing order. For the mercantile language of Venice infiltrates the romance world immediately after this profession of love and proves more powerful than any marriage contract binding members within the aristocratic body. News arrives to the effect that Antonio's ships have failed and that Shylock intends to enforce the terms of their agreement and the symbolic practices of sexual exchange in Belmont quickly give way before the economic contracts of Venice. The economic contract binding Antonio to Shylock combines with the more subtle bonding of male to male in a patronage relationship to demonstrate the power over and above the courtly discourse of Belmont.

The power of mercantile language can be largely attributed to its capacity for appropriating the signs and symbols of the grotesque body and the aristocratic body as well. It is in opposition to both that Shylock, the very embodiment of mercantile logic, understands his interests. Shylock seeks to profit from the voracious mouth of Venice – Lancelot Gobbo. In Shylock's service Gobbo is kept hungry, and Shylock only agrees to release him to join Bassanio's household with the expectation that Gobbo's habits will sap the strength of its aristocratic largesse. Shylock describes Gobbo as "a huge feeder" whom he sends "to waste" Bassanio's borrowed purse (II.v.46–52). As for aristocratic hospitality, Shylock turns that into an occasion to "feed upon/The prodigal Christian"

(II.v.14–15). At every turn, his language uses the figures of feast and festival to assault the aristocratic body. At the same time, such usage saps the vigor and joy of festival, as Shylock says to Jessica:

> Lock up my doors, and when you hear the drum
> And the vile squealing of the wry-neck'd fife,
> Clamber not you up to the casements then.
> Nor thrust your head into the public street
> To gaze on Christian fools with varnish'd faces;
> But stop my house's ears. . . . (II.v.29–34)

As he has Shylock play one off against the other, then, Shakespeare does not set the grotesque body in opposition to that of the aristocracy in this comedy. Rather, Shylock represents a source of power hostile to them both.

He uses the principle of scarcity against the insatiable hunger of the grotesque body. He also uses the principle of profit against the largesse of the patronage system. Both figures represent corporate bodies, their power deriving from the metaphysics of blood and the desires of the flesh respectively. By way of contrast, Shylock seeks to individuate the collective body, to substitute profit for metaphysics, and to convert flesh into gold. The perverse alchemy of Shylock's argument makes literal the substitution of flesh for money. He holds gold can breed gold just as Laban's sheep reproduced for Jacob's profit, and when Jessica elopes, adopting a logic quite antithetical to Bassanio's reading of the caskets – Shylock's speech confuses her with his precious metals: "My daughter! O my ducats! O my daughter! / Fled with a Christian! O my Christian ducats" (II.viii.15–16). Where Bassanio's casket speech presumes blood to be the only thing of value, mercantile language finds no value in blood or offspring but only in stones and metals. Shylock thus represents the loss of his daughter as a form of castration. "A sealed bag, two sealed bags of ducats," Shylock is reported to have cried, "And jewels, two stones, two rich and precious stones, / Stol'n by my daughter" (lines 19–21).

In seeking to translate flesh into gold, Shylock's mercantile language regularly attacks the body's desires. When he imagines his daughter, it is as a dead object encased with the gems and precious metals she has stolen, "I would my daughter were dead at my foot, and the jewels in her ear! Would she were hears'd at my foot, and the ducats in her coffin" (III.i.88–90). It is on these grounds, then, that the voices of street and festival make mockery of him. "Why, all the boys in Venice follow him, / Crying, his stones, his daughter, and his ducats" (II.viii.23–4) in celebration of his loss of power over the flesh. But despite his opposition to the pleasures of the flesh, Shylock's real threat lies in his opposition to the aristocratic body. Nowhere is this clearer than when he describes aristocratic bounty as "waste." It is important to distinguish Shylock from the forces that more commonly oppose aristocratic power. The Machiavel and the overreacher, for example, give voice to the aristocratic model for power; they only take issue with it in advocating merit rather than blood as the basis for possessing and dispensing aristocratic prerogatives. In contrast, the mercantile language of Shylock speaks solely of scarcity and profit. In this, it contradicts the economic principles at the heart of the aristocratic system. In Shylock's economy, power comes from the withholding of wealth and not from the power to endow.

Of all the ways Shakespeare could have chosen to overthrow the power of mercantile language, it is important that he chose the figure of the unruly woman.[47] Indeed everywhere in the romantic comedies this figure is brought by elaborate strategies of plot to serve the means of authorizing a traditional hierarchy. Jessica assumes the role of unruly woman when she dresses as a boy to escape her father. Portia adopts the role of a judge to break Shylock's hold on the Venetian economy. In Belmont, then, Shakespeare gives Portia the ribald language of the unruly woman to reorder the patronage system binding Bassanio to Antonio. When Shylock makes human flesh quite specifically the referent for the coin of the city, Portia inverts his strategy of interpretation. In doing so, what is more, she fixes words to their referent more securely than Shylock does. He refuses the offer of any alternate form of compensation as well as the request for a surgeon at hand to prevent Antonio from bleeding to death on grounds that "'tis not in the bond" (IV.i.262). Having eliminated the possibility of any flexibility in interpretation, he is vulnerable to an interpretation that observes the letter of the contract even more rigidly than his. In Portia's words:

> This bond doth give thee here no jot of blood;
> The words expressly are "a pound of flesh."
> Take then thy bond, take thou thy pound of flesh,
> But in the cutting it, if thou dost shed
> One drop of Christian blood, thy lands and goods
> Are by the laws of Venice confiscate
> Unto the state of Venice. (IV.i.306–12)

In this manner, her reading of the contract cancels out Shylock's contract by paradoxically equating the fulfillment of its terms with their violation. But while this rhetorical victory frees Antonio and therefore makes the practice of patronage once again possible in Venice, the problem with the language of romance in Belmont remains unresolved. It still appears helpless before the language of patronage relations in Venice. We might say then that Portia's triumph over Shylock only clears the stage for this other, more primary symbolic struggle.

The problem with the language of patronage in Venice is that it fails to understand itself as a substitute for the language of courtship. Thus both Bassanio and Gratiano are too ready to discount the symbolic power of the ring and glove they received when they plighted troth in Belmont. Bassanio says to Antonio just before the judge's decision is rendered,

> Antonio, I am married to a wife
> Which is as dear to me as life itself,
> But life itself, my wife, and all the world,
> Are not with me esteem'd above thy life.
> I would lose all, ay, sacrifice them all
> Here to this devil, to deliver you. (IV.i.282–7)

And Gratiano wishes his wife in heaven "so she could / Entreat some power to change this currish Jew" (IV.i.291–2). When the judge later asks for some token from Antonio's friends, Portia invokes that same language of love, saying to Bassanio:

> for your love I'll take this ring from you.
> Do not draw back your hand, I'll take no more,
> And you in love shall not deny me this! (IV.i.427–9)

The love to which she refers, of course, is that binding men to men in patronage relationships. Lest we should miss the point, Shakespeare reiterates it when Antonio declares the patronage bond is stronger than even the marriage vow:

> My Lord Bassanio, let him have the ring.
> Let his deservings and my love withal
> Be valued 'gainst your wive's commandement. (IV.i.449–51)

This contract brings the bond of patronage into direct conflict with the rules of kinship relations. They cannot coexist within the same system of social relations so long as the client of patronage uses the signs and symbols of courtship to acquire power from a source other than blood, that is, from wealth or even from law.

If not before, then by this point in the play, it is clear Shakespeare has created a problem which can only be resolved by a transvestite – a woman who in Belmont, though a maid, confers the power of her father, and who in Venice puts on patriarchal power with the robes of the law. Only in this way – by a female who assumes the mantle of patriarch – can all the contending forms of power in the play be taken up and embodied symbolically in a single person and language. Far from gratuitous, the last act – for all its playfulness – demonstrates the single source of power in all symbolic forms, particularly that of speech. It is significant that it is ribald speech – speech usually reserved for negotiating sexual relationships in the tavern – that Shakespeare gives Portia, like Petruchio before her, as the language through which to display the full range of her power to determine meaning and, with meaning, the true order of social relationships. She uses the ring – first given to Bassanio to empower her father's authority in Belmont, then taken from him as a sign of his fealty to his patron in Venice – as a sign of the material body and, more specifically, of the body's openness and susceptibility to impregnation.

Her playful use of the ring in the last act thus captures in a single figure the semiotic transformation wrought by the drama as a whole, making this punning on Portia's part something on the order of Shakespeare's signature on his work. With it, he makes what we must consider a characteristic cultural maneuver. He creates a situation where the courtly language of love appears to give way before symbolic practices associated with carnival, namely, the material practices of the body. This is to say that courtly dissimulation yields to a more literal meaning as Portia plays with the meaning of her ring:

> Since he hath got the jewel that I loved,
> And that which you did swear to keep for me,
> I will become as liberal as you,
> I'll not deny him anything I have,
> No, not my body nor my husband's bed. . . .
> I'll have that doctor for [my] bedfellow. (V.i.224–33)

Portia uses the ring to signify the ring of flesh, which, of course, Bassanio has given away out of love for his patron. To use the language of love in this situation is for Bassanio to cuckold himself willfully, provided one attaches his profession of love, in this case, to its referent. Or rather, Bassanio would have irrevocably broken the sacred vows of love and behaved in the manner of a bawd were it not for the fact that Shakespeare used Portia herself much like a pun, as the desired object of Bassanio's courtly speech in Belmont as well as the patron of Bassanio's patron in Venice.

Only because she fills both these roles – female and male respectively – and only because both are finally embodied in a woman, can the play mediate the contrary bases of power represented by Belmont and Venice. When she gives the ring to Antonio to give to Bassanio, she rescues Bassanio from his folly and reveals her own status as the pun: "Pardon me, Bassanio, / For by this ring, the doctor lay with me" (V.i.258–9). The play works its transformations through the figure of the unruly woman and her speech of street and tavern. The comic magic is effective because the tropes of courtly writing are bodied forth upon the stage in such a popular figure who threatens to act out the somatic consequences of these tropes. Even using such popular materials to mock the practices of court, however, Shakespeare adheres strictly to the metaphysics of blood. If Portia is a pun of sorts, it is to demonstrate that all meaning derives from her, just as surely as all political power derives from her and the patriarchal word that she embodies.

VIII

That heroines possessing the power of patriarchy should regularly appear on the stage during the 1590s and not later, obviously had something to do with the fact that a female monarch was on the throne. By this I do not mean to suggest that these heroines stood in any allegorical relation to Elizabeth. I am only suggesting that during this period it became possible to imagine patriarchal power embodied in a female, which obviously opened a whole new set of possibilities for representing power on the stage. Each of Shakespeare's heroines indeed enacts, problematizes, and resolves the issues of how power was distributed in England. This is no doubt one reason why such a politically literate audience as Shakespeare's attended the popular theater in the first place. Even as it expanded the possibilities for imagining power, however, the public theater actually served Elizabeth's interests by presenting visible and readily accessible signs of the metaphysics of blood.

In the concluding moments of *The Merchant of Venice*, Shakespeare seizes the occasion to bring forth the political configuration governing each of the romantic comedies. Portia gives her ring to Antonio, and he in turn gives it to Bassanio. Antonio promises to be the bond for Bassanio's fidelity, and Bassanio is once more given the patrimony left by Portia's father. For the third time in this play, then, we see the female invested with the patriarchal prerogatives of status, wealth, and power, and for the third time, too, we see the female transfer the patrimony to the man she desires. Her desire thus appears instrumental in the acquisition of such power. What is true of *The Merchant of Venice* in this regard is true of all of the romantic comedies. Each makes it seem that female desire for the male is the essential means of acquiring patriarchal power, and each comedy in turn poses a slightly different problem for which the self-subordination of an aristocratic woman offers the only comic (as opposed to violent) solution. To generalize further, at the beginning of each comedy it appears that power originates with the male. Portia's father, Petruchio, Don Pedro and Claudio, Duke Frederick and Oliver, are all cases in point. As my discussion of both *The Taming of the Shrew* and *The Merchant of Venice* has argued, there is a moment in every comedy which transfers this power to the aristocratic female. Portia restores – as if by magic – Antonio's ships and with them the proper order of political relationships. Rosalind apparently has the power to call down Hymen to sanctify her betrothal. Kate is not only the very pattern of wifely obedience but also the one who enforces her model upon other women. But even though Shakespeare endows each of his heroines with certain patriarchal prerogatives, this move always constitutes one step in a double move which relocates power in the male by way of marriage. Shakespeare thus restores the natural hierarchy of social relations as the wife subordinates herself to her husband. Having been so transferred from male to female and back again, however, the very nature of power changes. Because she authorizes the male, power appears to originate in the female. With her restoration of power to the male, furthermore, the social order becomes more flexible and inclusive. The comic form itself depends upon such a transformation which increases the aristocratic community through marriage without ever impugning the purity of its blood.

Shakespearean comedy thus materializes the double bind which organizes many of the cultural products of Elizabeth's reign. This double bind sets the imperative to seek membership in the community of blood against the imperative to keep the community pure. It is this double bind, I have argued, which shapes the Petrarchan fantasy as well as the comedies which so regularly parody the representation of sexual desire among the elite. Petrarchan writing always situates us outside of the community of blood. By definition it always fixes the gaze on that which is metaphysically other than the gazer as the male attempts to make himself desirable to a female of a significantly higher station by representing his desire for her in extravagant terms. By way of contrast, Shakespearean comedy foregrounds the instrumentality of female desire. The multiple marriages at a comedy's conclusion make it seem as if desire had brought about a politically homogeneous community. At the same time, desire also preserves the sexual hierarchy, for the subordination of wife to husband invariably invokes that of subject to king. On stage, furthermore, the dress of the various candidates for the hand of the heroine would have indicated all the distinctions of rank and the matching and mismatching of partners in a visually political game.

Given that the transfer of power from aristocratic female to a male counterpart is such a crucial feature of these comedies, given too, that this transfer depends on the desire of the aristocratic female, it was perhaps inevitable that as Shakespeare worked and reworked with the materials of Elizabethan writing he would eventually focus exclusively on the nature and instrumentality of female desire itself. I would like to consider *Twelfth Night* as the play in which the playwright strips away other political issues to consider the dilemma arising when the aristocratic female lacks the kind of desire that elsewhere in the comedies provides the glue for a social world that is both homogeneous and hierarchical.

If nothing else, Petrarchan language authorizes the metaphysics of blood. And therein lies the upside-downness of Orsino's position in *Twelfth Night*. As Duke of Illyria, he embodies all the magic of blood. In using the language of the aspiring courtier, then, Orsino uses figures of speech to negotiate sexual relations which completely overturn his position of political superiority in relation to Olivia. His opening speech, "If music be the food of love, play on," aestheticizes love by dislodging it from its political body. Thus Orsino's courtier dialect makes him appear, as if he were politically disenfranchised. Though empowered politically by virtue of his noble birth, the joke is that Orsino finds himself in the female position of being the desired object, only lacking the female's power to inspire desire. That is to say, he finds himself in the position of not being the object of desire but the desiring subject. The relationship may fulfill the ideals of courtier writing, but it also demonstrates how restrictive that kind of writing is; it places one outside of the empowered community. The more Olivia withholds herself, the more Orsino desires her, and thus he invests her with the power that should normally be his. This comic dilemma becomes demonstrably clear as Shakespeare marshalls the clichés of the Petrarchan lover, to represent the state to which Olivia's withholding has reduced Orsino. It is as if Orsino were no more than a Lucentio upon first gazing at the silent Bianca:

> O, when mine eyes did see Olivia first,
> Methought she purg'd the air of pestilence!
> That instant was I turned into a hart,
> And my desires, like fell and cruel hounds,
> E'er since pursue me. (I.i.18–22)

Rather than occupying a position of political power where he would be the object of the gaze, Orsino has placed himself in the role of the gazer. He has put himself in a position where his value depends upon Olivia's desire, and given her the power to refuse him. It is of course foolish for an aristocrat to discount the value of his blood, and dangerous to imagine the aristocratic body divided in this manner. Orsino has allowed himself to become yet one more competitor. We might note that, despite Orsino's tendency to lose sight of this point, desire always has its political significance in this play. Shakespeare never allows his audience to forget that the absence of desire in Olivia is tantamount to political disruption.

Her rejection of Orsino calls into question all the criteria for determining one's political station. Sir Toby explains, "She'll none o' th' Count. She'll not match above her degree, neither in estate, years, nor wit; I have heard her swear't" (I.iii.109–11).

If Orsino perversely assumes the role of courtier at the beginning of the play where he should be the one to stand aloof, at play's end he fails to sue for the hand of Viola, a fact which has disturbed those modern critics who wish Shakespeare had written a sentimental romance rather than a Renaissance romantic comedy. Neglecting to display any sign of desire for his intended, Orsino merely says to Cesario, "Boy, thou hast said to me a thousand times / Thou never shouldst love woman like to me" (V.i.267–8). It is Viola who then assumes the role of courtier in repeating her earlier professions of love:

> And all those sayings will I over swear,
> And all those swearings keep as true in soul
> As doth that orbed continent the fire
> That severs day from night. (V.i.269–72)

Though it flies in the face of our own sense of normal behavior, Cesario's performance reinscribes sexual relationships within the prevailing hierarchy of political relations. At this moment in the play, one might say, Shakespeare has rewritten Olivia as the Viola who steps forth to fill the role of desiring subject. This gesture restores the social order as female desire authorizes aristocratic blood.

Orsino is not Shakespeare's only means of inverting the courtier fantasy; Cesario does much the same thing. A young courtier in the service of the duke, Cesario has to speak the language of aristocratic love in order to win the desire of the previously unavailable lady, Olivia. In this case, however, courtier language again misfires as it succeeds in winning the love of a woman for a woman. Shakespeare uses the figure of the transvestite to question the role of female desire, its object, and thus by implication the nature of the bond uniting the aristocratic community itself. As a transvestite, Cesario embodies all the features of the trope which personifies the courtier. As Puttenham explains,

> the Courtly figure *Allegoria* which is when we speake one thing and thinke another, and that our wordes and our meanings meete not . . . his principall vertue . . . is when we do speake in sence translatiue and wrested from the one signification, neuerthelese applied to another not altogether contrary. . . . (p. 155)

Indeed, Olivia falls in love with Cesario when she regards his words allegorically: "I am not that I play," (I.v.184) and "What I am, and what I would, are as secret as maidenhead: to your ears divinity" (I.v.215–17). Not only does he declare himself the figure of false seeming, Cesario also uses the Petrarchan strategy of appealing to the lady's pity. Cesario explains that were he so rejected by her as Orsino has been, he would respond with cantos "of contemned love" to

> Hallow your name to the reverberate hills,
> And make the babbling gossip of the air
> Cry out "Olivia!" O, you should not rest
> Between the elements of air and earth
> But you should pity me! (I.v.272–6)

Sounding very much like Sidney's Astrophel, Cesario offers Olivia a text which echoes her name. To accept this invitation to hear her name sounded in poetry is for Olivia to succumb to self-love. The courtier's verse allows her to imagine Cesario as the perfect mirror of herself, to wit, Shakespeare has the page protest once again "I am not what I am." And he has Olivia respond with a figure that similarly dissolves the boundary between self and other, not the boundary between the sexes, we should note, but that between different social positions: "I would you were as I would have you be" (III.i.142). Under similar conditions, Sebastian agrees to marry Olivia as if he were being dreamed by another:

> For though my soul disputes well with my sense,
> That this may be some error, but no madness,
> Yet doth this accident and flood of fortune
> So far exceed all instance, all discourse,
> That I am ready to distrust mine eyes,
> And wrangle with my reason that persuades me
> To any other trust but that I am mad,
> Or else the lady's mad; yet if 'twere so,
> She could not sway her house, command her followers, . . .
> With such a smooth, discreet, and stable bearing
> As I perceive she does. (IV.iii.9–20)

On the basis of this reasoning he willingly accepts Olivia's invitation to marry.

And in such fashion Olivia fulfills the comic heroine's function of empowering the object of her desire, first declaring love to Cesario, then marrying his twin brother. The fact she marries Sebastian does not pose a problem. For Shakespeare, at least, such doubling provides the corrective to the doubling of desire which courtly poetry engendered. Sebastian is, after all, of the same blood as Viola/Cesario and the original for whom Viola substituted herself when she assumed her disguise in the first place.

When Olivia first falls in love with Cesario, furthermore, she reads the signs of this lineage in his lineaments. It is such a reading that draws out her desire. Mulling over the answer to her query about Cesario's parentage, she says,

> "Above my fortunes, yet my state is well:
> I am a gentleman." I'll be sworn thou art;
> Thy tongue, thy face, thy limbs, actions, and spirit
> Do give thee fivefold blazon. (I.v.290–3)

Thus she reads the body as a genealogical text whose nature reveals a noble birth beneath a page's dress. To pursue this line of thinking is to credit Olivia with reading the body quite accurately in Elizabethan terms, for what makes it desirable is first and foremost the iconic value of blood. Clearly that is what is meant when she says,

> Methinks I feel this youth's perfections
> With an invisible and subtle stealth
> To creep in at mine eyes. (I.v.296–8)

To fall in love with Cesario inverts the order of things only if Cesario is a page, but not if he is of noble lineage – even if he should be a she. With the discovery of her birth, the problem posed virtually disappears; not sex, but blood makes all the difference. Thus when Sebastian appears on the stage to reveal that Olivia has been "betrothed to a maid and man," Orsino quickly assures the countess, "Be not amaz'd, right noble is his blood" (V.i.264).

If it was Olivia's failure to value blood that initially disrupted social relations, then Malvolio's desire to marry above his rank dramatizes the other side of the Elizabethan double bind. He reveals the paradox inherent in the Petrarchan fantasy. In doing so, furthermore, he draws punishment without pity because his willingness to believe he could improve his station through marriage challenges the basis of membership in the aristocratic community more surely than Olivia's failure to desire Orsino. Malvolio more than Orsino or Cesario, has all the necessary social ingredients for a Petrarchan lover. From outside the empowered community, he fantasizes that access to power depends on the arbitrary nature of a female's desire which appears to operate according to some logic other than the metaphysics of blood. He believes, as he says, " 'Tis but fortune, all is fortune." He draws encouragement for the fantasy "To be Count Malvolio" from an incident where female desire went against the rules of status: "the Lady of the Strachy married the yeoman of the wardrobe" (II.v.35–40). But at the prompting of a counterfeit letter which makes

Olivia resemble this lady, Malvolio undertakes a form of self-fashioning that clearly parodies rather than fulfills the Petrarchan fantasy:

> I will be proud, I will read politic authors, I will baffle Sir Toby, I will wash off gross acquaintance, I will be point devise the very man. . . . I will be strange, stout, in yellow stockings and cross-garter'd. . . . (II.v.161–71)

Olivia could misread Cesario and yet not err because she read the lineage in his lineaments correctly. What she desired in him and what she finally gained in Sebastian was her own aristocratic likeness. Malvolio misreads her desire, however, in comparing his situation with that of the yeoman of the wardrobe who was beloved of the Lady of the Strachy. He thinks the desire of such women hinges upon the courtier's performance – his dissimulation – rather than the value inherent in the performer himself. This, the play's third dramatization of the Petrarchan fantasy in the play, demonstrates that contrary to the logic of the courtier's self-fashioning, it is the value inscribed at birth within the lover's body – more than his style of self-presentation – which gives rise to desire. In this respect, Malvolio is a counterfeit while Cesario is the genuine coin, and one proof of his lack of gentle heritage resides in his inability to understand himself as such. Malvolio's snobbery betrays his lack of breeding as clearly as does his ability to carry off the courtier's performance without making mockery of it.

Malvolio can only imagine the community to which he aspires as one that arbitrarily excludes him. On this basis, he takes it upon himself to enforce the principle of exclusion when acting as the overseer of Olivia's household. Malvolio appropriates the voice of the community to which he wants to belong, however, and uses it to assault certain practices of courtly life. Intolerant of déclassé kin such as Sir Toby, inhospitable to such guests as Sir Andrew, and disapproving of the presence of Feste the clown, Malvolio threatens to close down those ceremonies and processionals which celebrate the aristocratic body. He would deny to the privileged community the very forms of power which it uses to order society without recourse to violence.

Sir Toby Belch, Feste, Sir Andrew, and Maria in turn take up the oppositional practices of disguise and inversion to drive Malvolio out of the society. Their opposition is political rather than aesthetic. They punish him for his presumption; they mock his seriousness; and they turn his desire to madness. Here, as in the other comedies, the carnivalesque operates in concert with the interests of an idealized aristocratic community to punish the figures opposing that ideal. After doing its work, however, knavery must be contained and solemnized. For in this fashion can Shakespeare stage a purer, more idealized representation of the aristocratic community and also produce a larger, more expansive vision of society. Once their energy and aggression has demolished the element threatening the purity of the aristocratic body, namely, the presumptions of Malvolio, Shakespeare strips the disruptive features from Sir Toby and his crew. Sir Toby is ready to set aside carnivalesque practices for a more moderate mode of behavior once Malvolio has been punished. "I would we were well rid of this knavery," he says of the mock imprisonment of Malvolio, "If he may be conveniently deliver'd, I would he were, for I am now so far in offense with my niece that I cannot pursue with any safety this sport . . ." (IV.ii.67–70). When Sir Toby once more misreads Cesario's lineaments – taking Sebastian for the page – the fat knight is given a ritual beating about the ears. He finally renounces disruptive play to join the lovers in solemnizing his own marriage to Maria.

Earlier romantic comedies imply what *Twelfth Night* makes explicit. The problem and resolution of each depends upon the transfer of patriarchal power to a woman. Nowhere is this comic move so bold as in the case of Cesario/Viola who wins Olivia's gaze where the page wished only to woo for his master. But this shift in power from male to female – Orsino to Olivia – is part of a circuit of exchange which relocates power in the male through the marriage ceremony which concludes all of the comedies. When the male figures – Petruchio, Theseus, Orsino, Bassanio – do come to embody patriarchal power, however, the power they embody has changed. In the transfer of this power from male to female and back again, romantic comedy transforms it. Having passed into the body of a woman, power becomes her gift to give. As such, it assumes a more humane and less violent form. The illusion that the edge of monarchy's sword has thus softened materializes upon the stage as the threat of civil violence gives way to ceremonies of state. These – the wedding dance and feast – are modelled upon and incorporate materials of popular festival indigenous to England. They invoke and contain the disruptive power of nature. For the reason that they bear traces of the spontaneous and joyful as well as transgressive elements of festival, they acquire the symbolic force of a natural hierarchy – or myth, if you will – where they originally appeared arbitrarily exclusive and opposed to human desire.

IX

It is my contention that the comedic representation of power both drew upon and helped to constitute a political iconography that was employed elsewhere in the theater as well as in the society at large. A brief look at *Henry V* will demonstrate how Shakespeare could use the representation of power he employed in the comedies to serve other generic purposes. That he could do so indicates something of the political force the comic representation had acquired. It is surely significant that when Shakespeare sought ways to imagine the conclusion to the second tetralogy, he activated the strategies of romantic comedy to represent forth the good society. More to the point, he chose to dramatize the conquest of France as Henry's wooing of Katherine. Observing the cultural logic of his romantic comedies, Shakespeare personifies the power of the French nation in the French princess. French armies may be miraculously defeated and French noblemen perform acts of fealty to the English king, but to show that Henry has taken possession of France itself and can therefore lay claim to rule its territory, Shakespeare brings forth the iconography of power from the comedies. Only with such a dramatic language, we might conclude, could he even momentarily transform the violent contests of chronicle history into a tableau of stasis and hierarchy.

For Shakespeare and his audience, genealogy is the true history of state power; *Henry V* is about nothing if not that. Having displayed the quality of his blood in Henry's military prowess and his diplomatic instincts, Shakespeare has the victorious king play the lover. Let us therefore consider, by way of concluding this chapter and opening the next, how an English king's successful wooing of the French princess confirms the value of blood. Let us consider, further, why it is essential to understand power as ultimately residing in blood and distributed through marriage, which is to make the female the chief form of currency in a system of political exchanges. Successful as he is, Henry's success is limited to what can be gained by military conquest and diplomacy. Therefore, of all the conditions that might put an end to French resistance, Henry insists that Katherine's hand should be "our capital demand." With this, Shakespeare sets in motion the comic strategy which makes patriarchal power the gift a woman gives to the suitor she favors. Only here, in *Henry V*, it is King Henry who recasts the political conflict in these terms, endowing the French princess with the power to reclaim France. The transfer of political power to the female and back again appears to have a salutary effect. There is the illusion that France resembles the object of Petrarchan desire because France will somehow ennoble this rude English king. If his adopting the role of suitor for Katherine's hand invokes the Petrarchan situation, however, Henry's manner of wooing also sets him apart – and in opposition – to his non-aristocratic counterpart, the courtier. He rejects the position assumed by "fellows of infinite tongue that can rhyme their way into ladies' favors," a kind of speech which inverts the tropes of aristocratic verse and invokes the oaths of the tavern: while Henry pretends to play the role of the subject:

> Marry, if you would put me to verses, or to dance for your sake, Kate, why, you undid me: for the one, I have neither words nor measure; and for the other, I have no strength in measure . . . before God, Kate, I cannot look greenly, nor gasp out my eloquence nor I have no cunning in protestation; only downright oaths, which I never use till urg'd, nor never break for urging. If thou canst love a fellow of this temper, Kate, . . . that never looks in his glass for love of any thing he sees there, let thine eye be thy cook. I speak to thee plain soldier. If thou canst love me for this, take me! if not, to say to thee that I shall die, is true; but for thy love, by the Lord, no; yet I love thee too. (V.ii.132–52)

By thus refusing to enter into the poetic game of self-fashioning, of course, Henry displays his power of dissembling all the more forcefully. For the conquering "Roi d'Angleterre, Héretier de France" (V.ii.339) to speak as a "plain soldier" at once realizes and overturns the courtly paradigm. Only Henry's desire for her can invest Katherine with the symbolic power that accompanies acceptance of his suit for her hand. The thematics shaping the chronicle histories will not allow one to ignore the fact that she is already subject to him. The comedic ending, however, insists on the fact that Katherine and Henry are of the same lineage. It remains only for her to desire him, and his rule over France will acquire the sanctity of a natural and ceremonial bond in place of the crude and rapacious qualities of the common soldier which might cling to him as the conqueror.

Thus there is a way in which Katherine's acceptance of Henry's suit, in being only symbolic, actually packs some political punch. In playing out the wooing scene, she enables the transformation of English authority as he embodies it. It is necessary to heal the breach created by the English conquest of France, the comic ending suggests, but it is obviously important to insist upon national difference as well. Thus we encounter in this chronicle history play yet another situation of a woman who modifies the Petrarchan ideal. Katherine has the capability of existing simultaneously as self and as other in relation to the English political body, much as the heroines of romantic comedy had stood in relation to the community of blood. We see in her, however, something that is less apparent in them: the politics of nationalism which the figure of the aristocratic woman invariably served as she appeared on the popular stage. Katherine is like Henry, a descendent of the crown, or at least her children will be, and this returns us to the whole issue of Elizabeth's marriage with which I opened my discussion of the politics of romantic comedy. In the case of *Henry V*, the male line of the French–English liaison would remain English, leaving no possibility of conflict between the French and English forms of patriarchy. The English line should dominate the French just as the husband should dominate the wife and the sovereign should rule over the subject. It is clear that Katherine embodies all these forms of otherness – France, wife and subject – which the ending of the play inscribes within the hierarchy of English patrilineage as if by a natural process. She is not only female and thus naturally subordinate to her husband, provided he be of lineage comparable to hers, she is also French and as such unnaturally subjected by his language.

It must be noted, finally, how their courtship alters the Petrarchan fantasy so that desire aims at overcoming national differences rather than the distinctions of blood. When Henry asks Katherine to teach him terms for wooing her, for example, she claims, "I cannot speak your England" (V.ii.102). But it is not for nationalist reasons in any narrow and obvious sense that find English so alien to the French tongue. Katherine cannot conduct a courtship in English because it – like the monarch himself – appears to her to possess all the features of the grotesque body. After hearing the English terms for "le pied" and "la robe," for example, Katherine exclaims, "Le foot et le count! O Seigneur Dieu! ils sont les mots de son mauvais, corruptible, gros, et impudique, et non pour les dames de honneur d'user" (III.iv.52–4). When she assents to him "in broken English," it is not only a nation in the person of the Princess who accedes to Henry but a whole notion of power that understands itself in opposition to the "other" social body, the people, as well as to the signs and symbols of this elite view. Henry rejects the language of courtly love, which would certainly translate into French well enough, in order to endorse an alternative representation of power which incorporates and hierarchizes what is popular, wild, and unruly even as it masters what is courtly, polished, and French.

2

RITUALS OF STATE
*History and the Elizabethan
strategies of power*

To discuss the politics of Shakespeare's history plays, I must again draw
two kinds of comparison: one comparison allows one to understand this
particular dramatic form in relation to others that we consider literary:
romantic comedy, tragedy and the court masque. My objective in this is to
determine what figures allow the materials of chronicle history to
authorize the state in characteristically Elizabethan ways. But this in turn
requires me to make another kind of comparison, one that understands
aesthetic strategies as political strategies. To argue that theatrical
spectacles displayed the power of the state, I will show how the figures
organizing materials for the stage also shaped policies of state. I will use
Henry VIII and *Hamlet* as test cases in proving this point. In addition to
isolating the political strategies which major chronicle history plays share
with romantic comedy, one can also see why *Henry VIII* is a play of
another kind even though it draws upon the materials of chronicle
history. By the same token, *Hamlet* must be placed with the chronicle
histories in terms of its strategies of representation rather than with the
Jacobean tragedies in terms of which literary tradition has identified it.

I will not be concerned with the march of literature, on the one hand,
nor with the history of institutions of state on the other. It is the
representation of power that commands my interest in this chapter, by
which I mean specifically that cultural logic or general economy of
meaning within which the monarch's body was inscribed and achieved
value. I will show that the theater which idealized state power did not
observe either its own logic or that of any individual author's development. Quite the contrary, as the inherited prerogatives of the monarch
were challenged, first by a contending faction within the aristocracy, and
later by dissenting voices outside the oligarchy, literature had to employ

radically discontinuous artistic strategies to remain politically consistent. Indeed, we find that a whole set of literary genres fell out of favor with the accession of James I, and new forms provided the appropriate means of situating oneself in proximity to political power. Along with romantic comedy, Petrarchan poetry, prose romance, and other genres as well, the chronicle history play enjoyed a period of unprecedented popularity during the 1590s. And just as clearly as it shared their popularity, the chronicle history play also participated in the demise of many of these Elizabethan genres; with few exceptions, such plays ceased to be produced after *Henry V* (1599), the most notable exception being *Henry VIII*.

II

To explain why history plays became virtually unwritable after 1600, I would like to consider what this dramatic form shared with romantic comedy and Petrarchan poetry that enabled these genres to address the interests of the same audience and then hasten into obsolescence together. For all their differences, chronicle history uses the same strategy to produce political order out of political conflict as romantic comedy uses to reinforce the dominant rules of kinship. Both represent patriarchal hierarchies in a state of disorder, in this way creating two bases for authority, and thus two competing hierarchies of power, which only the monarch can hold together in harmonious discord.

   If we recall for the moment the example of *A Midsummer Night's Dream*, a play surely characteristic of Shakespeare's romantic comedies, we can see that the problem which authority has to master is a problem with authority itself. It is the problem of authority grown archaic. At the outset, the law seems arbitrary in that it seems to serve only the will of the father. A comedic resolution does not require the law to be less arbitrary, for arbitrariness can be a perfectly acceptable feature of monarchal power. Rather, a comic resolution requires either the independence of the law or the generosity of the father. It requires, in other words, a more inclusionary order. Oberon represents the traditional alternative to patriarchal law, the elements of carnival. Thus we find his introduction into the play triggers a series of inversions.[1] As if Titania's playing the role of an unruly woman were not enough to define this as the role of fairie, Puck sets this principle of disorder to work among the Athenians – both lovers and mechanicals – who have wandered into the woods. Such inversions – of gender, age, status, even of species – violate all the categories organizing the Elizabethan social world. Relationships consequently assume the nightmarish proportions of Renaissance madness, which occurs as desire exists whenever transgressions of patriarchal law exist in absolute opposition to political authority.

But the romantic comedies demonstrate that festival breaks down the hierarchical distinctions organizing Elizabethan society only – in the end – to be taken within the social order where it authorizes a new form of political authority. This strategy of double inversion contains political disorder within the framework of festival where it can be further aestheticized, as illustrated by "the story of the night told o'er," Bottom's "dream," as well as the mechanicals' production of the tragedy of Pyramus and Thisbe. When Theseus and his party come upon the sleeping couples lying intermingled on the ground, the duke surmises, "No doubt they rose up early to observe / The rite of May . . ." (IV.i.132–3). By identifying the lovers as revelers, Theseus does more than decriminalize their transgression of the law; he identifies their state of disarray with the order of art. "I know you two are rival enemies," he says to the young men, "How comes this gentle concord in the world . . . ?" (IV.i.142–3) At the same time, however, by including filial disobedience within a field of permissible illegalities, Shakespeare has changed the construction of political authority. What had been a violation of the father's law now becomes a scene of harmony. And when Egeus presses Theseus to punish the youthful offenders, the duke overrules the father in what strikes many as an arbitrary gesture. While both Egeus and the duke have been arbitrary in their exercise of authority, the power of legitimate authority is distinguished from the patriarchal authority by the monarch's willingness to generously forgive where Egeus, despite the lovers' show of obeisance, would be penurious and harsh.

If Theseus authorizes certain inversions of power relations by permitting them to exist within the frameworks of festival and art, it is also true that the introduction of disorder into the play ultimately authorizes political authority. Once Theseus includes the rites of May within the domain of the permissible, the revelers in turn fall on their knees before him. Thus configured together, revelers and duke comprise a harmonious political body where the power of the monarch exists independently from that of the patriarch. The equation of juridical power with patriarchal power gives way to a new set of political conditions where competing bases for authority are held in equipoise by the duke. This form of authority constitutes an improvement over the punitive power he threatened to exercise at the play's opening. The entire last act of the play consequently theorizes the process of inversion whereby art and politics end up in this mutually authorizing relationship. This process is reproduced on the stage in the form of an Elizabethan tragedy – *Pyramus and Thisbe* – which has been converted into a comedy as rude mechanicals play a range of parts from those of noble lovers to the creatures and objects of the natural world.

The popularity of inversions which bring the law into contradiction with patriarchal authority cannot be fully understood unless one sees how Elizabeth used these forms of authority against one another. It is not enough to say that the transfiguration of authority in romantic comedy resembles Elizabeth's actual style of exercising the power of the monarch. To be sure, she used her power as a patron to curb the power of the ruling families and set economically-based authority in opposition to that based on blood. But the facts would indicate this strategy was more than personal ingenuity on her part. They indicate her characteristic strategies for expressing power were no less dependent upon the political conditions of the time than the form of a comedy such as *A Midsummer Night's Dream*.

The Acts of Parliament of 1536 and 1543 gave Henry VIII the power to determine succession. His will not only specified the crown would pass to Edward, Mary and Elizabeth in that order, it also determined that, if his children should die without issue, the crown would pass to his younger sister's children in the Suffolk line and not to her older sister's children in the superior hereditary Stuart line.[2] Henry thus treated the crown as property, governed by the same common-law rules against alien inheritance as any other piece of English property. By exploiting his legal prerogative to authorize this line of descent, Henry used the civil authority of a property owner to define the monarchy as such a juridical form. This tautology set the dominant principle of genealogy against the one which was invoked later by supporters of Mary Queen of Scots and her line. During Elizabeth's reign, both Catholic and Stuart spokesmen insisted on the traditional view of the monarch as two bodies, a body natural and a body mystical, in the same body.[3] Theirs was a monolithic view of power that saw the body politic as the corporate body of the crown in perpetuity. The mystical body purged the body natural of attainder; it joined the king with his royal predecessors to constitute them as one and the same corporate person; and the metaphysical body was joined to the natural body of the king, they argued, like an affair of the heart in a marital pre-contract of the blood royal.

A similar logic operates in *A Midsummer Night's Dream* as the law and the father temporarily come into contradiction in the last act of the play. In this instance, however, the splitting of one form of power into two competing voices is hardly the dramatic problem. It is rather the comedic resolution to a problem which develops when authority assumes an absolute and monolithic form. Since Elizabeth's ascendancy could be justified according to her father's will and primogeniture both, her very person temporarily reconciled the competing viewpoints formulated during the debates concerning her succession. Elizabeth was a paradox, in other words, by virtue of the contradictory definitions of monarchal authority her succession had occasioned. Much the same contradiction resolves the dramatic conflict of *A Midsummer Night's Dream* with the divergence of Theseus's authority from that of Egeus. Indeed, in turning back to courtly poetry, we find the same strategy for idealizing power obtains as the patron is endowed with the attributes of the reluctant lover. The puns characterizing the Petrarchan mode of poetry effectively create a gulf between the power of property (in the form of economic favors) and that of blood (through marriage into the aristocracy), even as the two modes for representing power are brought together in one figure of speech.

III

If the Petrarchan lyric or romantic comedy are shaped by strategies for idealizing the state, this rhetorical behavior should be all the more evident in the chronicle history plays. The obstacle one encounters in identifying these strategies in the material of chronicle history is not quite the same as the obstacles that stand in the way of historicizing romantic comedy. Shakespeare's use of political rather than sexual subject matter entices many to make the history plays allude to contemporary events. While such a procedure anchors "the text" to events taking place in a "context," such an allusory, or allegorical construction prevents us from seeing the drama as a symbolic activity of a piece with and giving shape to the events we call history. It is fair to say that the form of the history play is so completely one with certain Elizabethan controversies, that the materials of chronicle history could no longer be so assembled once the official strategies for mastering those controversies changed.

Richard II exemplifies the strategies by which Shakespeare stages the struggle for legitimate authority. It is significant that few if any monarchs in the entire sequence of history plays are represented at the outset of their dramas with a more secure claim to the throne. Yet within the first two acts Shakespeare creates the impression that no monarch is more irresponsible and finally more threatening to the stability of the state. He makes Richard appear as a tragic version of the patriarch who exercises his authority for penurious and exclusionary ends. In contrast with the anointed king, then, Shakespeare makes the displaced and dispossessed Bullingbroke into the figure who rescues the principle of genealogy and links it to the law.

Shakespeare first has Richard act as if he had absolute authority over the law by virtue of his solid claim to the throne. At the same time, Richard disregards the other principle that secures his position. In the opening scenes, the king is unwilling – or, more likely, unable – to entertain Bullingbroke's charge that Mowbray was responsible for Gloucester's murder. There is even the possibility Richard is complicit in that crime, which would implicate the king in a crime against the state. An impossible semiotic dilemma would arise in the event of such a conflict within the body politic between the monarch's two bodies. The notion that the bearer of blood could also betray the state requires one to imagine the state and the blood as separate entities. Although several of the sources for the play suggest the possibility of Richard's implication in his uncle's death, then, Shakespeare leaves the whole issue in a cloudy state. Otherwise, he would have to represent Richard II as the monstrous form in which Richard III steps forth.

In *III Henry VI* as well as in *Richard III*, Richard's monstrosity is stressed at the very moment he wages personal war on the monarchy. When Richard has murdered King Edward, boasted to the imprisoned King Henry of killing the king's son as well, and stabbed Henry repeatedly, the dying monarch describes Richard as a monster. His regicidal behavior fits a body that also is a disfiguration of the family line, ". . . an indigested and deformed lump, / Not like the fruit of such a goodly tree" (V.vi.51–2). Richard then muses on his figure using Henry's terms: having been born with teeth, he says, "I should snarl, and bite, and play the dog" (V.vi.77). He sees his behavior as the providential equivalent for the deformation of his natural body: "Then since the heavens have shap'd my body so, / Let hell make crook'd my mind to answer it" (V.vi.78–9). By this, he makes his monstrous form become the figure for the fratricidal desire that works against the aristocratic body through the entire first tetralogy. At the end of *Richard III*, the victorious Richmond enters with the crown to describe the victory in these terms, "The day is ours, the bloody dog is dead" (V.v.2). It is important to note that even as Shakespeare represents this king quite literally as a monster, the playwright still has this monster preserve the iconic relationship between the two bodies of the monarch. In being so disfigured in his body the power of blood will also be restored to its natural form with Richard's defeat.

In *Richard II*, Shakespeare suggests quite a different order of problem is plaguing the state, namely its failure to exercise force. In assuming the authority of blood is absolute, Richard neglects those displays of political authority which establish the absolute power of the monarch over the material body of the subject. To settle the charges about Mowbray's role in the murder of the Duke of Gloucester, Richard stages a trial by combat, only to cancel this ceremony before it gets underway. His subsequent banishment of Mowbray and Bullingbroke demonstrates the monarch's right to exercise royal power arbitrarily. But with a consistency that suggests he could not do otherwise, Richard avoids those occasions where scenes of violence ordinarily would be staged. Even late in the play, Shakespeare does not allow Richard to do battle where he would show an ability to exercise the force of state. Hearing of the uprising led by Bullingbroke, Richard instead invokes the metaphysics of kingship to protect his crown. It is from his position as the magical body of England that he urges the earth,

> Feed not thy sovereign's foe, my gentle earth,
> Nor with thy sweets comfort his ravenous sense,
> But let thy spiders, that suck up thy venom,
> And heavy-gaited toads lie in their way,
> Doing annoyance to the treacherous feet,
> Which with usurping steps do trample thee. (III.ii.12–17)

He believes angels will fight on his behalf, that stones will become soldiers for the anointed king, and that "the king's name" is worth "twenty thousand names" (III.ii.85). In contrast with Richard III, then, Richard II threatens to break the bond between the king's two bodies.

Although Shakespeare raises the matter of Gloucester's death, he stops short of making it the central issue. Instead, he uses Gaunt's deathbed speech to represent Richard as "the careless patient" who fails to prevent the spilling of royal blood. Of equal importance is Richard's insensitivity to the dangers of leasing the royal lands, for both policies – or lack of policy – cause the body politic to fall dangerously ill. Giving up his control over royal land threatens the very basis of the monarch's authority ("This land . . . Is now leas'd out – I die pronouncing it – / Like to a tenement or pelting farm" [II.i.57–60]). The danger, of course, is one and the same as that troubling the participants in the succession debate. By so representing Richard, Shakespeare has the king undermine the bond among the claims to power which Elizabeth embodied. In Gaunt's opinion, Richard threatens to destroy the equipoise between the king's two bodies by making that body subject to contract. "Landlord of England art thou now, not king," the dying Gaunt charges, "Thy state of law is bond-slave to the law" (II.i.113–14). Besides the spilling of aristocratic blood and the leasing of the aristocratic body, Shakespeare represents yet another assault by Richard on the institutions of power, his arrogant disregard for the principle of primogeniture. When the king seizes Bullingbroke's inheritance following the death of Gaunt, York rightly accuses him of challenging the principle on which his own power rests. ". . . How art thou a king," York asks, "But by fair sequence and succession" (II.i.198–9). This act threatens the entire nobility and provides as great a threat to the body politic as the "grievous taxes" that have stripped the common people bare and "quite lost their hearts" (II.i.247).

In the comedies, as we have seen, such a split in the body politic is repaired as the state contains all the heterogeneous elements of carnival. This makes the hierarchy of state seem less at odds with nature, at once more inclusionary and less arbitrary in its laws. Although we do not usually think of Henry Bullingbroke in such terms, Shakespeare does give him the features of inversion which necessarily challenge the law. In preparing for battle against Mowbray, Bullingbroke is "lusty, young, and cheerly drawing breath" (I.iii.66). As Henry leaves England, Richard accordingly describes his rival as one who enjoys the popular support of the "craftsmen," "an oyster-wench," and a "brace of draymen." These elements, Richard notes, regard Henry as if "England [were] in reversion his, / And he our subjects' next degree of hope" (I.iv.35–6). Even the support enabling Henry to challenge the king – in its mixing of ages, sexes and social ranks – sounds more like a carnivalesque troop than a disciplined military force. And indeed, Scroop employs figures of inversion to describe the raggle-taggle supporters of Bullingbroke:

> White beards have arm'd their thin and hairless scalps
> Against thy majesty; boys, with women's voices,
> Strive to speak big, and clap their female joints
> In stiff unwieldy arms against thy crown;
> Thy very beadsmen learn to bend their bows
> Of double-fatal yew against thy state;
> Yea, distaff-women manage rusty bills
> Against thy seat: both young and old rebel. . . . (III.ii.112–19)

This is not the figure of a revolutionary army assaulting the traditions of patriarchy. To the contrary, as E.P. Thompson has noted, such are the elements of an essentially conservative form of riot staged to demand better adherence to a patriarchal ideal.[4] In *Richard III*, then, Richmond's troops successfully overthrow the tyrant Richard to return England to a stable England. To Richard III, however, these soldiers appear as, "A sort of vagabonds, rascals, and runaways, / A scum of Britains and base lackey peasants . . ." (V.iii.316–17).

I would like to suggest that the history plays all turn on this use of the materials of carnival. The popular energy embodied in carnival legitimizes authority, provided that energy can be incorporated in the political body of the state. In effect, such energy lends the power of autochthony to a rigidly hierarchical form of patriarchy. In this respect, it is significant to find Richard describing Bullingbroke in language more appropriate for a Falstaff than an English king; Bullingbroke is "a thief," as well as "a traitor," one "Who all this while hath revell'd in the night" (III.ii.47–8). It is especially significant that Bullingbroke embody these features as he rescues the principle of inheritance which underwrites Richard's right to wear the crown. Bullingbroke repeats his uncle's words as he lays claim to a title and, with it, to the authority of the blood, "Wherefore was I born? / If that my cousin king be King in England, / It must be granted I am Duke of Lancaster" (II.iii.122–4). If Richard had dissociated the power of blood from the exercise of force, then Henry restores the body politic to wholeness. His England incorporates the robust features of festival, while Richard's is a state that lets the family blood and leases the royal land. Gaunt characterizes Richard's body politic as a place where Edward III's "son's sons . . . destroy his sons" (II.i.105), and it "is now bound in with shame, / With inky blots and rotten parchment bonds . . ." (II.i.63–4). It is for this reason that the figure of carnival is associated with Henry, while the figure of a mutilated England characterizes Richard's monarchy. The rhetorical contrast between them shifts legitimate authority from Richard to Henry.

The shift begins when Bullingbroke arrests Bushy and Green on charges of treason for assaulting the king's body. Not even the loyal York questions Henry's authority in this, for Bushy and Green have,

> . . . misled a prince, a royal king,
> A happy gentleman in blood and lineaments,
> By you unhappied and disfigured clean. . . . (III.i.8–10)

They "disfigured" Richard, we should note, by dividing the king from the queen, thus breaking "the possession of a royal bed," as well as by dividing Bullingbroke from the king. As Henry says, "you did make him misinterpret me." While critics have puzzled over the charge of divorce, (there is no evidence in the play or in the chronicles of any such divorce), the play simply suggests that anything dividing the aristocratic body against itself disfigures the king. Assaults on Bullingbroke's estate constitute the same treasonous act of disfigurement, then, as Bullingbroke further details the crimes of Bushy and Green:

> . . . you have fed upon my signories,
> Dispark'd my parks and fell'd my forest woods,
> From my own windows torn my household coat,
> Ras'd out my imprese, leaving me no sign,
> Save men's opinions and my living blood,
> To show the world I am a gentleman. (III.i.16–27)

This representation of aristocracy divested of its natural body indicts not only Bushy and Green, we must note, but also Richard. In allowing the body of England to be split apart and himself disfigured, he has disfigured the official iconography of state. He has become the "other" against whom popular support may be legitimately invoked.

Richard has been called the poet king by critics who want to read him in the nineteenth-century manner, as a poet king who was a political failure, rather than as a sixteenth-century monarch who destroyed the sign of his own legitimacy.[5] In actuality, it is Henry IV rather than Richard in whom Shakespeare invests the power of the artist, not a power detached from matters political, that is, but the power to incorporate disruptive cultural elements within the official rituals of state. Henry successfully stages Richard's resignation of the crown and the procession and coronation that legitimate his own claim to the throne.[6] York contrasts Richard's poor appearance to Bullingbroke's triumphant processional; while Henry drew everyone's gaze, he says Richard appeared

> As in a theatre the eyes of men,
> After a well-graced actor leaves the stage,
> Are idly bent on him that enters next,
> Thinking his prattle to be tedious. . . . (V.ii.23–6)

Another occasion for Henry to display his authority occurs when Aumerle, his conspiracy discovered, begs forgiveness, and Henry grants it. With this, Shakespeare completes the contrast between Richard and Henry. Richard lacks the power of generosity as well as the capacity for ruthlessness. Henry possesses both and can manifest either power in extreme as he so chooses. No less important than granting his cousin Aumerle forgiveness is Henry's condemnation and pursuit of all those who plotted against him. He vows, "Destruction straight shall dog them at their heels . . ./ They shall not live within this world, I swear" (V.iii.139, 142). Thus in one scene he shows both sides of the coin of power: he vows to exercise unlimited force in the interest of the state, and he displays generosity in the interest of the blood. It is significant that by staging this scene of forgiveness for Aumerle's parents, the Duke and Duchess of York, Henry recasts his authority in a comedic form. "Our scene is alt'red from a serious thing" (V.iii.79), he observes, when the Duchess begs an audience to plead for her son. Having just examined the comedies, one should find this scene a familiar one. By this stroke, we might say, Shakespeare acknowledges the conceptual link between his two major Elizabethan genres.

IV

In certain respects, *Henry V* can be called a piece of political hagiography.[7] As if omniscient, Henry discovers domestic conspirators and punishes them. He secures his borders against Scottish invaders, unifies the dispirited and heterogeneous body under his authority, and wins the battle of Agincourt, thus taking control of territory which had been claimed by French inheritance law and contested by English laws of succession. The stability of the state having been won, and the promise of its continuance having been established by the king's marriage with the French princess, the Epilogue to this tetralogy takes on the features of a comic resolution:

> Thus far, with rough and all-unable pen,
> Our bending author hath pursu'd the story,
> In little room confining mighty men,
> Mangling by starts the full course of their glory.
> Small time, but in that small most greatly lived
> This star of England. Fortune made his sword;
> By which the world's best garden he achieved,
> And of it left his son imperial lord. (lines 1–8)

The history play stabilizes the conflict among contradictory origins of power, it appears, only to define that stasis as nothing else but a moment of equipoise within a competitive process. The hagiographical theme of this play understands power as the inevitable unfolding of order. But to idealize political authority, Shakespeare evidently found it necessary to counter this theme with a contrary one.

In this other logic of history, history is nothing else but the history of forms of disorder, over which Henry temporarily triumphs. He alone embodies the contradictions that bring disruption into the service of the state and allows a discontinuous political process to appear as a coherent moment. Thus the Epilogue continues on past a comedic resolution to remind the Elizabethan audience that the very marriage which secured the peace with France and established the line of succession eventually led to the Wars of the Roses:

> Henry the Sixt, in infant bands crown'd King
> Of France and England, did this king succeed;
> Whose state so many had the managing,
> That they lost France, and made his England bleed.... (lines 9–12)

Providence temporarily comes under the control of the monarch. Working against political order, however, providence offers a tide that one can ride into power but against which he must struggle vainly in order to remain there.[8] This leveling force effectively unseats every hierarchy. This seems to be the point of Richard III's rise, of Henry Richmond's victory over Richard, of Bullingbroke's successful challenge to Richard II, but particularly of Hal's defeat of Hotspur and his subsequent victory over the French. In each case, state authority does not descend directly through blood. Rather, it pursues a disrupted and discontinuous course through history, arising out of conflicts within the reigning oligarchy as to which bloodline shall legitimately rule. Together these chronicle history plays demonstrate, then, that authority goes to the contender who can seize hold of the symbols and signs legitimizing authority and wrest them from his rivals to make them serve his own interests. What else is accomplished, however perversely, by Richard III's incarceration of the young princes? Or Bullingbroke's public ceremony in which Richard is forced to hand over the crown? And surely Hal's self-coronation in *II Henry IV*, preemptive though it may be, dramatizes the same principle, that power is an inversion of legitimate authority which gains possession, as such, of the means of self-authorization.

Such a rhetorical strategy guarantees the figures of carnival will play a particularly instrumental role in the idealizing process that proves so crucial in legitimizing political power. It cannot be accidental that the *Henriad*, which produces Shakespeare's most accomplished Elizabethan monarch, should also produce his most memorable figure of misrule. The complete king was by birth entitled to the throne. A youth misspent in low-life activities at the same time lends him the demonic features of the contender, a potential regicide, whose legitimacy has yet to be recognized. The various conflicts comprising *I* and *II Henry IV*, in actuality cohere as a single strategy of idealization. In opposition to legitimate authority, Hal takes on a populist energy. In contrast, the law of the father seems to have atrophied and grown rigid to the degree that it can be inverted by the likes of Falstaff, whose abuses of legitimate authority, like those of Oberon, take on a menacing quality when unconstrained by the forest glade or tavern. Falstaff frequently anticipates the lawlessness he will enjoy when Hal assumes authority and authority is therefore not "as it is with the rusty curb of old father antic the law" (I.ii.61). Upon hearing of Henry IV's death, again (in *Part II*) he looks forward to the dissolution of the state: "I know the young king is sick for me. Let us take any man's horses, the laws of England are at my commandment" (V.iii.135–7). Thus Shakespeare uses the figures of carnival to represent a source of power contrary to that power inhering in genealogy. However, the various confrontations between licit and illicit authority comprising the *Henriad* more firmly draw the distinction between aristocracy and populace even as they appear to overturn this primary categorical distinction.

The figures of carnival ultimately authorize the state as the state appears to take on the vigor of festival. We see this, for example, in Vernon's account of Hal and his men preparing to do battle with Hotspur:

> Glittering in golden coats like images,
> As full of spirit as the month of May,
> And gorgeous as the sun at midsummer;
> Wanton as youthful goats, wild as young bulls.[9] (IV.i.100–3)

The same process transfers what is weak and corrupt onto the tavern folk where it is contained and finally driven even from that debased world. Criminalizing the popular figures of inversion is as necessary to the poetics of power as incorporating a certain popular vigor within the legitimate body of the state. This capability of making rebellion serve the interests of the state by including it within the state is the proof of noble blood and the principle toward which the tetralogy moves. Legitimate order can come into being only through disruption according to this principle, and it can maintain itself only through discontinuous and self-contradictory policies.

If Henry V appears to be Shakespeare's ultimate monarch, it is because historical sources provided the author with material that met the Elizabethan conditions for idealization. Yet these semiotic conditions for producing the ideal political figure are precisely what make Henry V so resistant to modern criticism's attempts at appropriating him for a post-Enlightenment humanism.[10] The king's identity coalesces and his power intensifies as he unifies those territories that are his by hereditary law. But as this occurs, one finds that the figure of the monarch breaks apart and disappears into many different roles and dialects. He uses the strategies of disguise and inversion to occupy a range of positions from soldier to lover, as well as several roles in between. As a consequence, the king is virtually everywhere. He occupies the center of every theater of social action and in this way constitutes a state that to modern readers appears to have no center at all, neither a continuous political policy nor an internally coherent self. To make sense to an Elizabethan audience, we must therefore assume the king's body did not have to behave as if it were that of a self-enclosed individual. Rather the histories suggest that body had to behave, semiotically speaking, as if blood had conspired with the disruptive operations of providence to produce it. In becoming so many functions and dialects of a single political body, he makes the various social groups he thus contains lose their autonomy. At the same time, the people acquire an ideal identity as they are embodied by the king.

The most successful monarch of the Elizabethan stage plays displayed his power by incorporating political elements – people, land, dialects – within the body politic. So, too, the power of the monarch achieved legitimacy as recalcitrant cultural materials were taken up and hierarchized within the official rituals of state. Figuratively speaking, this notion of power argued against the idea of patriarchy whose authority was based purely on primogeniture and the metaphysics of blood. But since no challenge to patriarchal authority was successful unless the claimant also happened to possess the blood, the exercise of force alone could hardly convert the energy of the populace into a display of legitimate power. Thus a monarch's ability to convert carnivalesque activity into banqueting and procession was the sign of his entitlement to political power.

V

Hamlet marks the moment when the Elizabethan strategies for authorizing monarchy became problematic. While he still thinks in terms of Elizabethan figures for power, Shakespeare appears to question their adequacy in representing the transfer of power from one monarch to another. History plays could not be written after *Hamlet*, I will argue, because this whole matter of transferring power from one monarch to another had to be rethought in view of the aging body of the queen, Elizabeth. That body was, as I have said, a political figure in its own right. Its decay without an apparent heir precipitated serious speculation about the transfer of power, and such speculation gave rise to narrative strategies to figure out how the continuity of the metaphysical body might be preserved.

During the Christmas celebrations of 1600, Elizabeth made a public show of dancing with Duke Bracciano. John Chamberlain writes, "The Queen entertained him very graciously, and to show that she is not so old as some would have her danced both measures and galliards in his presence."[11] But the signs of her age were everywhere to be seen. At the opening of Parliament in 1601, it was reported, "her robes of velvet and ermine had proved too heavy for her; on the steps of the throne she had staggered and was only saved from falling by the peer who stood nearest catching her in his arms. . . ."[12] The degree to which the condition of her body represented that of the state is apparent in Sir John Harrington's description of the scene at court written during the same year:

> the madcaps are all in riot, and much evil threatened . . . the Queen is quite disfavoured, and unattired, and these troubles waste her much. She disregardeth every costly cover that cometh to the table and taketh little but manchet and succory potage. Every new message from the City doth disturb her . . . The many evil plots and designs have overcome all her Highness' sweet temper. She walks much in her Privy

Chamber, and stamps with her feet at ill news, and thrusts her rusty sword at times into the arras in great rage. . . . The dangers are over, and yet she always keeps a sword by her table.[13]

"The many evil plots and designs" in Harrington's account were just that, plots of a political drama organizing the court as well as the stage during this period. Some of these circulated at various European courts among members of the diplomatic corps who imagined the crown of England as an aging and still heirless Elizabeth. In Spain, France, and Italy there was serious debate about naming the Spanish Infanta to the English throne. France was deeply worried, Spain intrigued by the possibility, and the Pope ambivalent. Meanwhile, the North German princes were encouraging a Protestant to be named heir, and Denmark, of course, openly announced it expected Elizabeth to name James. Scottish representatives on the continent actively promoted rumours of various scenarios. A typical example is reported by John Petit who, writing to Peter Helms from Antwerp in 1598, says:

If I were not acquainted with Scottish brags, I might believe England was already more than half theirs. They say the King of Denmark's brother . . . is to bring men from Denmark to do wonders in England; that the Queen, having promised the King of Scots, at his marriage with the Dane, to declare him her successor she must perform it. . . .[14]

Prominent members of Elizabeth's own court envisioned other narratives in their secret correspondence with James VI of Scotland.[15] Still further possibilities were produced by the gossip of an anxious populace quick to imagine the worst possible conclusion to events. And yet other dramas were acted out in the form of failed conspiracies or foolhardy rebellions, the Essex rebellion constituting the most famous attempt to determine the line of power.

In declaring the line of succession, the queen would determine history itself, and any plot other than hers was treason. Such questions, however, had to be discussed with discretion. The Act of 1571 prohibited debate on the matter of succession outside of Parliament, and after 1571 Parliament itself became extremely reluctant to debate the matter. Despite the fact that James was the most likely candidate, he was far from being the only contender. Yet even though the issue could never become the topic of open debate, Thomas Wilson's *The State of England, Anno Dom. 1600* provides a useful indication of the central role this issue played in thinking about the nature of the state and one's relation to political authority. While many Englishmen felt the crown would go to James, Wilson cautions, "to determine thereof is to all English capitally forbidden. . . ." For as he explains, "The crown is not like to fall to the ground for want of heads that claim to wear it, but upon whose head it will fall is by many doubted. . . ."[16] Because there were so many heads ready to claim the crown (if one follows Wilson's argument there were at least three with reasonable claims), we may safely assume the matter of succession was the single most important concern among the literate classes.

Elizabeth's physical condition seemed at regular intervals to open a gap between the two notions of kingship her physical presence had success-fully mediated for some forty years. We might be tempted to say this is also true of chronicle history plays which pit the claims of blood against the effective exercise of force. But Shakespeare invokes the possibility of such a threat to the body politic only to demonstrate that the monarch's two bodies cannot exist as separate entities. It is significant, then, when we find that the very presupposition allowing Shakespeare to play out a dialectics of power in the earlier plays was regularly called into question between 1599 and 1601, the years when it is most likely *Hamlet* was being written.[17] When, in August of 1599, London feared a Spanish invasion, John Chamberlain explained to Dudley Carleton how the appearance of military commanders at the Paul's Cross Sermons was read by the London crowds:

> The Lord General with all great officers of the field came in great bravery to Paul's Cross on Sunday . . . and then was the alarm at the hottest that the Spaniards were at Brest . . . .
>
> The vulgar sort cannot be persuaded that there was some great mystery in the assembling of these forces, and because they cannot find the reason for it, make many wild conjectures and cast beyond the moon: as sometimes that the Queen was dangerously sick. . . .[18]

Rather than appearing to them as the routine attendance of military men at Paul's Cross the "vulgar sort" took the presence of military force in the city to mean that the queen was certainly failing. With the loss of her natural body, they must have assumed, the magical power of the Crown was also in question, and the nation, therefore in a state of extreme peril. What is most important for purposes of this argument, however, is the fact that between 1599 and 1601 people could obviously imagine state authority as two separate bodies.

One could speculate that the Essex rebellion was founded on this same presupposition. However one reads his motive, furthermore, the twelve-hour rebellion forced the government and the populace at large to question whether history resided in the exercise of human force or in the Crown's power. Angry at the queen for her support of Cecil, angry at her, too, for reprimanding him when he granted wholesale knighthoods in Ireland, angry at being denied the opportunity to dispense patronage in England, and angry at the recent Star Chamber proceedings against him, Essex is said by Camden to have complained bitterly that Elizabeth was "grown an old woman and as crooked in mind as in her carcase."[19] Clearly Essex conceived of the aristocratic body and the change of government to be susceptible to the exercise of force. Even after the government discovered his plans, Essex believed the mere display of his colors and the support of relatives, friends, clients, and household retainers would gain him the popular voice and military force to achieve authority. He obviously had Bullingbroke's method of challenging Richard II in mind, for he requested Shakespeare's company to revive *Richard II* the night before the rebellion.

While Essex undoubtedly believed the queen's body embodied the magic of blood, he did not see the exercise of force or the power of the law as one and the same force as her magic. Rather, his display seems to have been aimed at controlling the magical body. Following his arrest, the indictments charged Essex specifically with attempting "to usurp the Crown," and the Earls of Essex, Southampton, Rutland, and Sandys, with conspiring to depose and slay the queen.[20] In secret letters to James, Essex had indeed declared he intended to seize the queen and force her to name James as her successor. Two days after his conviction, Essex changed his story, claiming his purpose had been to seize the queen, use her authority to change the government, and then call a parliament that would condemn his opponents for mismanaging the state.[21] In both versions of the story, the iconic relationship between the monarch's two bodies was in question. Whether he intended to overthrow the queen – which is unlikely – or simply to force her to name the successor of his choice, Essex was insisting that with the mere display of power he could command the natural body, which would in turn determine the mystic line of succession.

VI

Hamlet rehearses this dilemma of a state torn between two competitors, neither of whom can embody the mystical power of blood and land associated with the natural body. Hamlet's claim to power derives from his position as son in a patrilinear system as well as from "popular support." It is this support which Claudius consistently lacks and which, at the same time, prevents him from moving openly against Hamlet. Following the murder of Polonius, for example, Claudius says of Hamlet, "Yet must not we put the strong law on him./ He's lov'd of the distracted multitude . . .'' (IV.iii.3–4). But this alone does not guarantee authority. Hamlet is not by nature capable of exercising force. To signal this lack, Shakespeare has given him the speech of Stoical writing, which shifts all action onto a mental plane where any show of force becomes self-inflicted aggression. We find this identification of force with self-assault made explicit in Hamlet's speeches on suicide as well as those in which he berates himself for his inability to act.

In contrast with Hamlet, Claudius's authority comes by way of his marriage to Gertrude. Where he would be second to Hamlet and Hamlet's line in a patrilineal system, the queen's husband and uncle of the king's son occupies the privileged male position in a matrilineal system. Like one of the successful figures from a history play, Claudius overthrew the reigning patriarch. Like one of the successful courtiers in a romantic comedy, he married into the aristocratic community. What is perhaps more important, he has taken the position through the effective use of force. Thus Shakespeare sets in opposition the two claims to authority – the exercise of force and the magic of blood – by means of these two members of the royal family. Because each has a claim, neither Hamlet nor Claudius achieves legitimate control over Denmark. Each one consequently assaults the aristocratic body in attempting to acquire the crown. It is to be expected that Claudius could not legally possess the crown, the matrilinear succession having the weaker claim on British political thinking. Thus the tragedy resides not in his failure but in the impossibility of Hamlet's rising according to Elizabethan strategies of state. This calls the relationship between the metaphysics of patriarchy and the force of law into question.

Claudius's criminality is never the problem. What more heinous crime could be committed against the aristocratic body than a fratricide that is also a regicide? Add to this that both Hamlet and his father's ghost consider this crime incestuous in that it allows one member of the king's family to marry another. But even when they acquired state power under the most questionable means, and even when the magic of blood seemed to locate power elsewhere, the monarchs of the chronicle histories could authorize force and sanction their blood by certain displays of power. Thus we see them incorporating popular energy in the processions of state. In particular, we find them including alienated members of the aristocracy. We may observe this in rituals of forgiveness as Bullingbroke uses to forgive Aumerle, for example, or Henry's vow to banish Falstaff while promising to those that do reform themselves, ''We will, according to your strengths and qualities, / Give you advancement'' (V.v.69–70). *Henry V* concludes in comic fashion with courtship and promises of marriage, much as *Richard III* ends with Richmond's prayer, ''O now let

Richmond and Elizabeth,/ The true succeeders of each royal house,/ By God's fair ordinance conjoin together" (V.v.29–31). All these gestures stress the patron's generosity rather than his power to subordinate. It is important, then, that Claudius cannot seize hold of these signs and symbols of power that would authorize his reign. If Hamlet cannot translate the claims of blood into the exercise of force, it is also true that Claudius cannot command the symbolic elements of his culture which testify to the magic of blood. This is especially apparent in the contrast Shakespeare draws between the patron's feast and the revels Claudius attempts to stage. Significantly, Hamlet must explain to a startled Horatio that the sudden noise of trumpet and cannon do not signal a military invasion but rather announce Claudius's revels:

> The King doth wake to-night and takes his rouse,
> Keeps wassail, and the swagg'ring up-spring reels;
> And as he drains his draughts of Rhenish down,
> The kettle-drum and trumpet thus bray out
> The triumph of his pledge. (I.iv.8–12)

Add to this the fact that Shakespeare has Hamlet describe Claudius to Gertrude in terms that specifically invoke the figure of misrule:

> A murtherer and a villain!
> A slave that is not twentieth part the [tithe]
> Of your precedent lord; a vice of kings,
> A cutpurse of the empire and the rule,
> That from a shelf the precious diadem stole,
> And put it in his pocket . . .
> A king of shreds and patches . . .(III.iv.95–102)

As he leaves, Hamlet urges his mother not to let "The bloat king tempt you again to bed . . ." (line 182). To call Claudius a "bloat king," a "lecherous" man, "a cutpurse of the empire," "a vice of kings," is for Shakespeare to cut this usurper out of the same cloth he used in fabricating Falstaff. Thus Claudius acquires the features of illicit power which the history plays subordinate, if not purge, in sanctifying power.

Rather than authorizing the state, then, Shakespeare lines up the benign image of carnival – a populist support – in opposition to Claudius. When Laertes returns to demand justice for the murder of his father, he exhibits the same features of popular authority which Shakespeare gave the heroes of his chronicle history plays and attributed to Hamlet as well:

> young Laertes, in a riotous head,
> O'erbears your officers. The rabble call him lord,
> And as the world were now but to begin,

Antiquity forgot, custom not known,
The ratifiers and props of every word,
[They] cry, "Choose we, Laertes shall be king!" (IV.v.102–7)

In light of the power these features have to authorize force in the history
plays, then, we must sit up and take note when the figure of popular
energy is caught up in Claudius's conspiracy to turn the banquet table
into the scene of Hamlet's death. Transformed, these materials testify to
the hierarchizing power of the aristocracy. Untransformed, however,
these materials represent what is outside the aristocratic body and most
threatening to it.

The staging of a play within a play, say, in *A Midsummer Night's Dream*
and *The Taming of the Shrew*, as well as in *Hamlet*, serves another purpose.
Shakespeare makes these stagings part of the official rituals of state even
when directed by pranksters and rude mechanicals. Furthermore, the
dramatic performance so nested within the dramatic performance of the
play as a whole invariably concerns itself with ruptures or disturbances
within the aristocratic body itself. When Hamlet stages *The Murder of
Gonzago*, it is his attempt to locate and purge a corrupt element within the
aristocratic body. In this respect, he does not resemble Laertes playing the
revenger of Senecan tragedy but acts in his capacity as would-be
sovereign. Shakespeare gives Hamlet the state's power to discover and
punish a crime against the sovereign's body. In refusing to display his
power by staging some spectacle of punishment, we should recall, Richard
II weakened his hold on the throne, while Henry IV strengthened his by
taking such action upon acquiring the crown.

The play within the play is Hamlet's attempt to reenact his uncle's
assault on the sovereign's body and thus establish the truth of regicide
which would authorize Hamlet's claim to the throne. He explains:

> I'll have these players
> Play something like the murther of my father
> Before mine uncle. I'll observe his looks,
> I'll tent him to the quick. If 'a do blench,
> I know my course. (II.ii.594–8)

Hamlet means the play to "tent," or probe Claudius as with a dagger that
opens an infected wound. Thus he would inscribe upon his uncle's body
the truth of his crime against the king. Of torture and confession which
precedes the spectacle of punishment, Foucault writes, "the secret and
written form" – torture and confession – "reflects the principle that in
criminal matters the establishment of truth was the absolute right and the
exclusive power of the sovereign."[22] Let us make the statement still

stronger and say that the monarch's ability to establish truth is as important as his ability to incorporate the state within his body politic. Both are means of authorizing forms of violence which otherwise would have to be considered acts of insurrection and regicide. But Hamlet's play fails in two respects to materialize as a spectacle of punishment which would display the authority of Hamlet over Claudius. Because the play is only a play, first of all, and not an official ritual of state, its truth is bracketed as a supposition rather than a reenactment of the truth. It is another instance of Shakespeare's giving Hamlet a mode of speech that cannot constitute political action because it automatically translates all action onto the purely symbolic plane of thought and art. Only here it is the Senecan mode of tragedy that turns the exercise of power into a purely symbolic gesture, not his use of Stoic discourse.

Even as a symbolic gesture, secondly, the play fails to hit its mark. Hamlet has chosen to produce *The Murder of Gonzago* for its political truth. The play he says will be "something like the murther of my father" (II.ii.595). Indeed, the play does reenact that fratricide in that it portrays the aristocratic body turning against itself to inflict a mortal wound. But Hamlet's gloss on the play gives us to understand he has chosen a play portraying the murder of an uncle by his nephew:

> This is one Lucianus, nephew to the king. . . .
> 'A poisons him i'th' garden for his estate. His name's Gonzago. The story is extant, and written in very choice Italian. You shall see anon how the murtherer gets the love of Gonzago's wife. (III.ii.244–64)

Rather than a crime against a patrilineal system of descent, then, *The Murder of Gonzago* portrays a crime which would be precisely equivalent to fratricide in a matrilineal system of descent where uncle and nephew rather than first and second sons constitute the most competitive male relations. This is not to say that Shakespeare has the play betray Hamlet's intentions and reveal the secret wishes – thus the thought crimes – of its director. Quite the contrary, Shakespeare has carefully worked out the configuration of family relations within and without this play. As he did so, Shakespeare deviated from the source by casting the murderer as a nephew to the duke.[23] By this deliberate revision of his source, Shakespeare equated Hamlet's punishment with Claudius's crime. This is to say that both acts of violence assault the sovereign's body rather than establish the absolute power of the aristocratic body over that of its subject. Both turn out to be self-inflicted wounds. As the play concludes by heaping up the bodies of the royal family where the banquet scene should have been, this truth materializes: that the murder of one member of the aristocracy by another is an assault on the entire body, in other words, an act of suicide.

That Hamlet's act of vengeance against his uncle constitutes a crime against the state is dramatized in another way as well: in the language that Hamlet speaks. Where he spoke a Stoic discourse (e.g. "To be or not to be . . .") before staging his play, afterwards Hamlet speaks in the contrasting terms of Senecan tragedy:

> 'Tis now the very witching time of night,
> When churchyards yawn and hell itself [breathes] out
> Contagion to this world. Now could I drink hot blood
> And do such [bitter business as the] day
> Would quake to look on. (III.ii.387–92)

This is the language which Nashe identified a decade earlier as that of the "English Seneca" which characterized earlier productions of "whole Hamlets."[24] By giving him this familiar stage speech, Shakespeare distinguishes Hamlet's exercise of authority from the rituals and processionals concluding the chronicle history plays. At the same time, such speech identifies Hamlet with Claudius whose exercise of force turns into Senecan tragedy, first, in the murder of Hamlet's father which initiated the action of the play, and then in the murder of Hamlet with which the play concludes. Thus Hamlet's play figures out the power of the state on a symbolic plane in the very terms that Claudius uses to enact his authority. Neither can act in a way that establishes the family line according to the strategies of state governing the chronicle history plays.

One might be tempted to declare a generic difference between *Hamlet*, as a tragedy, and the history plays on just these grounds, but I will argue against the wisdom of doing so for those who want to understand Shakespeare's genres as political strategies. Even as he raises questions concerning the iconic relationship between the queen's two bodies, Shakespeare cannot imagine legitimate power in any other way. Given the fact that neither Claudius nor Hamlet could embody the state in a way that effectively hierarchized power – this, chiefly because each had equal claims to power – neither one could become the legitimate sovereign of Denmark. In light of their failure, the arrival of Fortinbras marks *Hamlet* as an Elizabethan play. Nowhere to be found in the sources, his name implies a natural ability to exercise force. Shakespeare also endows Fortinbras with aristocratic blood, though not that of the Danish line. In this, he obviously resembles the figure who emerges at the end of all the major history plays as the product of human history and providence as well. Most perfectly realized in *Henry V*, this figure acquires authority not only through material conflicts which display the effective exercise of force, but also through the metaphysics of blood which he embodies.

VII

Interrogation of the relationship between the monarch's two bodies would not end with the death of Elizabeth and James's ascent to the English throne. We may in fact see Jacobean drama as an attempt to deny there could be any relationship between the two bodies. Jacobean drama, including Shakespeare's own, is obviously troubled by Elizabethan representations which seem to grant the possibility of acquiring power through human force and artifice in violation of the doctrine of blood. In this respect, Jonson's masque of *Oberon* written for the investiture of Henry as Prince of Wales, provides a useful comparison between the Elizabethan and Jacobean strategies for idealizing political authority. Jonson evidently found it advantageous to revise the Elizabethan figure of misrule and thus the kind of artistic authority associated with him. One purpose of the masque was the undoing of the opposition between the carnivalesque and the law of the father, an opposition as we have seen, upon which such a comedy as *A Midsummer Night's Dream* depends for its comic resolution. It should come as no surprise, then, to find that various forms of carnival, particularly those associated with May Day festivities, became increasingly controversial during Elizabeth's reign. These were evidently viewed as practices that resisted the strategies of the Reformation and, as such, were held to be sacrilegious by radical Protestant factions. Reformers also argued that such activities interfered with economic productivity. Moreover, its figures of inversion and boundary dissolution necessarily presented a challenge to the government. The Elizabethan response was mixed. On the one hand, as Peter Stallybrass has argued, when Elizabeth's accession day, November 17, became a national holiday, the state was clearly trying "to harness and appropriate the forces of misrule."[25] On the other hand, Elizabeth was careful not to arouse opposition to the central administration, either by actively supporting traditional festival celebrations or by enforcing rules that would suppress them. At the same time, her government frustrated legal efforts to enforce the practice of Sabbatarianism which gained support in the industrial centers and urban areas.[26] These were the same towns enacting legislation against theatrical performances and entertainments, and it is this legislation which reveals the political motivation most germane to my project.

Margot Heinemann summarizes the letters from the lord mayor and aldermen of London to the Privy Council in 1597 listing their objections to the theater. Not only did they condemn plays for drawing people away from sermons on Sunday, she notes, but the city fathers also felt such entertainments were a source of social disruption:

they encouraged apprentices to absent themselves from work . . . they caused traffic jams and spread infection in time of plague: and they gave an opportunity for the unemployed and idle to meet in riotous assemblies. Indeed, unruly apprentices and servants had admitted that they foregathered at stage plays to organize their "mutinous attempts", "being also the ordinary places for masterless men to come together".[27]

Even as they condemned the popular theater on the same grounds regularly justifying opposition to May Day celebrations and saints' day observances, these same men felt perfectly justified in producing elaborate forms of public and private entertainment:

> The Aldermen themselves freely staged shows, plays, and masques privately in their own houses. They lavished thousands of pounds on Lord Mayors' pageants to impress Londoners with the wealth and glory of their city, and to preach, through allegorical tableaux, the virtues of industry and thrift.[28]

Evidently it was not theater per se that disturbed the town fathers. What was at stake was not the nature of the performance — not a moral issue — but a political one: who had control of the means for representing power? Only those performances could be authorized in London which in turn authorized the governing powers of the city.

In contrast to Elizabeth, James made it a matter of royal policy not only to seek control of the theater but also to advocate the celebration of festivals and the practice of various Maytime sports. In the *Basilikon Doron*, he approves of the practices of the traditional festivities, and in the infamous *Book of Sports* (1618), he argues that participating in sports and festivities did more than improve the health of the laboring poor and make them fit for the army. It actually prevented the populace from engaging in subversive political activities. In declaring his position openly, he necessarily defined his authority in opposition to radical Protestantism where Elizabeth had successfully avoided such confrontation. As Leah S. Marcus notes:

> During the early years of the seventeenth century . . . attitudes toward the maygames became sharply and dangerously polarized: to advocate such pastimes became tantamount to a declaration of loyalty to the king and conservative Anglicanism; to preach or write openly against the pastimes came to imply alliance with the growing factions of puritan and parliamentary dissidents.[29]

What more effective way, then, of revising the figures of Elizabethan literature than using revels to represent the investiture of the heir to the

English throne and Oberon to portray the future monarch of England? What better way to dramatize the new concept of political power than using Oberon to symbolize a rebirth of the powers of blood? In Jonson's masque, he thus inhabits a palace along with the noblest knights of history now "Quickened with a second birth."[30] Representing that of the prince, Oberon's costume incorporates the signs of Roman, Arthurian, and Jacobean nobility, and two white bears draw his chariot toward the center of power to the accompaniment, significantly, of this song:[31]

> Melt earth to sea, sea flow to air,
>   And air fly into fire,
> Whilst we in tunes to Arthur's chair
>   Bear Oberon's desire,
>   Than which there nothing can be higher
> Save James, to whom it flies:
> But he the wonder is of tongues, of ears, of eyes. (lines 220–6)

As the father of Prince Henry, James is the origin of his son's power. In the guise of Oberon, the son acknowledges the principle of genealogy as he places all the powers traditionally opposing the patriarch – those of youth, nature, and the tradition of romance – in the king's service.[32] Thus we learn Oberon and his knights pay homage to James, "To whose sole power and magic they do give / the honor of their being . . ." (lines 49–50). It is worth noting that the costume which Inigo Jones designed for the fairy king in this masque alludes to the three monarchies James claimed to unite within himself. It was as if the masque brought all of the traditional signs of authority under the governance of the contemporary monarch for the sole purpose of identifying that monarch as an historically earlier and mythical form of political authority.

VIII

Henry VIII, Shakespeare's belated history play, consequently resembles the dramatic romances and masques that come into favor under James more than it does a chronicle history play as we know it.[33] Operating in violation of the very strategy he so perfectly realized right through the end of the Epilogue of *Henry V*, Shakespeare makes genealogy one and the same thing as providence in *Henry VIII*. The events which constitute this model of history are those which reproduce Henry VIII and thus perpetuate the power of blood, Henry's divorce from Katharine, for example, and the union with Anne from which Elizabeth is subsequently born. Operating under this imperative, the playwright has no cause to engender sympathy for Katharine or endow his monarch with it. He may in fact equate the unproductive mate with Wolsey and Buckingham – all three oppose legitimate political authority – because they obstruct genealogy. Buckingham represents a contending line of succession, and Wolsey's populist energy serves only his own ambitions. These, we must remember, were the very figures that lent the Elizabethan hero power and enabled him to seize the throne. As these figures came to define the forces conspiring against the Tudor and Stuart lines, however, Shakespeare rather obviously turned them to the task of revising Elizabethan strategies for authorizing power.

The strategies shaping his Elizabethan plays are no less tautological than those he revises. It is worth noting that Henry VIII, unlike the political heroes of an earlier stage, does not have to overpower those who possess the symbols of authority in order to make his line legitimate. Quite the contrary, in possessing the blood, his body is a living icon in relation to which all other signs and symbols acquire meaning and value. This is acknowledged when the king removes his mask after he and his revelers – having disguised themselves as shepherds and dressed in golden costumes – intrude on Wolsey's banquet. Not only is the monarch's presence felt by Wolsey and his guests before the king appears in his own person, but once he does reveal himself as king, the festivities reorganize around him as if around the sun. Wolsey simply cedes his position to one "More worthy this place than myself, to whom / (If I but knew him) with my love and duty / I would surrender it" (I.iv.79–81). Henry need not struggle with these opponents because they possess no force except that which he confers upon them. It is as if they exist only to demonstrate the absolute supremacy of his blood by their utter subjection to its mystic power. Wolsey's famous advice to Cromwell just before the deposed cardinal departs echoes the last words of Katharine and Buckingham by acknowledging Henry as the source of all earthly power:

> Serve the King, and – prithee lead me in.
> There take an inventory of all I have,
> To the last penny, 'tis the King's. My robe
> And my integrity to heaven, is all
> I dare now call my own. (III.ii.450–4)

This is the triumph of the hagiographical theme: to locate the essence of the fully-realized figure in the original. In perfectly realizing this political strategy, however, history gives way to a slow procession of tableaux which convert all the dialectical motion of history into the same static and hierarchical figure of political power.

Shakespeare's use of the carnivalesque in this play offers a means of comparing the later strategy for idealizing power with that lending the materials of chronicle history their Elizabethan form. As his identity makes itself known, the king instantly assumes Wolsey's role as the king of misrule. Referred to as a "keech," or lump of suet, by Buckingham, Shakespeare endows the cardinal with features of the grotesque body. Rather than threaten the monarch, his illicit practices are taken over by Henry as the legitimate prerogatives of the state:

> Let's be merry,
> Good my Lord Cardinal: I have half a dozen healths
> To drink to these fair ladies, and a measure
> To lead 'em once again, and then let's dream
> Who's best in favor. Let the music knock it. (I.iv.104–8)

The disruptive powers associated with the erotic, the demonic, and the folk never constitute a field of contention in this play. Indeed, we find all that is politically threatening caught up, sexualized, and aestheticized in the official ceremony of Anne's coronation:

> Such joy
> I never saw before. Great-bellied women,
> That had not half a week to go, like rams
> In the old time of war, would shake the press
> And make 'em reel before 'em. No man living
> Could say, "This is my wife" there, all were woven
> So strangely in one piece. (IV.i.75–80)

Such a strategy for harnessing populist energy clearly maintains the absolute identification of power and genealogy.

It is no mere accident of history, then, that the ending of *Henry VIII* presents such a striking contrast to the Epilogue of *Henry V*. The blessing of the infant Elizabeth heralds the fulfillment of divine prophecy and guarantees the corporate nature of the Crown in perpetuity. It certainly does not usher in a period of controversy and misrule over which a new contender will triumph. The poetics of Jacobean politics aim at transforming all such change into continuity. For achieving this end, chronology may be discarded and even gender differences effaced to present change as repetition and conflate successive monarchs into a single identity. When Henry demands of the midwife attending Anne, "Is the Queen deliver'd? / Say ay, and of a boy," the old lady answers, "Ay, ay, my liege, / and of a lovely boy. The God of heaven / Both now and ever bless her! 'tis a girl / Promises boys hereafter" (V.i.162–6). Cranmer's blessing over the infant Elizabeth in the last moments of the play places still more emphasis upon sameness over difference and upon continuity over change. This speech echoes with the language of biblical prophecy as

Cranmer foresees her reign of peace and prosperity. Her death in turn will be, he says,

> . . . as when
> The bird of wonder dies, the maiden phoenix,
> Her ashes new create another heir
> As great in admiration as herself,
> So shall she leave her blessedness to one . . .
> Who from the sacred ashes of her honor
> Shall star-like rise as great in fame as she was,
> And so stand fix'd. (V.iv.39–47)

The fulfillment of this prophecy is none other than King James, whom this speech has united with both Elizabeth and Henry VIII in the corporate identity of the Crown.

IX

If nothing else, Shakespeare's inability to write an Elizabethan chronicle history play for a Jacobean audience indicates the degree to which Renaissance drama was a political activity. Shakespeare drew upon the same sources and worked under the general imperative to idealize political authority throughout his career. As political circumstances changed and presented the monarch with new forms of opposition, then, the strategies for legitimizing that authority had to change accordingly. In the Elizabethan history play, art authorizes genealogy. That is, to legitimize blood one must acquire the signs and symbols of authorization, which is to question the iconicity of the king's body and entertain the possibility of its arbitrary relation to the laws and ceremonies of state. Shakespeare's only Jacobean history play declares itself a contradiction in terms by emphatically canceling out this notion of power. Genealogy authorizes art in this play, and the production of art consequently comes squarely under a political imperative to display wealth and title.

The chapters that follow – on Shakespeare's tragedies and dramatic romances – will consider the major Jacobean genres as formal manifestations of the political imperative which both limited James and provided him with ways to display himself as the natural embodiment of metaphysical power. My analysis will rest, as it has to this point, on the assumption that culture, in providing certain figures of legitimate authority, has much more to do with a monarch's style of exercising power than does his individuality in our modern psychological sense of the term. Accordingly, we find the Jacobean theater revising Elizabethan materials under the pressure from new political resistance to traditional figures of patriarchy. James's succession to power appears to have ended the competition among various families for control of England. This was in part due to James's shrewd decision to arrange marriages between the major families, a practice he first began in Scotland where he successfully brought peace to the feuding clans. When he came to England he continued the same policy. But the end of the Elizabethan style of competition among rival court factions was as much a response to new resistance forming against his style of patriarchy. This challenge to the ideology of the court no doubt encouraged the court to think of itself as a unified and hierarchized body not unlike the figure enacted by the court masque. In opposition to this form of authority was that embodied by parliament, whose claim to power had nothing to do with blood; it derived instead from the contractual relationship between the people and the state.

It is not my point to argue that the Jacobean theater in general did not differ in its fundamental ideology from the Elizabethan theater. It represents the differences between them by Shakespeare's revision of his earlier strategies for authorizing power, and I consider this "artistic development" as two poles of imaginative possibilities for representing essentially the same form of power. Both poles presuppose the desirability of a pure aristocratic body. Although Shakespeare renounces the artistic strategies which distinguish romantic comedy and chronicle history from his other dramatic genres, this does not mean the politics of the theater had changed. It remained a place for displaying state power. His shift in genres occurred, I will argue, as he developed strategies to authorize essentially the same fantasy of power that motivated his earlier dramas. But those strategies had to change as the conditions for producing such a fantasy altered significantly in the years preceding 1604.

Accordingly, we find the Jacobean Shakespeare dragging Elizabethan materials upon a stage of punishment to purge them of their inclusionary ethos. This effectively canceled out the desirability of marrying into power. In dismantling the Elizabethan heroine, then, Shakespeare was not inviting his audience to understand her as undesirable by virtue of mixing male and female features. The Elizabethan woman of Shakespeare's romantic comedies has the power to give herself in marriage. Such a challenge to traditional patriarchal prerogatives was considered politically subversive under James where it was perfectly in keeping with the Elizabethan strategy of authorizing the monarch's power. In the romances, we find much the same reactionary strategy at work to purify the iconography of state. Here again the objective is to rule out any possibility of exogamous desire so as to eliminate the possibility of power flowing outward through the body of the woman. In apparent contradiction with the logic of Elizabethan sexuality as exemplified by Petrarchan verse, the dramatic romances formulate a mythological family through whom priority is granted to the metaphysics of blood over the natural body of power and an efficacious use of force. I will allow these deliberately sketchy descriptions to stand by way of an introduction to my chapters on the Jacobean Shakespeare, where I hope to give them textual substance and the force of political logic.

3

THE THEATER OF PUNISHMENT
*Jacobean tragedy and the
politics of misogyny*

Elizabeth Tudor knew the power of display. She also knew how to display
her power as queen. This is not to say that even so powerful a monarch as
she could determine the conditions for effectively displaying political
power. Upon her accession, if not well before, Elizabeth found herself
thoroughly inscribed within a system of political meaning. Marie Axton
explains:

> for the purposes of the law it was found necessary by 1561 to endow the
> Queen with two bodies: a *body natural* and a *body politic*. (This body
> politic should not be confused with the old metaphor of the realm as a
> great body composed of many men with the king as a head. The ideas
> are related but distinct.) The body politic was supposed to be *contained
> within the natural body of the Queen*. When lawyers spoke of this body
> politic they referred to a specific quality: the essence of *corporate
> perpetuity*. The Queen's natural body was subject to infancy, error, and
> old age; her body politic . . . was held to be unerring and immortal.[1]
> (emphasis mine)

The "lawyers," as Axton observes, "were unable or unwilling to separate
state and monarch."[2] Elizabeth also insisted upon identifying her body
with England on grounds she embodied the mystical power of the blood.
Her natural body both contained and stood for this power. It did so at a
moment when England was ready to understand power in nationalist
terms and Elizabeth was bent on displaying her power accordingly. Her
sexual features figured into a representation of the monarch's body and
redefined the concept of the body politic in certain characteristically
Elizabethan ways. At the same time, I will insist, the monarch's sexuality
was always just that, the *monarch's* sexuality.[3] As such, the features of

Elizabeth's body natural were always already components of a political figure which made the physical vigor and autonomy of the monarch one and the same thing as the condition of England. The English form of patriarchy distributed power according to a principle whereby a female could legitimately and fully embody the power of the patriarch. Those powers were in her and nowhere else so long as she sat on the throne. They were no less patriarchal for being embodied as a female, and the female was no less female for possessing patriarchal powers. In being patriarchal, we must conclude, the form of state power was not understood as male in any biological sense, for Elizabeth was certainly represented and treated as a female. The idea of a female patriarch appears to have posed no contradiction in terms of Elizabethan culture. This chapter pursues several implications of this iconic notion of the queen's body by way of considering the conditions for political display.

First, I shall cite one or two examples to suggest how far a Tudor monarch could go in maintaining his or her iconographic status. Accounts of the debate on the Act of Supremacy reveal that some members of Parliament felt that to name a woman Supreme Head of the Church was more than most Catholics and many Protestants would tolerate. Although her brother and father had assumed the title of "Supreme Head" of the Church of England, Elizabeth agreed to revise the title she bore to "Supreme Governor." This was just one of many occasions where she allowed her image to be sexed. But when sexuality was used in any way to compromise her patriarchal prerogatives, the queen reacted in an entirely different manner. In 1576, for instance, the recently appointed Archbishop Grindal wrote her to request that "you would not use to pronounce so resolutely and preemptorily, *quasi ex auctoritate*, as ye may do in civil and extern matters. . . ."[4] The queen immediately sequestered Grindal and would have removed him entirely from his post, had he not "forstalled the arrangements . . . by dying, still in office."[5] Where she would tolerate minor changes in title, then, she would brook absolutely no challenge to the power inherent in her blood. By the same token, upon assuming the throne, she renewed the practice initiated by her father and continued by her brother which installed the royal coat of arms over the chancel arch of the churches of England. Her coat of arms thus replaced the religious images which had been condemned in the iconoclastic reform of the English Church. "Honor toward this royal emblem, if not civic veneration," writes John Phillips, "was now demanded from Englishmen. . . ."[6] As the church came to house the secular emblems of state, the queen's sexual body acquired the power of a religious image. Bishop Jewel, for one, referred to her as "the only nurse and mother of the church."[7] Elizabeth treated sex as her particular signature upon the body politic which in no way changed the essential nature of its power.[8]

The identification of the queen's sexual body with the political body was no less absolute than the iconic bonding of the political body to the sacred authority of the Church. Roy Strong discusses the royal coat of arms as but "one of a series of material objects which were universally regarded as emanations of royal power. In this way," he continues, "the royal arms erected in churches as manifestations of the royal governorship of the *Ecclesia Anglia* become 'portraits' of the Queen."[9] Strong includes this emblem with the paintings and engravings that represented her natural body. Among these portraits, I would like to take special notice of the Ditchley portrait that shows Elizabeth standing upon the map of England, as well as a Dutch engraving of 1598 which, in similar fashion, portrays her body enclosing Europe against the Pope and the power of Spain. Such portraits as these made explicit, in Peter Stallybrass's words, "the conjunction of imperial virgin and cartographic image to constitute together the terrain of Elizabethan nationalism."[10] Even when the bond between her body and the body politic was not represented in territorial terms, however, this bond was still apparent in portraits where the surface of her body was ornamented with the power and wealth of the state. That Elizabeth wanted her subjects to know they were admiring England's power in gazing upon her image is apparent in her response to the industry which sprang up for the purpose of representing the queen. In 1563 a proclamation was drafted calling for one painter to have access to the queen "to take the natural representation of her majesty," and "to prohibit all manner of other persons to draw, paint, grave, or portray her majesty's personage or visage. . . ."[11] Though apparently never enforced, this proclamation "was designed to counter the production of debased images of the Queen."[12] Along with others drafted during her reign, this measure suggests that it was not royal vanity that made her fret over "deform'd" images and counterfeit portraiture but her awareness of the queen's image as a kind of political coin whose iconic value had to be protected.

There is evidence to suggest that Elizabeth's loyal subjects were not the only ones to accept the iconic nature of her representation. Her enemies apparently believed that because her image "partook in some mysterious way of the nature of the sitter it was also potentially dangerous." Strong bases this speculation, as he explains, on the fact that "Throughout the reign efforts were made to dispose of the Queen by stabbing, burning, or otherwise destroying her image."[13] Burghley was sufficiently worried about such attacks on the queen's image to treat them as dangerous offenses. But the way in which an assault on Elizabeth's personal iconography constituted an assault on the body politic itself is explained still more clearly by an incident in *Richard II*. As I explained in the preceding chapter, Bullingbroke declares he is executing Bushy and Green for the crimes of "disfiguring" the king. Such an act of treason evidently extends to assaults on any member of the aristocracy if it extends to the signs and symbols of royal blood. Thus Bullingbroke charges the pair with "disparking" his own lands, defacing his coat of arms and razing his imprese, "leaving me no sign," he says, "Save men's opinion and my living blood / To show the world I am a gentleman" (III.i.25–7).

In a system where the power of the monarch was immanent in the official symbols of the state, the natural body of the monarch was bound by the same poetics of display. That Elizabeth knew the power of such display is evident in her willingness to help finance and stage a passage through London the day before her coronation.[14] Unlike the more important pageants which had been financed for her sister by foreign communities in London, Elizabeth excluded from the passage either the support or the participation of "any foreign person."[15] This point was emphasized in the account of the passage that was published almost immediately afterwards. Her pageant therefore provided an exclusively English context for displaying her power. This well-known description of her passage through London to Westminster the day before her coronation suggests the degree to which the signs and symbols of power were all understood in reference to her body:

> if a man shoulde say well, he could not better tearme the Citie of London that time, than a stage wherein was shewed the wonderful spectacle, of a noble hearted Princesse toward her most loving People, and the People's exceding comfort in beholding so worthy a Soveraigne, and hearing so Prince like a voice, which could not but have set the enemie on fyre, since the verture is in the enemie alway commended, much more could not but enflame her naturall, obedient, and most loving People, whose weale leaneth onely uppon her Grace and her Government.[16]

The staging of this official passage, like that of a royal progress, not only brought forth the queen's body and displayed it in the context of her considerable entourage. It also called forth elaborate pageants, tributes, opulent shows of all kind in response to the queen's appearance. These to be witnessed by large numbers of people. To speak of the queen's body in such terms is not to speak of the desiring subject or the object of desire she has become in historical narratives written in the nineteenth and twentieth centuries. To the contrary, the aesthetic performances centered in the figure of the queen were entirely political, as they aimed at identifying the monarch's body with English power in all its manifestations.[17]

II

Displaying the monarch's body was so essential to maintaining the power of state that the aesthetics of such displays shaped the theater which grew up during Elizabeth's reign. On 16 May 1559, she imposed a "temporary inhibition of plays," and her Privy Council assumed jurisdiction over all theatrical performances. While her brother had also imposed a temporary restraint on the production of plays during periods of social unrest, no other Tudor monarch maintained such tight control over the plays and players as Elizabeth.[18] By 1572 only barons or personages of higher degree were allowed the privilege of maintaining "minstrels or players of interludes." This legislation was amended, but not changed substantially, in 1576, in 1584–5, and again in 1597–8.[19] It would appear that only members of the peerage could be trusted with so powerful a political medium. After the mid-1570s, the very existence of the elaborate machinery of playhouses, acting companies, and censorship procedures was obviously associated with the political interests of the queen. Ann Jennalie Cook suggests that "the entire rationale for the existence of dramatic companies was that they provided essential recreation for the sovereign. In theory," she continues, "public performances merely provided an opportunity for rehearsal and perfection of plays before they were presented at Court."[20] I simply want to take this notion more literally than Cook does. Her research shows a theater audience largely composed of the so-called privileged playgoers who identified their interests with those of the queen.[21] But it was as much, if not more, the treatment of the aristocratic body on stage as it was the constitution of the audience, I will argue, that made the public theater and the Inns of Court drama resemble other displays of state power. It is easy for us to imagine how, for such an audience, the staging of chronicle history and even tragedy made openly political statements. Though perhaps not so obvious to a modern reader of Renaissance literature, the romantic comedies and Petrarchan lyrics were bound by the same imperative to identify the queen's body with that of the state. More than any other monarch, we should recall, Elizabeth regulated the sexual relations of her court. In such an environment as this, a drama was never more political than when it turned on the body of an aristocratic woman.

I will use the much abused play *Titus Andronicus* to make my point. As thoroughly unnatural as its staging of sexual relations seems today, *Titus* plays on the whole notion of the state as the body of an aristocratic female. Titus's daughter is raped and disfigured in the second act of the play. Shakespeare's stage directions suggest he brings her on stage after the rape mainly in order to call attention to her mutilated condition. The sheer spectacle of a woman, herself dismembered, carrying her father's amputated hand in her mouth has not earned this play a particularly high place in a canon based on lofty ideas and good taste. The mutilation of Lavinia's body has been written off as one of the exuberant excesses of an immature playwright or else as the corrupting influence of another poet.[22] But I would like to consider these sensational features as part of a political iconography which Shakespeare understood as well as anyone else, one which he felt obliged to use as well as free to exploit for his own dramatic purposes. With this purpose in mind we might understand the otherwise outrageous scene in which Titus receives his own hand along with the heads of his two sons from Saturninus, the emperor. Seeing the human members which have been severed from himself, Titus issues this memorably gruesome command,

> Come, brother, take a head,
> And in this hand the other will I bear;
> And, Lavinia, thou shalt be employed;
> Bear thou my hand, sweet wench, between thy teeth. (III.i.279–82)

To tell her father she has been raped as well as mutilated, Lavinia has to rifle through a volume of Ovid with her handless arms until she finds the account of Philomel. Shakespeare's stage direction reads, "*She takes the staff in her mouth, and guides it with her stumps, and writes*" (s.d., IV.i.76).

What is important in this – as in the other scenes where Lavinia's body appears as synecdoche and emblem of the disorder of things – is that Shakespeare has us see the rape of Lavinia as the definitive instance of dismemberment. I write this knowing it defies the logic inherent in the figure of rape. We are accustomed to think of rape as a boundary violation where the outsider forcibly penetrates some sacred cultural territory – the sanctuary of the home or the enclosure of the individual, if not the autonomy of the aristocratic community – and calls these concepts into question. But Shakespeare uses rape for this purpose neither in *Titus Andronicus* nor in *The Rape of Lucrece*. He does not allow us to name rape as the crime when we find rape reinscribed upon Lavinia's body as the crime of dismemberment. Indeed amputation displaces penetration as Lavinia's stumps point back to the story of Philomel in order to make the fact of rape known. What Shakespeare does stage, then, is the fact of dismemberment as a highly self-conscious revision of his classical materials. I would like to suggest that this peculiar turning of rape into dismemberment is a singularly Elizabethan move. The mutilation of Lavinia's body simply restates her father's murder of his own son, the decapitation of her two brothers, her father's self-inflicted amputation, his dicing up of the emperor's stepsons for their mother's consumption, and all the slicing, dicing, chopping and lopping that heaps bodies upon the stage in *Titus Andronicus*. Lavinia's body restates and interprets this seemingly gratuitous carnage in a way that must have been clear to an Elizabethan audience in as much as her body was that of a daughter of the popular candidate for emperor of Rome, the first choice of wife for the emperor of Rome, and the betrothed of the emperor's younger brother. That as such she stands for the entire aristocratic body is made clear when Marcus Andronicus, inspired by the pile of bodies heaped at the banquet table, enjoins the citizens of Rome, "Let me teach you how to knit again / . . . These broken limbs into one body" (V.iii.70–2).

Dismemberment entails the loss of members. Thus the initial gesture of penetration does not seem to matter so much in Shakespeare's version of the Philomel story as the condition of Lavinia's body which both conceals and points to the initial act of penetration. Rather than make Lavinia serve as the object of illicit lust, Shakespeare uses her body as the site for political rivalry among various families with competing claims to power over Rome. For one of them to possess Lavinia is for that family to display power over the rest – nothing more nor less than that. By the same token, to wound Lavinia is to wound oneself, as if dismembering her body were dismembering a body of which one were a part, thus to cut oneself off from that body. To make certain we see this distinction between an earlier meaning of rape and his own, Shakespeare has Lavinia destroyed by the remaining hand of her father, but not because her rape has stained his blood. Before killing her, Titus asks the emperor for clarification on precisely this point:

> Was it well done of rash Virginius
> To slay his daughter with his own right hand,
> Because she was enforc'd, stain'd, and deflow'r'd? (V.iii.36–8)

Saturninus answers that Virginius was right to slay Virginia, but not for the reason Titus gives, not because she was "deflow'r'd" (Virginia was not), but rather, the emperor says, "Because the girl should not survive her shame, / And by her presence still renew his sorrows" (lines 41–2). Titus's farewell to Lavinia repeats the distinction between her "shame" and his "sorrow" which transforms the concepts of dishonor and pollution usually associated with rape into quite a different order of transgression: "Die, die, Lavinia, and thy shame with thee, / And with thy shame thy father's sorrow die" (lines 46–7). The play proves that the murder of his daughter is a self-inflicted wound on Titus's part. Like any claim on Lavinia's body that leads to its mutilation, this blow brings death to all those competing for power over Rome.

But Shakespeare's *The Rape of Lucrece* makes this theme of self-slaughter still more explicit. While her rape at the hands of Tarquin is reported rather than dramatically represented, the penetration of Lucrece's body by her own dagger repeats the rape in figurative terms which merit elaborate display. This display effectively translates penetration into dismemberment. It is Lucrece's mutilated body to which the poem draws our eyes, as Lucrece's father throws himself ". . . on her self-slaughtered body," and "from the purple fountain Brutus drew / The murd'rous knife" (1733–5). Not her penetration by the knife but its withdrawal, we should note, releases the flow of blood which transforms the female body into a grotesquely disfigured object. Shakespeare takes this occasion to render the female in emblematic terms which resemble the Ditchley portrait in its bonding of the cartographic image to the sexual body of the monarch. Here – in the rape of Lucrece – the female body displays such violation in terms that suggest it is the aristocratic body imaged forth as, for example, in the Ditchley portrait. It is the body figured as the state which has been ravaged:

> and, as it [the knife] left the place,
> Her blood, in poor revenge, held it in chase;
>
> And bubbling from her breast, it doth divide
> In two slow rivers, that the crimson blood
> Circles her body in on every side,
> Who like a late-sack'd island vastly stood
> Bare and unpeopled in this fearful flood. (1735–41)

Shakespeare's use of the terms "late-sack'd" and "unpeopled" together with a phrase like "self-slaughtered" is worth noting. By describing the mutilated woman in such apparently self-contradictory terms, he not only equates the health of the aristocratic body with that of the state, or island, he also specifies the nature of the threat to the nation's wellbeing. Lucrece is only *like* a "late-sack'd island" whose territory has been invaded and devastated by forces from without. She has actually been destroyed from within. The last scene of *Titus* makes the same turn on the whole notion of rape as the figure for an alien invasion. Upon encountering the heap of carnage on the stage, Aemilius asks Lucius, the new emperor:

> Tell us what Sinon hath bewitch'd our ears,
> Or who hath brought the fatal engine in
> That gives our Troy, our Rome, the civil wound. (V.iii.85–7)

Again, rape has become the penetration of a political body, in this case, by "the fatal engine" of the Greeks. In equating rape with civic disorder, however, once again Shakespeare couples seemingly contradictory terms. He identifies Rome's fate with Troy's in such a manner as to equate

Lavinia's rape with the wounding of the body politic. But then he adds a peculiarly Elizabethan twist and has Aemilius call the mutilated body of the state, Rome's "shameful execution on herself" (V.iii.76).

The same use of this material occurs in *The Rape of Lucrece* where Shakespeare compares Tarquin to Sinon (lines 1520–68), the Greek who convinced the Trojans they should accept the gift which bore lethal invaders in its belly. He also has Brutus address Lucrece's husband in terms that attribute the victim's "wretchedness' as much to her suicide as to Tarquin's initial assault on her body: "Thy wretched wife mistook the matter so,/ To slay herself that should have slain her foe" (1826–7). In both cases Shakespeare changes his sources to stress the element of self-destruction rather than the kingdom's suffering at the hand of an invader. In her story of Salutati's *Declamatio Lucretiae*, Stephanie Jed explains the politics inherent in the Lucrece story as it was taken up by Salutati. It became part of the Humanist project reshaping classical materials into a Florentine historiography during the fifteenth century in Italy. Particularly important to my argument is the relationship Jed draws between the figure of rape and the nationalist strategies which represent the birth and justification of state power as an act of self-purification and enclosure in the face of foreign penetration. In the Italian version of the story, as Jed explains it, rape is clearly a crime of pollution.[23] It finds an antidote in Lucrece's suicide and the Tarquins' expulsion, which cuts off the polluting members and strengthens Rome.

When he equates rape with dismemberment, then, Shakespeare is revising the whole ethos of the sources for stories of rape as well as those about Lucrece in order to make them English. Almost every editor has been willing to write off this peculiar behavior of the figure of rape in *Titus Andronicus* as a lapse on Shakespeare's part. In the notes to one edition of *Titus*, Frank Kermode is frankly puzzled by Shakespeare's use of the story of Virginius, a father in Livy's account, who slew his daughter in order to prevent her body from becoming the site of family dishonor. Kermode writes, "This Roman centurion killed his daughter to *prevent* her rape. Either the dramatist has got the story wrong or he is failing to convey the idea that Titus has a better case for killing Lavinia than Virginius had for killing his daughter."[24] Critics rarely muster the boldness to chastise Shakespeare in this way for the careless use of his source materials. Thus we must sit up and take note when so fine a critic as Kermode feels perfectly comfortable in doing this. Kermode obviously feels he is on stable cultural ground when he holds Shakespeare to a logic of rape. Kermode's thinking on sexual matters is obviously locked into the notion that penetration is the essential element of rape, as such it is conceptually the opposite of dismemberment, or the figure of castration. According to this more modern politics of the body, it can make no sense to equate rape with dismemberment because political power is never figured out in female form: the female body represents the absence of power. Page duBois makes this point more eloquently in an essay on *Coriolanus* where she contrasts the Freudian reading of Rome as a masculine site of power to the Rome one encounters in Shakespeare's *Coriolanus*. The power of Shakespearean Rome in that play is not only female — duBois argues convincingly that Shakespeare has inscribed Coriolanus's body with female features — but it is also dismembered. Coriolanus is cut off from mother, from Rome, and ultimately from himself, in a sequence that identifies these acts of mutilation as one and the same.[25] As duBois' critique of Freud also suggests, Shakespeare's way of sexing power points less to some sexual problem or to a lapse of craftsmanship in the poet than it does to his thinking within a poetics of sexuality that radically differs from our own. To understand the degree to which Renaissance sexuality has to be figured out as a different political formation, we might turn to another Renaissance revision of the classical text.

Shakespeare was not the only one to modify Livy's story of Virginius for the Elizabethan stage. Some twenty-five years before *Titus Andronicus*, a hybrid moral interlude with Senecan features was written under the title of *Appius and Virginia*. In this early Elizabethan play, Virginius claims he would rather commit suicide than see his daughter deflowered by Appius, but then Virginia corrects her father's suicidal inclinations by giving him this lesson in the logic of Livy's text: "If I be once spotted,/ My name and kindred then forth will be blotted;/ And if thou my father should die for my cause / The world would accompt me as gilty in cause" (vii.794–7).[26] There is a reason why the early Elizabethan Virginius does not have his politics of rape quite right; his deviation from the classical model allows the author of this interlude to draw the equation between her rape and his death, neither of which occur in the classical story. To be sure, this is not so clear a statement of Elizabethan ideology as the heaping of bodies upon the stage for which the mutilated body of the woman stands as both cause and emblem, but it is an Elizabethan use of the female body nonetheless. It identifies the power of the state with the state of the female body and sees the danger to the state arising from the competition of rivalrous forces within the aristocratic body rather than from that body's penetration by forces from without. Besides, the very name Virginia could in no way have been a matter of personal choice for an Elizabethan author. To use it was to invoke the official iconography of state, which constituted a political gesture whether one's use of the virgin was faithful to Livy's account or not. And should the audience not understand this from the start, the Tudor interlude informs them outright that Virginia is not only "A virgin pure" but also "a quene in life" (v.478). These changes in classical stories of rape were obviously made for an age which thought of state power as female. Under such circumstances, these representations – perhaps any representation – of the aristocratic female provided the substance of a political iconography which enhanced the power of the Elizabethan state.

III

It is in terms of its representation of the female body and its relation to the disposition of power in the play, that I would like to regard *Hamlet*, now as a tragedy. In considering it alongside the history plays, I noted how it shared with them certain strategies for authorizing power while setting these strategies against one another in irreconcilable conflict. Thus Denmark is Hamlet's patrimony, but he cannot control its territory; Claudius possesses the land with the crown, but he has not inherited these according to a patrilineal principle. The dilemma of the play therefore arises from and turns upon the meaning and disposition of Gertrude's body. Claudius acquired the throne of Denmark with his marriage to Gertrude. In this respect, her body can be equated with Denmark. To Hamlet, on the other hand, Gertrude's body is the vessel through which the royal blood of the Danish line has passed; she is not the political body incarnate even if she has been married to Old Denmark. Where competition operates to legitimize blood in Elizbethan history plays, the same form of rivalry leads inevitably to the mutilation of the political body in the tragedies. Hamlet marks an historical change in this particular component of England's political iconography. Where Lavinia provided the site for the various forces competing for Rome, Gertrude's body stages a conceptual shift in the representation of political disorder. Her body becomes the place where the iconic bonding of blood and territory breaks down into competing bases for political authority. The question is not a matter of which family embodies legitimate authority over the land, but rather one of whether blood or else the possession of territory matters more in constituting legitimate authority.

Hamlet defines the opposition to legitimate power rather differently than Shakespeare does in the play as a whole. Shakespeare has Hamlet change the nature of the assault on the political body by staging *The Murder of Gonzago* as an entertainment for the king, as well as the means of indicting his uncle. This play within the play represents the queen's body in terms that go still farther in contradicting the politics of the body characterizing Elizabethan England. *The Murder of Gonzago* ends before the logic of this representation can play itself out. Nevertheless, the dumb show which precedes the performance, in combination with Hamlet's gloss and his uncle's angry reaction to it, bears intimations of another politics of the body. Hamlet's gloss on the play tells of a nephew poisoning his uncle, the king, and then wooing the queen. The audience has seen the king murdered "for his estate," Hamlet explains, only to add, "You shall see anon how the murtherer gets the love of Gonzago's wife" (III.ii.263–4). After this statement, Claudius rises and effectively closes down the theater before the drama of illicit sexual relations can fairly get underway. Coming when it does, this interruption of the play within the play further distinguishes two acts of treason – the seizure of royal property and the possession of the queen's body – one from the other. It is more than a little interesting to note that the threat to the aristocratic body is a double threat which distinguishes two points at which the aristocratic body might receive a mortal wound. Where Shakespeare could pose a political threat of this same magnitude in his earlier Senecan drama simply by mutilating the female body, now it requires two separate assaults to lose the land and to destroy the sacred symbols of state. Thus Shakespeare has the Player Queen in Hamlet's script describe her own sexual behavior as an assault on the political body separate and distinct from that which destroyed the king's natural body: "A second time I kill my husband dead,/ When second husband kisses me in bed" (III.ii.184–5). This splitting of the political body on the basis of sex does not mean that sexual desire is any less political than it was in earlier drama. It only means – in *Hamlet* at least – that the politics of the body is susceptible to historical change.

The Player Queen in Hamlet's revised script opens up a new category of crime. Her body is no longer that of the state. Or perhaps it is more accurate to say this the other way around, that the political body is no longer a woman. Accordingly, the Player Queen ceases to be a source of legitimate power. Like Gertrude, she crowns a counterfeit monarch who possesses the land on a basis other than blood. In the play within the play, then, the female body becomes a place where the body politic can be corrupted as the queen displaces rather than embodies the blood. Furthermore, she corrupts the official iconography of state as she becomes an object of desire in her own right, a desire for the signs and symbols of power dissociated from the metaphysics of blood. I am suggesting that there are different conceptions of the female body which interact in *Hamlet* to the eternal fascination of modern readers. One of these is particularly difficult for us to imagine because it requires one to see the body politic as female. The second notion of the female body develops with the revision of the first under the pressure from Elizabeth's aging body and the subsequent formation of new political resistance to the patriarchal ideal.

This second notion of the body politic sees the female body – and by this I mean specifically that of the aristocratic female – as the symbol and point of access to legitimate authority, thus as the potential substitute for blood and a basis for counterfeit power. The first sees the body as one and the same as the political body. This view resists our attempts at privileging sexual differences over those based on blood, however intensely modern culture encourages one to see the aristocratic body as a sexual body first and only then as a political body. The second view of the body allows us to translate political relationships into sexual relationships as it cuts a clear difference between the body politic and that of the female. With the possibility that her body serves as the symbolic substitute for some original body, furthermore, comes the possibility of construing the aristocratic woman as an object of sexual desire rather than as the means to political power. But to regard Gertrude in the light of modern sexuality is to reverse the priorities of Jacobean thinking where sexual desire always has a political meaning and objective. We regularly perform this gesture of historical reversal when we read the political formations overlapping in *Hamlet* as events in an interpsychic melodrama where queens are no longer political figures but only Hamlet's mother. Instead, I would like to stress the figural discontinuity between Gertrude's body and that of the Player Queen.

The fate of Gertrude makes *Hamlet* an Elizabethan play. Upon the condition of her body depends the health of the state. Like Old Denmark before her, Gertrude dies from taking poison into her body, and the same poison strikes down Hamlet, Laertes and Claudius as well. Her death thus initiates the heaping of bodies which characterizes the Elizabethan Seneca; the wounding of one of its members is the wounding of the entire political body. In this case, however, the infiltration of that body with poison puts an end to the Danish line. This is the fate, experienced by one, that all members share. This, then, and not by a blow is how Shakespeare imagines a lethal assault on the body politic. But *The Murder of Gonzago* takes the logic of this figure one step further. In doing so, Shakespeare uses poison to threaten the political body in a manner which appears to contradict the politics of dismemberment. Merely by inciting desire, the queen's sexuality becomes a form of corruption equivalent to but not the same as the poison which is poured in the ear of the sleeping king. Thus Hamlet insists upon shifting the crime from the fact of regicide to the act of "incest," namely the sexual relations between Claudius and his brother's wife which Hamlet considers illicit.

The play within the play can be viewed as Hamlet's way of distinguishing the one crime from the other, a distinction which shifts the means of assault on the political body to the female. Such a shift can occur only if the queen is not the same thing as the patriarch. Then any misuse of her sexual body, however deliberate on her part, may be understood as a direct assault on the whole concept of patriarchy. Then, too, any diversion of patrilineage flowing through her may be understood as a violation of the metaphysics of blood. Hamlet's obsession with the misuse of the queen's sexuality, more than with his uncle's possession of the state, transforms the threat of dismemberment into that of pollution. In redefining the nature of the threat against the body politic, Hamlet is attempting to stage a Jacobean tragedy, for Jacobean tragedy shares his obsessive concern with the sexual behavior of the aristocratic female.

IV

Mutilation assumes a more central place in Jacobean tragedy. It is almost as if all the prominent playwrights of the day suddenly felt obliged to torture, smother, strangle, stab, or poison an aristocratic woman when assembling the materials for staging a tragedy. In drawing upon the Elizabethan Seneca, later tragedy consistently makes this move: it destroys the bond linking rape metaphorically to mutilation. Instead, Jacobean tragedy characteristically sets rape and mutilation in a relationship of problem to solution. This change is most clearly dramatized in the elaborate scenes of punishment which distinguish Jacobean tragedy from Elizabethan drama. Highly ritualized and particularly gruesome, these scenes of punishment call attention to themselves as self-consciously staged. The following summary of a well-known Jacobean scene is typical in all but one respect:

> A lecherous duke is forced to kiss the poisoned skull of a woman whom he murdered when she refused his advances. As the poison begins to take effect, assassins drive a knife through his tongue, pinning it to his jaw. Dying, the duke has to watch as the duchess cuckolds him with his bastard son. Meanwhile, assassins kick the duke's body relentlessly until the poison does its work.[27]

The only unusual detail in this scene is the gender of the victim. Spectacles of punishment are more usually staged upon the body of an aristocratic female.

Recall, for example, the scene where her swarthy husband slowly smothers the virtuous lady from a prominent Venetian family. In a different scene Shakespeare dramatizes the suicide attempts of another aristocratic lady. Initially unsuccessful at taking her own life with a dagger, this woman dresses in her "best attires, crown and all" and then clasps an adder to her breast. Given how regularly one encounters the many scenes of sexual abuse and mutilation in Jacobean drama, it is

sometimes difficult to remember they arise out of political problems –
from Machiavellian intrigues at court to international conflicts. Jacobean
tragedies offer up their scenes of excessive punishment as if mutilating the
female could somehow correct political corruption. The female in question
may be completely innocent, her torture gratuitous, yet in play after play
she demands her own death or else claims responsibility for her murder.
In one notable example, Shakespeare revives Desdemona long enough for
Emilia to ask who is responsible for the murder, to which Desdemona
answers, "Nobody, I myself." The Duchess of Malfi is duped into kissing a
severed hand, viewing the corpses of her children, and then listening to
the wild songs of a chorus of madmen. As assassins approach her with rope
in hand, she instructs them, "Pull and pull strongly . . ." (IV.ii.230).[28]
When murderers begin to stab Vittoria Corombona's maid, Webster
makes her mistress demand:

> You shall not kill her first. Behold my breast:
> I will be waited on in death. . . . (V.vi.214–15)[29]

And Chapman has the countess plead:

> Oh kill me, kill me,
> Dear husband, be not crueler than death.
> You have beheld some Gorgon. (V.i.126–9)[30]

This, at the crucial moment in *Bussy D'Ambois*.

The women on the Jacobean stage are tortured, hung, smothered,
strangled, stabbed, poisoned or dismembered for one of two reasons:
either they are the subject of clandestine desire or else they have become
an object of desire which threatens the aristocratic community's self-
enclosure. Their innocence notwithstanding, women in *The Revenger's
Tragedy* must be poisoned once they become the objects of adulterous
desires. The Count Montsurrey in *Bussy D'Ambois* tortures Tamyra for
her secret assignations, and Othello murders Desdemona because he
assumes she has been guilty of infidelity. True, he is wrong to doubt her
innocence. On the other hand, Desdemona has, like the Duchess of Malfi,
violated the law of her blood in so marrying. Her marriage to the Moor
echoes the mismating of the Egyptian and the Roman, the duchess and the
steward, the duke and the White Devil as well as those two queens who
lust for the bastard Edmund. In other words, it seems that women must be
punished excessively when they have blurred within their bodies the
distinction between what is properly inside and what must be kept
outside the aristocratic community.

To be sure, the purity of the aristocratic community is at issue in
Elizabethan drama, but not with such disastrous consequences for

women. At the end of various Elizabethan comedies, the community seems enlarged and less exclusive. But even though its boundaries appear to be permeable, the community still remains utterly unsullied. In Jacobean tragedy, in the other hand, the gap between the two social bodies – the aristocratic body and that of the people – appears to close, with the obvious aim of canceling out the Elizabethan desire to cross over. To do this, however, Jacobean tragedy makes it possible to enter the aristocratic body, as Othello, Malfi's husband, Vittoria Corombona, and countless others do. This fantasy is allowed to materialize on the stage only to demonstrate that such a transgression produces disease and obscenity, which must be purged in order to produce a pure community of aristocratic blood. Poison displaces the sword as the chief instrument of illicit power when poison, not slicing and chopping, is linked to rape. In *The Revenger's Tragedy*, for example, Vindice poisons the skull of his betrothed whom the duke has raped and murdered and then uses the skull to poison the rapist. Having been raped by the duke's stepson, Antonio's wife commits suicide with poison. This is as much as to say women in *The Revenger's Tragedy* are poisoned once they become objects of adulterous desire. *The Revenger's Tragedy* simply literalizes the metaphor which clings to all the women of Jacobean tragedy and defines the female body as a source of pollution. Mary Douglas provides a useful definition of this process:

> pollution is a type of danger which is not likely to occur except where the lines of structure, cosmic or social, are clearly defined . . . A polluting person is always in the wrong. He has developed some wrong condition or simply crossed some line which should not have been crossed. . . . Pollution can be committed unintentionally, but intention is irrelevant to its effects. It is more likely to happen inadvertently. . . .[31]

It is according to this sort of logic innocent characters are slaughtered while morally opprobrious conduct goes unpunished. All the possibilities for combination, metamorphosis, and inverted status relationships which exist in the green world of Elizabethan romantic comedy are closed down in Jacobean tragedy to fix the line between licit and illicit relations.

Let me elaborate for a moment on how the language of festival in Elizabethan drama differs from Jacobean usage, for herein lies the difference between two ways of constituting the pure community. In Elizabethan comedy the language of festival ultimately authorizes state power. In *A Midsummer Night's Dream*, the duke and his entourage come upon the sleeping lovers at the edge of the forest, but he does not see them as criminals attempting to escape his edict. He assumes they have come to participate in "the rites of May" celebrating his marriage. Here, as in the history plays, the figure of carnival appears to expand and diversify the social elements under the monarch's control. The mingling of bodies and various boundary transgressions associated with carnival could attribute permeability to the aristocratic community without calling its purity into question. It could be argued that *Romeo and Juliet* resembles *Titus* in its insistence that tragedy arises from internal division and not from threats to the enclosure of the aristocratic body. In Jacobean tragedy, however, any sign of permeability automatically endangers the community. On the Jacobean stage, the female body must still be understood in terms of the metaphysics of blood, but the female body no longer exists in the same iconic relationship with that of the monarch and the magical power of blood. If anything, Jacobean tragedy insists on this relationship all the more forcefully by imagining the state as nothing else but the blood, the blood in its purest form, that is, the blood of the patriarch. Such is Hamlet's ideal of the state over and against Claudius's more Elizabethan strategy of self-authorization.

In such a symbolic milieu, the signs of festival become those of filth, disease, rape and insurrection. When a scene of feasting and drinking on Cyprus was declared to celebrate the destruction of the Turkish fleet and Othello's marriage, the celebration turns into a riot. In Othello's words, all have turned Turk. The conversion of festival's figures into those of corruption is still more explicit in *The Revenger's Tragedy* where the invigorating food and drink of the banquet table turn poisonous in order to comprise a feast of death. His lover's skull masked and painted with poison provides Vindice with a tasty dish for the lecherous duke. Or consider the manner in which Webster stages the Duchess of Malfi's last supper:

> A masque of common courtesans
> Have her meat served up by bawds and ruffians . . .
> All the mad folk [to be placed] near her lodging
> There let them practice together, sing, and dance,
> And act their gambols to the full o' th moon. (IV.i.124–30)

Just as she is about to be strangled, the duchess expresses regrets for so small a legacy, because, in her words, "many hungry guests have fed upon me" (IV.ii.201). Thus Jacobean tragedy transforms the signs and symbols for representing popular vigor into those of the gloomy festival of punishment.

A closer look at one of these scenes of punishment will reveal a figurative logic that begins with tropes of doubling. All the mechanisms of punishment are set in motion by doubling the female. As he tortures his wife, for example, the Count Montsurrey claims it is actually her lust that murders what he calls her "twin": "The chain shot of thy lust is aloft / And it must murder; 'tis thine own dear twin" (V.i.91–2). Vittoria Corombona is doubled to become the White Devil because Duke Brachiano desires her. In similar fashion Desdemona is doubled when Iago creates the lusty and desiring Venetian court lady to stand as a substitute for the Moor's virtuous wife. The two Desdemonas can be clearly seen in the passage where Othello decides to murder her. He speaks of Desdemona as "A fine woman! a fair woman! a sweet woman!" (IV.i.178). But she is also the whore of Venice who must be punished, in his words: "I will chop her into messes. Cuckold me!" (IV.i.200).

It should not be surprising in this regard to discover that twinning and doubling occupy a major section in Renaissance books on monstrosity, a topic that held considerable fascination for Elizabethans. In his book on monsters and marvels, Ambroise Pare describes twins who share a single head, twins joined at the belly, and twins who have but a single anus between them. Or he describes the monstrous as a single figure with twinned arms on one side of the body, or that has double the number of legs, extra fingers, and extra members of other kinds as well. Particularly important among these stands the hermaphrodite. By virtue of possessing a second set of sexual organs, the hermaphrodite resembles other monsters in that he violates natural categories. In doing so, however, the hermaphrodite could also be used to clarify these differences. It was always necessary to determine which set of sexual organs was dominant and thereby remove the hermaphrodite from the status of a monstrosity. Pare explains that whenever both sets of sexual organs were fully formed in an individual, both ancient and modern law obliged these monsters to say "which they wish to use, and then they are forbidden upon pain of death to use any but those they have chosen."[32] By containing an extra member, we must infer, hermaphrodites not only violated the natural order, they also threatened to pollute the community. It was therefore necessary for them to suppress the supplementary feature.

The woman who will be mutilated assumes a central place in Jacobean theater, first of all, because she is sexually monstrous. Always a member of the aristocracy, she embodies the illicit desire for access to that political body. Whether forcibly taken from or given by the woman herself in adulterous passion, the female body can only be possessed illegitimately, and Jacobean drama represents this transgression as a sexual disfigurement. In desiring a male, she embodies male desire. Thus the female becomes monstrous by virtue of containing male parts; she may be described as a "Gorgon" or "Medusa." A variation on this theme occurs when Malfi's mismatched mate is called a "hermaphrodite." But whether or not this monstrosity arises from her own sexual desire, the desiring female is nonetheless monstrous. By forcible rape, by seduction, or by merely representing her as the desiring subject, her body is understood as taking in an extra member. In this way, Tamyra, the Duchess of Malfi, Desdemona, Cleopatra, Vittoria Corombona, and others obscure within themselves the boundary differentiating what belongs to the body politic from what must be kept outside. The breakdown of gender differences within the women of Jacobean tragedy represents this loss of political boundaries. Purifying the female body of its male sexuality resolves this dilemma symbolically in that it violently subordinates the female body to male authority, for this renews the symbolic power of the sexual body to authorize patriarchy. These scenes of punishment are simply the other side of the same cultural coin of power whose positive image is the generous patron.

From this historical vantage point, one can predict the direction which Hamlet's Senecan materials will take in enforcing the law of patriarchy. He as much as says he wants to turn the Elizabethan stage into a theater of punishment when he says he intends to have his actors

> Play something like the murther of my father
> Before my uncle . . .
> I'll tent him to the quick. If 'a do blench,
> I know my course. (II.ii.595–8)

The king brings an end to the play before it can identify the source of his power with the crime of pollution. But had Hamlet succeeded in turning the stage into an instrument of political power, he would have transformed an Elizabethan tragedy into one more characteristic of the Jacobean stage where extravagant scenes of mutilation displayed the legitimate exercise of patriarchal power.

In the second chapter of *Discipline and Punish*, Michel Foucault insists upon precisely this relationship between the power of display and the exercise of force. When his subjects forget that legitimate power is absolute, Foucault explains, the monarch stages spectacles displaying that radical dissymmetry of power. The scaffold provided such a theater of punishment where the monarch – never present in person but always present in the person of the law – demonstrated his ability to penetrate and control the natural body of the subject at the micro level of its parts. In the following passage, Foucault explains the poetics of punishment:

If torture was so strongly embedded in legal practice, it was because it revealed truth and showed the operation of power. It assured the articulation of the written on the oral, the secret on the public, the procedure of investigation on the operation of confession; it made possible to reproduce the crime on the visible body of the criminal; in the same horror, the crime had to be manifested and annulled. The nature of the threat posed by the criminal can only be intensified when the crime is a crime against the aristocratic body itself.[33]

Speaking metaphorically of his reason for staging a play, Hamlet means to inscribe the crime of regicide upon his uncle's body ("I'll tent him to the quick") and extract a confession from him ("If 'a do blench, I know my course" [II.ii.597–8]). Jacobean tragedy simply translates these metaphors of torture and confusion into sexual terms, accomplishing what Hamlet might have accomplished had the king allowed *The Murder of Gonzago* to continue.

Like the criminal's assault on the law, a wife's infidelity to her husband *is* an assault on the Crown. The punishment of unchaste aristocratic women therefore displays the truth of the subject's relation to the state. It displays the dissymmetry of this relationship as it imprints the crime on the subject's body, in this way demonstrating the state's absolute power over that body. Having noted this, we can return to one of the most self-conscious of the plays and examine the tropes of punishment as they operate there. These are the terms in which Tamyra would have us understand the forthcoming scene of her torture in *Bussy D'Ambois*:

Hide in some gloomy dungeon my loathed face . . .
Hang me in chains, and let me eat those arms
That have offended: bind me face to face
To some dead woman taken from the cart of
Execution. . . . (V.i.104–10)

This passage establishes a parallel between the husband-wife relationship and that of sovereign and subject. For a Jacobean audience this homology would have automatically made sense of Tamyra's crime and of the scene of her punishment: the wife's assertion of power against her husband must be understood in relation to the subject's assault upon the sovereign's power, but not in the manner of an allegory which makes one relationship stand for the other. As Foucault insists, both relationships should be taken literally. Whatever attacks the law of the sovereign also attacks him physically, since the force of the law is the force of the prince. Thus Tamyra's husband orders her to write the name of her go-between on a paper as he stretches her on the rack and stabs her arms repeatedly. Self-contradictory though his behavior may seem, her crime derives from the permeability of her body. It is therefore appropriate in Jacobean terms that her husband should cut openings upon her. Her crime authorizes his power as he makes that crime legible on her body. It was as if most of Jacobean tragedy conspired to effect legibility of precisely this kind, for such mutilation of the female body provides the symbolic antidote to the political problem represented by rape.

This is the nature of the contrast between the Elizabethan Lavinia and later versions of the Lucrece story. Produced in 1610, Fletcher's *Valentinian* understands rape as a penetration of the political body which pollutes it. This form of transgression differs sharply from the self-slaughter displayed by the dismembered body of the raped woman on the Elizabethan stage. Discovering Lucina's rape, her husband declares, "I am ruin'd," and urges her suicide as the means of liberating his family from her taint. At this point, it is worth recalling how Shakespeare's allusion to the Virginius and Virginia story modified the classical source according to the politics of dismemberment. The Elizabethan story made Virginia the actual rather than simply the intended victim of rape, as I have noted. Shakespeare also equates her rape with her father's suicide. These changes identify rape with dismemberment. In contrast, Webster's (and Heywood's?) *Appius and Virginia* holds true to the classical source exactly where Shakespeare's *Titus* deviates. It seems fair to say that the Jacobean version of this story returns the tale of rape to the original. First, it represents the threat of Virginia's rape as a potential source of her father's shame, which makes a rape into a crime against patriarchy. Then Webster solves the problem of the body's permeability by having the father slay his daughter before rape can occur. This act of mutilation purifies the land and preserves patriarchal authority against the illegitimate use of force that, in threatening to pollute the female body, also threatens the authority of his blood. Bathed in his daughter's blood, Virginius claims that "Lustful *Appius*, he that swayes the land, / Slew poor *Virginia* by this father's hand" (IV.ii.155–6).[34] Finally, Webster makes clear Virginia's slaughter eliminates the danger posed by the possibility of rape when he has Virginius address the mutinous troops, "I have bred a daughter whose chaste blood / Was spilt for you, and for *Romes* lasting good" (IV.ii.206–7). As they subordinated female to male by such extravagant means, these dramatists revised the sexual materials of the Elizabethan theater according to a Jacobean politics of the body.

V

To understand Renaissance sexuality in terms of a modern theme that opposes male to female will certainly blot out a complex political thematics of which gender was an integral component. By reading *Othello*, *King Lear*, *Macbeth*, and *Antony and Cleopatra* in relation to the Jacobean theater of punishment, my point is to dissolve the sexual theme into those which, in my view, determined the components of Jacobean drama and the nature of their relationship: kingship versus kinship; natural versus metaphysical bodies of power; the signs and symbols of state versus the exercise of state power. As I name them now, the force of these themes in Jacobean culture will be less than evident. As I demonstrate how they reshaped an earlier iconography into the stuff of Shakespeare's greatest tragedies, however, I hope this manner of historicizing Shakespeare will gain credibility, however estranging my treatment of his dramatic strategies — particularly those involving gender — may seem. My discussion of Shakespeare's plays will show how he picked up Jacobean themes and worked variations on them. I must quickly add that by this I do not mean to situate Shakespeare's writing in what is usually termed a "context." I refer here to the notion of "context" implicit in the modern distinction between "self" and "society," for example, or between *langue* and *parole*, or that of figure and ground. Rather than understanding the text in relation to an external context at all, I am interested in the historical process preserved for us in Shakespeare's use of certain cultural materials. More specifically, I am interested in how his later drama remodeled his Elizabethan materials for purposes of the Jacobean theater. To this end, I will try to describe the form of Shakespeare's Jacobean tragedies as the revision of the cultural strategies upon which his Elizabethan genres depended. He takes the materials of these earlier genres apart according to a later strategy for authorizing political power, I will argue, which makes them represent what we might call a more conservative form of patriarchy.

Even before we examine how Shakespeare develops a Jacobean thematics in his plays, it is possible to understand how this new basis for political meaning dismantles the Elizabethan synthesis. Where the history plays understood the body politic as embodied in the monarch's natural body, Jacobean tragedy questions this relationship. Each of the tragedies entails some violation of the metaphysics of blood arising from the Elizabethan assumption that power can be obtained by seizing hold of territory, law, and other instruments of state. Rather than sanctioning the line which succeeds in exercising power, however, Shakespeare's Jacobean drama invariably associates such power with degraded images of festival. Set in opposition to patriarchal authority, these images always mark power as illegitimate. As Jacobean drama opens the possibility of separating the metaphysics of blood from the natural body of the monarch, it demonstrates the consequences of loosening the bond characterizing an earlier political iconography in another way as well. These plays dramatize the consequences of detaching the symbols and rituals of state authority from the legitimate exercise of such power. This crisis is a crisis of representation itself. And this is perhaps Shakespeare's favorite theme. It lends his work a self-reflexive quality, which may explain why his language — more than that of other dramatists — has proved so susceptible to our attempts to make it literary. Even so, it seems to me that all the oppositions which organize the great tragedies — including that inherent in gender itself — cooperate to flesh out a problematic relationship between kinship and kingship. I would pursue this line of thinking still one step further and claim that all other themes — including that of gender — have to be understood in relation to kingship and kinship if we wish to understand Shakespeare's meaning historically.

If something can be said of all tragedies which allows us to specify them as Jacobean, it is this: they disrupt genealogy to question the possibility of representing the distribution of power in some system of relationships other than patrilineage. As they do this, however, Shakespeare's tragedies invariably show us how such a separation of politics and sexuality into different systems of relationships produces political disorder and the breakdown of family relationships. The separation of politics and sexuality would render the world incoherent, that is, if such a separation were actually possible. If Jacobean drama proves one single thing, however, it is that sexual relations are always political. Jacobean tragedies maintain the patriarchal principles despite extravagant assaults on the monarch's natural body, despite illicit seizure of the instruments of state, and despite misuse of the rituals and symbols of power. That all such challenges to the body politic are ultimately thwarted only testifies to the metaphysical sources of its power. That certain elements of an earlier iconography of state are caught up in assaults on the principle of blood only purifies that iconography to authorize a Jacobean ideal of patriarchy.

Hamlet wanted to stage a play which would transform his own situation into a drama dominated by this Jacobean logic of representation. But the political context of Hamlet's play — in other words, Shakespeare's play — proved more powerful than Hamlet's attempt to transfer the political relationships he resisted. It is to the Elizabethan dynamic of competition that he eventually succumbs as Shakespeare brings Hamlet's struggle on behalf of a later construction of patriarchy to an Elizabethan conclusion. Where Hamlet fails to transform the iconography of state, however, Shakespeare does allow protagonists who come after him to succeed. In a scene which must have had a blatantly political edge for his audience, for example, Shakespeare has the Venetian senate overrule the patriarch — represented by Desdemona's father — and authorize his daughter's right to give herself in marriage. Shakespeare then allows Iago to transform into political terms this political transgression against the law of the father. This is the stuff of Elizabethan comedy as Stephen Greenblatt has pointed out in calling attention to Iago's role as a plotmaker/playwright of a comic narrative.[35] In writing Desdemona and Cassio as characters of a romantic comedy, Iago revises the manner of representing sexual relations on the Elizabethan stage as he gulls Roderigo into thinking the rich young Venetian lady has tired of her "outlandish" husband. But this staging of sexual relationships transforms the stuff of comedy in another way as well. Iago's plot transforms comic materials into those of a Jacobean tragedy.

Resembling nothing so much as an Elizabethan heroine in her capacity for erotic desire as well as in her authority to give herself in marriage, Desdemona contains just the right features for a Jacobean rewriting of the female body. That the Jacobean politics of the body differs significantly from what came before becomes clear as Iago stages his romantic comedy: here the threat implicit in the daughter's initial act of rebellion against the patriarch displays its true nature. It is not only Roderigo whom Iago gulls into seeing the vigor of her Elizabethan eroticism as the poison of adulterous passion. Iago's magic as dramatist is such that he transforms the signs of Desdemona's chaste desire into those of a monstrous betrayal right before Othello's eyes. Self-possessed and capable of speaking the language of the court, Desdemona herself takes on Iago in a court game. "What wouldst write of me," she asks, "If thou shouldst praise me?" (II.i.117–18). Desdemona continues as if anticipating Iago's words will transform her own words, "How if she be black and witty? . . . fair and foolish?" (II.i.131–40). Ironically, too, it is this very power to write herself which Iago turns into a vice and Othello forcibly strips from her character as he strangles her.

When she first appears on the Jacobean stage, Desdemona is nothing if not the embodiment of power. In convincing the senate to side with her against her father, Desdemona seizes hold of two patriarchal prerogatives: the power to speak the language of the law, which in turn gives her the power to give her own body in marriage. The power to marry herself threatens to detach the sexual prerogative from other forms of patriarchal authority, and such a sexual challenge has to be construed as an assault upon patriarchy in Jacobean terms. It is only left to Iago to turn the features of her political rebellion into the signs of unchaste desire. Thus for Desdemona to speak to Lodovico of Cassio's fall from power proves to Othello that she is a "devil" and "the whore of Venice"; he translates her exercise of political patronage into an illicit use of her body. However wrong he may seem in regarding her as the embodiment of such monstrous desire, Othello is only reading Desdemona's political features according to the Jacobean politics of the body. But it is ultimately Shakespeare himself who deprives Desdemona of her capacity to speak with the authority of the law, just as he deprives her of any authority to determine the use of her body. His representation of her character differs from that of Iago only in that Shakespeare idealizes where his malevolent counterpart defames. Shakespeare does not differ from Iago in terms of the basis upon which gender distinctions should be made. Either way the female body loses its capacity to exercise patriarchal authority. These political features are returned to the male by way of Othello's vengeance, which operates, then, much as a theater of punishment.

The point I want to stress for purposes of this argument is Shakespeare's collaboration with Iago rather than his condemnation of the malcontent, the collaboration of the two, that is, in purifying political iconography. Thus by the end of the fourth act, Desdemona has completely lost the verbal powers she possessed as the sophisticated lady who challenged Iago in a courtly game of wit during the second act of the play. Grown newly naive, she must ask Emilia if there really are women in the world capable of cuckolding their husbands. True, Shakespeare uses her loss of verbal power as an idealizing strategy when he makes Desdemona seem all the more innocent as Iago poisons her character. But as she loses the power of speech, she also loses the control over her body she possessed at the opening of the play and, with it, the verbal power to argue for the legitimacy of her sexual behavior.

Othello may be wrong in taking Iago's interpretation of this comic heroine for the Desdemona whom Shakespeare portrays as the innocent instrument of the malcontent's assault on his ungenerous patron. But there is a way in which Iago's interpretation of her is correct. Even if Desdemona's relationship with Cassio was strictly business, such interest in court dealings as war makes her sexually monstrous according to the Jacobean understanding of power. She may have mingled the two in joining her husband on the iron bed of war, but her body becomes susceptible to misreading because she overturns the natural subordination of female to male when she married Othello in the first place. When she asks permission to accompany Othello to the frontier, she acknowledges that her own behavior was a violent assault on custom:

> That I [did] love the Moor to live with him,
> My downright violence, and storm of fortunes,
> May trumpet to the world. My heart's subdu'd
> Even to the very quality of my lord. . . .
> And to his honors and his valiant parts
> Did I my soul and fortunes consecrate.
> So that, dear lords, if I be left behind,
> . . . and he go to the war,
> The rites for why I love him are bereft me. (I.iii.248–57)

As Iago reminds the Moor, "She did deceive her father, marrying you."
(III.iii.205) If she can overthrow her father's authority, presumably she
can overthrow that of Othello as well. For this reason, we may gather, he
views her alleged sexual infidelity as the overthrow of his patriarchal
authority:

> I had been happy, if the general camp,
> Pioners and all, had tasted her sweet body,
> So I had nothing known. O now, for ever
> Farewell the tranquil mind! farewell content!
> Farewell the plumed troops and the big wars . . .
> Farewell! Othello's occupation's gone. (III.iii.345–57)

An Elizabethan to the end, Othello thinks first of dismemberment – "I will
chop her into messes," and then of poison. Poison would make him a
source of her pollution in symbolic terms, rather than the agent of
purification. But Iago's Jacobean turn of mind instructs Othello otherwise. It requires a punishment to make the crime legible upon the subject's
body. "Do it not with poison," he thus tells Othello, but "strangle her in
her bed, even the bed she hath contaminated" (IV.i.207–8). With this,
Shakespeare has Iago distinguish between the act of pollution and that of
purification. Mutilation, in other words, becomes the solution to the
assault on the authority of the monarch. Now completely given over to the
machinations of the Jacobean theater, Othello reenacts the crime upon the
female's body – more accurately, upon her mouth – by smothering her.
Much as it may seem to diverge from a form of mutilation that displays the
permeability of the body, this punishment also points right to the source
of the assault upon patriarchy, the woman's political voice. And true to
the poetics of punishment, the act which reveals the truth of his crime
radically subordinates the material body of the subject in a ritual
testimony to the power of blood. By this brief reading of *Othello*, I simply
want to suggest that a shift in the strategies of political display can be
inferred from Shakespeare's use of the female body. Desdemona poses a
specifically Jacobean assault on monarchy when she assumes authority
over her body and persuades the senate to assert the priority of a
contractual relationship over and against the will of the patriarch.

VI

If Iago's behavior perplexes a modern readership accustomed to thinking
in terms which root motivation in a private sexual domain, then Lady
Macbeth poses an equally troublesome case. Criticism has failed to come to
terms with Shakespeare's sudden transformation of Lady Macbeth into a

regicidal maniac driven by political ambition and subsequently condemned to madness. Criticism has no more success, in my view, with the
role he assigns to the witches. Even the most recent work on the play gives
us two unsatisfactory choices with which to rationalize this behavior.
While criticism seems to agree on Macbeth's spinelessness, it cannot
decide if he was too weak to act on his ambition without his wife's
prodding, or if he was too weak in putting up moral resistance to her.
From this we might conclude that Lady Macbeth is a castrating bitch or
else that Shakespeare is a misogynist. Both choices try to make sense of
unacceptable forms of behavior by ascribing a psychological cause. But
our reading of other Jacobean drama suggests, to the contrary, that such
forms of behavior become meaningful in relation to the monarch's body as
they revise or maintain its iconographic status and structure.

In *Macbeth*, *King Lear*, and *Antony and Cleopatra* Shakespeare takes the
signs and symbols of legitimate authority and inverts them. He hands
them over to illegitimate authority, but he does this in order to
demonstrate that the iconography of the stage cannot possibly be used
against the aristocratic body. At the outset of *Macbeth*, Shakespeare gives
Lady Macbeth the very same elements which other Jacobean playwrights
use to display the absolute power of the state. He shows how these might
be used subversively. First, he has Lady Macbeth deliberately double
herself by taking on the mantle of the punitive patriarch. To call attention
to this variation on a classic Jacobean move, then, Shakespeare has her ask
to be made monstrous: ". . . unsex me here, / And fill me from the crown
to the toe topful / Of direst cruelty! Make thick my blood . . . / Come to my
woman's breast / And take my milk for gall . . ." (I.v.41–8). Another
famous speech finds Lady Macbeth vowing to snatch the sucking infant
from her breast and crush its skull had she so sworn with such a vow as
Macbeth's vow to kill the king. The modern impulse is to read this
testimony to her ambitions as the inversion of maternal instincts. But what
– we should ask – if Shakespeare were not working within a modern logic
of the body. What if the maternal bond, though important, gave way
before a higher and more important bond? Such a figure of speech might
make a different kind of sense, for example, in a culture where genealogy
matters more than the individual, and where children matter most who
carry on the royal lineage.

Next Shakespeare has Lady Macbeth turn festival practices to the
purpose of staging a regicide; Lady Macbeth subdues Duncan's guards
with "wine and wassail" to insure the assassination's success. And she
herself appropriates the carnivalesque energy to murderous ends. "That
which hath made them [Duncan's guards] drunk hath made me bold,"
and, she adds, "What hath quench'd them hath given me fire" (II.ii.1–2).
To complete the inversion of the figures of legitimate authority, Macbeth

uses the techniques of ritual punishment to stage this Jacobean scene upon Duncan's body. There is, for instance, the requisite blessing of the executioner, and the identification of Macbeth, the would-be monarch, with the hangman. This comes by way of Macbeth's description of the king's guards who were startled from their drunken stupor: "One cried, 'God bless us,'" and the other said "amen" as if "they had seen me with these hangman's hands" (II.ii.24–5). Like the scene on the scaffold in Foucault's account, the monarch – though never really present in person – is there in the wounds on the subject's body which dramatize its total subjection to state power. That Macbeth shares the role of counterfeit king with his lady becomes apparent as her behavior fulfills that of the monarch in ritual punishment too. To implicate her as the one whose invisible force commanded this spectacle, Shakespeare has her return after the murder to "gild the faces of the grooms" with blood (II.ii.53).

Having turned the practices of legitimate power to illegitimate ends, Shakespeare immediately begins to return the iconography of the theater to the monarch. It is as if the language of the play were inherently incapable of speaking against legitimate authority. This process of purification begins with Duncan's murder. Usually, the scene of punishment inscribes the crime upon the body of the criminal, but here the situation is completely reversed. It is Macbeth's ambition that is written on Duncan's body. And it is Macbeth himself who describes the monarch's corpse in a way that declares the executioner's crime rather than that of his victim: "His silver skin [was] lac'd with golden blood,/ And his gash'd stabs look'd like a breach in nature" (II.iii.112–13). Shakespeare has not described this scene in terms that would render it a rite of purification, but to the contrary, has described Duncan's murder as a violation of nature.

Next, Shakespeare takes back the figures of festival and disallows their use in authorizing illegitimate power. That is to say, he denies Lady Macbeth the privilege of a state banquet. Banquo's ghost disrupts the banquet, and Macbeth abruptly calls it to an end. More than that, once Macbeth assumes the throne, Shakespeare withdraws the very materials for staging such festivities. Thus an anonymous member of the aristocracy laments the barren kingdom and hopes for the successful insurgency of Macduff, Northumberland and Siward:

> . . . by the help of these (with Him above
> To ratify the work) we may again
> Give to our tables meat, sleep to our nights;
> Free from our feasts and banquets bloody knives;
> Do faithful homage and receive free honors;
> All which we pine for now. (III.vi.32–7)

All of these are aristocratic privileges which Shakespeare removes from Scotland during the reign of the tyrant Macbeth. Finally, Shakespeare turns the doubling of Lady Macbeth against her. If she invoked the trope of doubling in order to accomplish her regicidal ambitions, then doubling becomes her punishment too. Nowhere is this more clear than in her madness. Lady Macbeth's language quite literally rebels against her, and she speaks as if another person inhabited her body. Where she was unsexed and filled with cruelty before, now she is obsessed with her pollution. "Out, damn'd spot! out," she cries out in her delirium, "What, will these hands ne'er be clean?" (V.i.35, 43) In this manner, she reenacts the details of the murder in a parody of ritual purification.

In recovering the use of these theatrical practices for legitimate authority, Shakespeare does more than restore the throne to its rightful heir. He mystifies the notion of kingship, reinvigorates the signs and symbols associated with the exercise of legitimate power, and makes the theater speak a more conservative ideology. We see this transformation in the supernatural materials of the play, particularly in the witches. Admittedly an unusual feature of the play, it has always been assumed that the witches' presence has something to do with King James's interest in demonology. Initially, they speak a subversive prophecy – an antipatriarchal truth – that seems to authorize Macbeth's treason. But then every one of their prophetic figures of speech is turned around to work on the side of patriarchy. In the march of the trees from Birnam wood to Dunsinane castle, for instance, Shakespeare materializes the fantastic representation of Macbeth's downfall. In similar fashion, he fulfills the witches' prophecy that Macbeth can be overcome only by one not of woman born. As the figures of impossibility are realized and each otherworldly prophecy fulfilled, nature and culture both appear to conspire in restoring patriarchal authority.

In this light, we might consider the difference between the murdered Duncan and Malcolm, his legitimate successor. Malcolm's passivity contrasts sharply with the heroic features of such Elizabethan warrior kings as Bullingbroke, Henry V, or Fortinbras. When Macduff confronts Malcolm to lead the assault on Macbeth, Shakespeare goes to great lengths to stress both the passivity and the purity of Malcolm. After first testing Macduff, Malcolm confesses:

> I am yet
> Unknown to woman, never was forsworn,
> Scarcely have coveted what was mine own,
> At no time broke my faith, would not betray
> The devil to his fellow, and delight
> No less in truth than life. (IV.iii.125–30)

We might say that Shakespeare established Duncan as the benevolent and generous king only to kill him off and replace him with this purer, more mystical patriarch. This is not a restoration of the patriarch but a displacement with a more conservative mode, for what Shakespeare emphasizes through the violation of genealogy is that the mystical body of the monarch has become embodied in a natural body that denies its own physicality. By so displacing Duncan with Malcolm, Shakespeare makes it seem as if nothing can disrupt the progress of the crown from Banquo to James; all the elements of nature, like those of the theater, join to put Malcolm on the throne.

Most other Jacobean tragedies presuppose this same connection between sexual relations and the condition of the political body. In staging *Macbeth*, Shakespeare simply literalizes the homology which makes unruliness on the part of an aristocratic woman into an assault on the sovereign's power. He allows Lady Macbeth to overrule her husband in order to show that such inversion of sexual relations is also an inversion of the political order. Her possession of illicit desire in its most masculine form – the twisted ambition of the malcontent – leads directly to regicide. Such an explanation for Lady Macbeth's behavior has all the virtues of simplicity. It accounts for her centrality in the play as well as the force of her character and this, even though she all but disappears during the second half of the play.

The same homology between kinship and kingship accounts for the curious means Shakespeare uses in the play to restore the world to its natural hierarchy. Perhaps most obvious among these is the gendering of patriarchal prerogatives. If Macbeth's assault on genealogy began with his wife's possession of certain male features associated with political ambition, then the play creates a clear distinction between male and female in restoring the proper dissymmetry of monarch and subject. Like Desdemona, Lady Macbeth grows docile and unworldly as she loses the power to speak as a court lady. But this is not to relegate Machiavellian twistings of desire and turnings of plot to the domain of the male. Quite the contrary. Shakespeare thrusts Malcolm forward as the ideal patriarch on grounds he is as pure in his way as the self-castigated Lady Macbeth is in hers. Malcolm confesses his virginity – "I am yet / Unknown to woman" (IV.iii.125–6) – and declares that the forms of sexual desire are "strangers to my nature." Thus he confesses to a lack of desire to ever mingle his blood with that of a woman. And as if this were not enough to make the point, Shakespeare's agent for restoring Malcolm to his rightful position of patriarch must be a man "not of woman born." This radical resexing of power completes the process of restoring the correct order of relationships. In realigning kinship with kingship, the notion of a female patriarch has become something of a contradiction in terms, as the possession of any of the political features of the patriarch by a female constitutes the overturning of some primal natural order.

Against such usurpers alone can the technology of punishment be legitimately applied, as it is when Lady Macbeth, having misused this technology in applying it to Duncan, turns it round on herself in her madness. For Macbeth, we should note, another form of subjection obtains. As the male on the throne, he possesses the technology of the executioner and all the power to stage scenes of punishment. Thus, we might surmise, Shakespeare cannot very well detach that function from the Crown without contradicting the whole purpose of a genre that aimed at purifying political iconography; the Crown must be purified of the taints of ambition and the competitive strategies for translating such desire into legitimate authority. Though derived from Lady Macbeth, all these Elizabethan features inhere in the Crown under Macbeth's reign of terror. In confusing gender distinctions, they polluted the political body. To remove such a taint from the Crown itself requires a special strategy of purification. At least such is the inference we must draw when Shakespeare stages a scene of tyrannicide to restore the natural relationship between sovereign and subject. If Macbeth has appropriated the technology of punishment, in other words, Macbeth himself must be removed by some other means before these techniques can be used once again to inscribe his crimes against legitimate authority upon the criminal's body. A good deal of the play's impact and its tribute to James comes about as Shakespeare signals the entire reversal of Macbeth's reversal of legitimate power relations by having Macduff hold up the severed head of the tyrant. This gesture belongs with those which distinguish and purify gender, as well as with those which set nature in league with culture in a grand plot to vindicate blood. All these operate to privilege blood – and thus the metaphysical body of power – over the accidents of competition and the momentary subordination of one member of the aristocracy to another.

Like *Macbeth* and *Othello*, *King Lear* perplexes readers in those places where what is done can only be for the purpose of purifying the iconography of the Elizabethan theater. This is to suggest *King Lear* has proved troubling to critics mainly because of the political consequences which unfold when the monarch divests himself of the patriarchal prerogatives traditionally inhering in his body. This attempt on Lear's part to retain only this symbolic status as king initiates events which defy our notion of psychological motivation. For Shakespeare's audience these scenes must have been disturbing too. But the seventeenth-century theater-goer would have been disturbed for the very reason that the political meaning of dramatic events was sharply apparent. For us, in contrast, that meaning has been lost over the course of time, its traces further obscured by several centuries of literary interpretation, and the behavior displayed on the stage consequently cries out for a "depth" interpretation.

Aside from its obvious kinship to such a work as *Gorboduc*, Shakespeare's play draws most heavily upon another Elizabethan source, *The True Chronicle Historie of King Leir* for the Lear story. Sidney's account of the blind king of Paphlagonia in *The Countess of Pembroke's Arcadia*, inspired much of the Gloucester story. Shakespeare obviously felt obliged to revise these Elizabethan materials for a historically later audience, for the Jacobean Lear forfeits the Crown's prerogative to control the exchange of daughters along with the power to distribute property. Gone, too, is an Elizabethan teleology that reunited an internally divided state by means of outside intervention. It is this notion of providence, among other things, that makes the source *King Leir* at one with other Elizabethan chronicle history plays. However outnumbered, the army of Gallia succeeds in the Elizabethan *Leir* when, as Cornwall says, "The day is lost, our friends do all revolt, / And joyne against us with the adverse part . . ." (lines 2616–17).[36] In Shakespeare's revision of the story, however, neither Edmund nor Cordelia can be successful in these earlier terms. When they try to play the upstart challenger and redemptive outsider respectively, each fails to seize the kingdom. They collapse before the forces which providence has lined up in support of patriarchal power.

Shakespeare's most telling revision of Elizabethan materials has to do with the division of the kingdom and the events that unfold as a consequence, for it is with this that he raises the whole issue of what the monarchy is. In *King Leir* the crown is merely property: it can be divided, willed, used as surety for a loan, and – as the play takes pains to demonstrate – treated as dowry to be divided equally among the three daughters for their jointure. As property, it could be subjected to laws governing the distribution of property or even be seized by force. As in the history plays, the crown goes to whoever could seize the signs and symbols of kingship and also command popular support. Like the resolution of any other Elizabethan chronicle history, then, the outnumbered and undervalued King of Gallia successfully overcomes the combined British forces to win the kingdom for Leir; true power displays itself in the effective exercise of physical force through competition and is subsequently ratified by an outpouring of popular support for the displaced king.

The older play, of course, is a chronicle history and not a tragedy. Yet even when it entertains the possibility of a tragic complication, in doing so *Lier* takes a peculiarly Elizabethan turn. The threat to the kingdom, for one thing, is imagined as the dismemberment of the aristocratic body. Leir's prophetic dream of his murder reveals each of his daughters, in his words, "brandishing a Faulchion in their hand,/ Ready to lop a lymme off where it fell/ and in their hands a naked poynyard,/ Wherewith they stabd me in a hundred places . . ." (1490–3). As it is figured forth in terms of dismemberment, such a threat to the old king is overturned with Cordella's restoration of the wounded body to "perfit health." Cordella's return at the end of the play prophetically reunites various parts of the state that have been fractured by competition. By way of contrast, Shakespeare's Jacobean version of the story interrogates the very notion of the Crown as a corporate essence in perpetuity. His Lear thus poses a threat to legitimate authority that had never been at issue before. Out of this historically later contest between the king's two bodies, a Jacobean thematics can be said to emerge. The metaphysics of the Crown itself is called into question so that it may be displaced on the state as a ubiquitous presence which exists prior to and ontologically different from any of its natural embodiments.

VII

When James came to the throne, in the words of Marie Axton:

> Poets and dramatists worked up pageants for James's coronation, translating into icons the legal theory which had supported the new King. Their pageant iconography declared that it was not the land, or the estates of Parliament, but the King who represented the power of government and the perpetuity of the realm.[37]

As the new phoenix as well as "England's Caesar," James was celebrated as the literal embodiment of the Crown in perpetuity, in contradiction to the facts of history. Writing of James's coronation pageant, Jonathan Goldberg has suggested that the major trope of this pageant – indeed of James's entire reign – was that of "revival"; James encouraged a belief in "the monarch's ability to live beyond himself."[38] He welcomed representations of himself as the British equivalent of the Roman emperor, and coins were struck to emphasize this connection. He enjoyed the title of *Rex Pacificus* and was represented as the prince of peace, the new Augustus. "In a Roman matrix," Goldberg argues, "James generated his 'style of gods,' claiming deity as the emperors had done before him."[39] In this environment, poets, playwrights, members of court, and members of parliament, along with all those who saw the pageants or read accounts of them, would have been aware of a new insistence on the iconic nature of the king's body. James himself maintained that bond was a much more literal one than Elizabeth had believed. He claimed not only to have the only body whose blood united all of Britain but also to exist in unbroken continuity with the tradition of monarchy. And this Stuart mythology extended beyond the first heady public pageant for the new king. The same year *King Lear* was probably produced, 1605, Anthony Munday's lord mayor's pageant, *The Triumphs of Re-United Britannia*, included an account of the myth of Brutus and his founding of England in which the monarch was celebrated as "our second *Brute*, Royall King *James*."[40]

In the first scene of *King Lear*, no one suggests Lear has violated the most important prohibition of his culture. Nor does anyone suggest that Lear is destroying the whole iconography of nationalism centered in the monarch's body. But this is indeed the threat such behavior on the part of a monarch actually poses, for the terrible consequences of violating the patriarchal prerogative subsequently play themselves out on the stage. As in *Othello*, so in *Lear*, too, the fundamental cultural truth that tragedy affirms remains largely unstated. It is defined through its violation. Like the Elizabethan drama which preceded it, *Lear* insists on the iconic nature of the monarch's body, but the basis for establishing that iconic bond has changed. There is nothing explicitly illegal in what Lear proposes in the opening scene. The will of the monarch is the law. When the will of the king is to divest monarchy of power, the carnage that ensues implies that it is a primal law of nature that has been violated. By dividing up the nonarchy, the powers which had been united in the monarch are separated into functions each of which – curiously enough – loses its efficacy once isolated from the others. Kent provides a handy summary of those features once bound together in Lear:

> Royal Lear
> Whom I have ever honor'd as my king,
> Lov'd as my father, as my master follow'd,
> As my great patron thought on in my prayers. . . . (I.i 139–42)

When he disperses his patrimony, Lear acts as if patronage no longer originates in the monarch; when he denounces Cordelia and hands her over in a dowerless marriage, he effectively renounces his role as *pater familias*; when he banishes Kent, he overturns the principle of fealty; and – perhaps more seriously than these – when he determines the rules of inheritance according to his will and not according to the principle of primogeniture, he appears to deny the metaphysics of the body politic and the special status of the king's blood. By dismantling his iconic body, Lear disperses these powers in a way that pits them against one another. This initiates a series of conflicts which threaten the stability of the state as well as the coherence of its signs and symbols.

It is precisely this separation of forms of power that makes Lear's retainers – seemingly a minor element in the play – a major issue which divides Lear and his daughters. When he resigns his throne, the retainers operate only as the symbols of a power once located in Lear. Detached from the legitimate right to exercise power, they suddenly pose a potential threat to legitimate authority. Rather than point to the harmony of a social order that is centered in the king and the displays of his court, then, Lear's retainers take on the features of carnival and inversion. Goneril says to Lear, "your insolent retinue / Do hourly carp and quarrel, breaking forth / In rank and not-to-be endur'd riots" (I.iv.202–4). As a rationale for stripping him of his retainers, she poses the problem in these terms:

> Here do you keep a hundred knights and squires,
> Men so disorder'd, so debosh'd and bold,
> That this our court, infected with their manners,
> Shows like a riotous inn. Epicurism and lust
> Makes it more like a tavern or a brothel
> Than a grac'd palace. (I.iv.241–6)

Rather than represent them in a stately processional mode, then, Goneril describes Lear's court in the very terms Shakespeare once used to represent Falstaff's carnivalesque excesses.

The history plays always included potentially disruptive forms of popular power marked by the features of carnival. Monarchs were successful to the degree they incorporated these carnivalesque elements within the official rituals of state. It has to be a significant moment, then, when the king's own retainers assimilate the dissolute features of a disruptive social force where once they would have opposed such a force in the name of political order. As the signs of state power, one finds that Lear's retainers exhibit a kind of invertibility which turns them back into the subversive forces of tavern and brothel that once opposed aristocratic signs of power. It is as if Shakespeare has allowed the components of kingship to devolve into the semiotic stuff of which they were made. But it is not in fact the inversion of patriarchal order that makes Lear's retainers so threatening. Shakespeare stresses that they have grown suddenly dangerous in that they threaten to revive an earlier form of monarchy. Goneril, for one, fears the retainers might exhibit fealty to the person of the monarch over and above the newer bureaucracy she has installed. To her such a possibility smacks of conspiracy against the state: "Each buzz, each fancy, each complaint, dislike, / He may enguard his dotage with their pow'rs, / And hold our lives in mercy" (I.iv.325–7). To those who rule, signs of loyalty to the old king have become signs of illegitimate power.

Shakespeare appropriately links the king's retainers in metonymy with the disloyal Edgar. These two signs of legitimate authority – the embodiment of aristocratic blood in the legitimate heir and the display of a household retinue – come together as a narrative designed to explain the plot on Gloucester's life by his legitimate son:

> Reg.   What, did my father's godson seek your life?
>   He whom my father nam'd, your Edgar?
> Glou.   O lady, lady, shame would have it hid!
> Reg.   Was he not companion with the riotous knights
>   That tended upon my father?
> Glou.   I know not, madam. 'Tis too bad, too bad.
> Edm.   Yes, madam, he was of that consort.
> Reg.   No marvel then, though he were ill affected:
>   'Tis they have put him on the old man's death,
>   To have th' expense and waste of his revenues. (II.i.91–100)

These few statements concerning Lear's retainers may stand for the larger drama of disintegration of which they constitute but one part. As the material forms of state power are detached from their symbolic center in the natural body of the monarch, their essential nature undergoes a sudden change, a change as sudden, that is, as the one which turns the king's retainers into a potential agency of misrule. His power having rested on land and title, when he renounces these, Lear also loses control over his daughters.

Violation of the principle of primogeniture, I have suggested, constitutes the most serious assault on the principle of patriarchy, for this violation challenges every Stuart king's right to sit. In particular, to deny primogeniture is to undermine the Stuart argument on the metaphysical body of power. In opposition to this argument, Lear behaves as if the sitting monarch alone determines the disposition of the crown without regard to primogeniture or to the laws of nature. This dissociation of kinship from kingship reverberates to the very core of Renaissance culture to challenge the belief which locates the metaphysical authority of the crown within the natural body of the aging monarch. For this reason, as soon as Lear cancels out primogeniture, Gloucester finds Edgar's malevolence plausible. This story of the legitimate son turned against his father in rivalry no longer violates the law of nature once Gloucester construes nature itself not only as portending but even as authorizing such a sundering of the patriarchal bond:

> These late eclipses in the sun and moon portend no good to us. Though the wisdom of nature can reason it thus and thus, yet nature finds itself

scourg'd by the sequent effects. Love cools, friendship falls off, brothers divide: in cities, mutinies; in countries, discord; in palaces, treason; and the bond crack'd twixt son and father. This villain of mine comes under the prediction; there's son against father: the King falls from bias of nature; there's father against child. (I.ii.103–12)

Once Gloucester sees nature as a disorderly force which opposes the traditional order of state, he can not only misconceive the bastard as the legitimate son; he can also dispossess Edgar of birthright, blood, and family.

At this point, it should be noted that the crimes which make Lear's daughters monstrous are not, at least in the first half of the play, crimes of pollution. The crimes which make Goneril and Regan monsters are all crimes of ingratitude. Ingratitude, which might also describe Macbeth's offense, is characteristically a male crime arising from a patronage relationship in which the ungrateful client mistakes his patron's generosity for a lack of aristocratic largess. By making women into figures of "monster ingratitude," Shakespeare both links them to and distinguishes them from those other women who are brutalized on the Jacobean stage. The fact that Lear's daughters are not initially subjected to spectacular scenes of torture for assaulting the king's body confirms again the political function such iconography served on the stage. The scene of punishment which fulfills the Jacobean pattern in this play is certainly the blinding of Gloucester. Cornwall gives the order, as Regan accuses the old duke of pollution,

> Corn. Bind him, I say.
> Reg. Hard, hard. O filthy traitor. (III.vii.32)

Gloucester recognizes his role in the drama which ensues – "I am tied to th' stake, and I must stand the course" (III.vii.54), just as Cornwall plays out the part of his tormenter: "Fellows, hold the chair, / Upon these eyes of thine I'll set my foot" (III.vii.67–8). Like Iago, Cornwall and Regan are writing their own death warrant on the body of Gloucester, but like Desdemona, he has offended a higher law. When he disowned his legitimate son and declared the bastard legitimate, Gloucester committed the same crime against the blood as that committed by the Duchess of Malfi or by Desdemona: he has included an extra member within the aristocratic body. In the scene of his punishment, then, Shakespeare completes the transposition begun when Lear's daughters became monsters of ingratitude. Having displaced the crime of ingratitude onto the female, Shakespeare locates pollution in the body of the male. This sexual transposition makes pollution and ingratitude into two forms of the same crime against the aristocratic body. Each one is a crime against patriarchy which explicitly challenges the metaphysics of the blood. By undergoing ritual punishment, Gloucester purifies the aristocratic body.

When Lear strips off his clothes to reveal himself as "unaccommodated man," Shakespeare boldly reveals the natural body of the king as one that appears to bear little value in its own right. It has been stripped of retainers, patronage, patrilineal authority, the ability to raise an army, the power of the *pater familias*, and all the other features which attract the gaze of power. In and of itself, it is powerless. Lear has already equated clothing with his retainers, when he says to his daughter,

> Thou art a lady;
> If only to go warm were gorgeous,
> Why, nature needs not what thou gorgeous wear'st,
> Which scarcely keep thee warm. (II.iv.267–70)

Observing this same principle, Shakespeare strips Lear of the symbolic surface he acquired by virtue of his blood and offers us a parodic version of kingship. He makes Lear hold a trial with a joint stool as defendant, for example, wander the countryside with a crown of wildflowers, and hold forth in a delirium on matters of government and the law. We can see how thoroughly Shakespeare has drained Elizabethan materials of their political power by such gestures. He does not consolidate power in a contender for the throne as the Elizabethan pattern would have had it. Instead, Shakespeare scatters the rituals of state after emptying them of all social content. To be sure, both *Gorboduc* and the Elizabethan *Leir* dramatize the conflicts arising from a divided kingdom. But theirs is just that, a kingdom internally divided, not one dispersed according to rules of kinship quite at odds with those which determine kingship. Lear gives Albany and Cornwall territory, "sway," "revenue," and the execution of the rights and powers of the monarch. Attuned to Elizabethan representations of disorder, we might presume such behavior would divide the kingdom against itself, but these are not the terms in which Shakespeare's Jacobean tragedy unfolds. He seems much more interested in depicting the consequences of severing the iconic bond between the powers inhering in the blood and the blood itself.

Detached from their legitimate source of power in his body, the instruments of state turn against the monarch. That they operate to subvert patriarchy creates a framework where the threat to legitimate power takes the form of pollution rather than dismemberment. By privileging kinship over kingship, Lear produces an unruly state where women can rule men, where daughters can rule their fathers, and where bastards can dispossess the aristocracy. That such disorder arises from the pollution of blood becomes explicit, finally, when the two unruly daughters lust for the bastard Edmund. And true to the logic of pollution too, *King Lear* itself enacts a purification of the blood that is first and foremost a purification of Shakespeare's sources. Shakespeare's play strips these sources of their Elizabethan features just as it strips Lear of all the cultural trappings of state power. Once scattered, the components of the monarch's body cannot be reassembled in quite the same way. We do not see contenders for the throne displaying and finally authorizing their use of its power. In marked contrast with Elizabethan strategies, Shakespeare devalues the natural body of power in such a way as to lend state authority a metaphysical source.

Unlike the Elizabethan chronicle history of *King Leir*, the restoration of patriarchal authority does not evolve out of some struggle among Lear, his daughters, and their husbands to see who shall possess the land. Shakespeare declared his difference from the Elizabethan materials both by making Gloucester suffer the ritual punishment usually reserved for the female and also by making Gloucester the figure who initiates the repair of the metaphysics of patriarchy. The blinding of Gloucester allows the mystical bond to assert itself between father and legitimate son. Thus recentered in the father-son matrix, the drama unfolds which makes the political world coherent. "Thy life's a miracle," (IV.vi.55) Edgar tells the blind man. But even as Edgar describes for him the supernatural form of intervention that prevented Gloucester's suicide, the son himself performs the miraculous rescue of the father before the audience's eyes. This is not to indicate duplicity or bad faith on Edgar's part, of course. The gesture simply makes Gloucester the object of his son's sense of patriarchal duty. Having so invested him with such meaning, Shakespeare has Gloucester pay fealty in turn to King Lear. This scene makes certain one knows that Gloucester cannot address what he cannot see – the natural body of the monarch as the blind duke does homage to the disembodied voice of his "royal lord." Then Shakespeare brings Cordelia on stage to acknowledge Lear as her father.

It is worth noting what happens to Lear's unruly daughters as patriarchal order returns to the world. After the blinding of Gloucester, Shakespeare suddenly removes Regan and Goneril from the sphere of male patronage relations where they were represented as malcontents. He reinscribes them within more properly female roles where they become monstrous women. Thus he uses them to draw sexual differences, much as he does in Desdemona and Lady Macbeth; with the reassertion of patriarchy as a metaphysical principle, the two ambitious daughters are suddenly seized by desire for the bastard Edmund. Nor is there precedent for their inexplicable lust in the sources. It is a curious moment in the play when the daughters give themselves over to libidinous desires which had not been part of their character for the three acts preceding the onset of this passion. As they are redefined in Jacobean terms, furthermore, it is as if the political threat represented by their sexual rebellion has already found a resolution. All threats to patriarchy disappear as these women are stabbed and poisoned for harboring illicit desire and, in the bastard's words, "wedded" with him "in death."

As if it were not enough to have remodeled all this theatrical machinery in *Lear*, Shakespeare even revises the traditional Elizabethan contest between contenders for power. This scene operates according to the logic of purification as well, which is to say there is no contest at all. The duel is staged for only one reason: to display the dissymmetrical power relations between bastard and legitimate son. In acknowledging his defeat, Edmund also acknowledges the legitimacy of his utter subjection on the basis of blood when he interrogates Edgar, "But what are thou/ That hast this fortune on me? – If thou'rt noble, / I do forgive thee" (V.iii.165–7). Shakespeare gives Edgar the lines which define his power over Edmund as that of blood, and blood, as defined patrilineally: "I am no less in blood than thou art, Edmund; / If more, the more th' hast wrong'd me. / My name is Edgar, and thy father's son" (lines 168–70). Shakespeare assures us that only those survive at the end of the play who have maintained belief in the primacy of blood over all other signs, instruments, or manifestations of power. Edgar is not alone in this. Albany remains true to the patriarchal principle throughout the play, for he claims to recognize the aristocratic blood beneath Tom's disguise. "Thy very gait," he tells Edgar, "did prophesy/ A royal nobleness" (lines 176–7). Upon Cordelia's death, it is Albany who returns the crown to Lear, renouncing his own claim with these words:

> . . . For us, we will resign
> During the life of this old majesty,
> To him our absolute power. (V.iii.299–301)

But if the patriarchal principle is really at stake, and if the play dramatizes the impossibility of separating kinship from kingship for Britain to remain Britain, then why does Cordelia have to die? The question is even more vexing when one realizes that not one of the historical sources felt obliged to kill her off in this apparently gratuitous fashion. To the contrary, without exception they insist that she restored her father to the throne and upon his death, then reigned for several years.

To ask why Cordelia, in my reading of the situation, has to die, is virtually to provide the answer: because the patriarchal principle itself rather than the identity of the monarch's natural body is in question.

England's kinship system allowed modification of strict patrilineage that made the requisite term "father"; the blood could be – and Shakespeare's audience well knew it had recently been – embodied in a female. But the relationship of power to gender is obviously *not* the issue this play asks an audience to consider. Rather, in reestablishing the bond between kinship and kingship, this play wants us to think of them both in male terms. Thus the Gloucester/Edgar relationship provides the site where the power of patriarchy re-enters the world. For the same reason, Albany remains in line for the throne even though he is not, strictly speaking, a blood relation, and even though in *Gorboduc* Albany plays the valevolent character. No doubt his Scottish title made Shakespeare prefer Albany over Cornwall as the one to survive, thus implicitly linking him to James even though his birth does not make the duke a particularly strong contender for the crown. Were Cordelia rather than Albany and Edgar to remain at the end of the play, the crown would descend to her upon Lear's death; either that or the play would challenge the metaphysics of blood all over again in giving the crown to a male. It is more than coincidental, then – or rather it is coincidental in precisely the way that ideology arranges the coincidence of such events – that no direct heir to the throne of Britain remains alive at the end of *King Lear*. Under such conditions, the power of state reverts to a male. But still more important than this, for lack of a natural embodiment, power reverts back to its metaphysical source – the patriarchal principle itself. What matters most in maintaining the order of the state is loyalty to the principle of blood – the metaphysical body of power – and not the individual who wields it. For this is the form of power that Shakespeare displays by his revision of Elizabethan materials.

VIII

We might consider *Antony and Cleopatra* as both the easiest and the most difficult of Shakespeare's tragedies for us to read. The language of the play translates so well into modern cultural terms that more than one critic has read the play as if it were a Renaissance version of a modern romance on the order of *Wuthering Heights*. For this very reason, it proves most difficult to understand this play in relation to other Jacobean tragedies and the poetics of display which gave them their form. The sexual relationship between Antony and Cleopatra displaces the political struggles within the Roman empire to the point where sexuality – at least from a modern perspective – appears to transcend politics in the play. Even the most dedicated historical critic feels hard pressed to think otherwise and therefore to maintain his or her concern for the vicissitudes of state power in this play. But, I will argue, this temptation to say the play is about love rather than politics is a form of seduction which Shakespeare himself has built into *Antony and Cleopatra*. He sees to it that his audience feels the seduction of a world independent of patriarchal power all the while knowing such a world is impossible. Where the modern reader feels the utopian attraction of a private world free of ideology, however, the early seventeenth-century theater-goer would have rejected it because of the undesirable political features inherent in such a utopia.

Contrary to novelistic strategies, Shakespeare's drama sets up the possibility of detaching sexuality from politics only to demonstrate the preposterousness of thinking of the body this way. *Antony and Cleopatra* resembles *King Lear* in the respect that kinship and kingship constitute a single strategy for distributing political power and thus for understanding the operations of such power in the world. But if *Antony and Cleopatra* seems somehow more mythic in its presentation of this theme, it is because the play self-consciously interweaves the various themes of Jacobean culture and works through the same problematic terms of its most important categories – sexuality and politics. Like other assaults on the political body – the senate's willingness to overrule Desdemona's father, Lear's attempt to divide his kingdom among his daughters, or Lady Macbeth's usurpation of patriarchal prerogatives – Antony's profession of love flies in the face of political reality to threaten the most basic law of Renaissance culture:

> Let Rome in Tiber melt, and the wide arch
> Of the rang'd empire fall! Here is my space,
> Kingdoms are clay; our dungy earth alike
> Feeds beast as man; the nobleness of life
> Is to do thus [*embracing*] – when such a mutual pair
> And such a twain can do't, in which I bind,
> [On] pain of punishment, the world to weet
> We stand up peerless. (I.i.33–40)

In making this statement, Antony obviously calls for a complete separation of love from nationalism, but his claim for the legitimacy of this relationship ultimately requires much more in the way of a cultural transformation than this. In his affection for, or his dotage on the Egyptian queen – depending on whose view one adopts – nobleness springs neither from aristocratic birth nor from the metaphysics of blood. It is engendered by the queen's embrace. Their relationship, in short, requires nothing less than a semiotic apocalypse. The basis of meaning itself – and with it the mating and mismating of terms – will henceforth be decided according to nature rather than the distinctions culture makes between nations or even between east and west. Any Jacobean audience would, I think, have recognized instantly the nature of the delusion. Antony can not actually separate politics from sexuality in this speech or for that matter anywhere else in the play. The very desire to have sovereignty over one's sexual relations and therefore to construct a private world within the public domain is an inherently political act. The play clearly demonstrates that by desiring a Cleopatra rather than a Fulvia or an Octavia, Antony does not remove himself from political history. Rather, the consequences of his desire change the course of history itself.

In the Elizabethan plays, union with the aristocratic female was always a political act. In fact, desire for the female and desire for political power could not be distinguished one from the other. But in Jacobean drama, we have noted, the iconic bond between the aristocratic female and the body politic is broken. No longer conceived as a legitimate means for access to membership in the corporate body, the aristocratic female has the potential to pollute. Nowhere is this clearer than with Cleopatra. Using her, Shakespeare undertakes his most thorough revision of that figure of the autochthonous female which had uses so central to Elizabethan representations of power. Cleopatra is Egypt. As such, however, she embodies everything that is not English according to the nationalism which developed under Elizabeth as well as to the British nationalism later fostered by James. It is perhaps difficult for us to see Cleopatra as such a threat to the political body. She contrasts Egyptian fecundity, luxury and hedonism to Rome's penury, harshness and self denial. The fact is, however, that no matter how well we romanticize her, Shakespeare has represented her in much the same terms Bakhtin uses to identify the grotesque – or popular – body in Renaissance culture. Shakespeare clearly endows her with all the features of carnival. These define her as the ultimate subject and object of illicit desire as Enobarbus's well known description suggests,

> Age cannot wither her, nor custom stale
> Her infinite variety. Other women cloy
> The appetites they feed, but she makes hungry
> Where most she satisfies; for vilest things
> Become themselves in her, that the holy priests
> Bless her when she is riggish. (II.ii.234–9)

A body that incorporates the basest things represents the very antithesis of aristocratic power. It is that which threatens to pollute the aristocratic community. Egypt's queen thus resembles other Jacobean females who in desiring or being desired become a source of pollution. That such a sexual threat poses a threat to the political body is repeated in several different variations. His sexual bond to Cleopatra strips Antony of his military judgement, deprives him of prowess in battle, and deceives him into committing suicide.

Unlike this Jacobean rendering, Elizabethan versions of the Antony and Cleopatra story like the sources for *King Lear*, represent the threat to the body politic in terms of division and inversion. *The Tragedie of Antonie* (1595), the Countess of Pembroke's translation of Garnier's play, begins with the following, "After the overthrowe of Brutus and Cassius, the libertie of Rome being now utterly oppressed, and the Empire settled in the hands of Octavius Caesar and Marcus Antonius. . . ."[41] In Daniel's *The Tragedie of Cleopatra* (1599), the action begins after Antony has committed suicide. Tragic consequences develop, then, from competition for political supremacy. In his version of this story, however, Shakespeare makes certain that the threat to Rome comes from an external rather than internal source. This is the first condition for the staging of pollution and its resolution, the scene of punishment. First Labienus with Parthian troops attacks Roman garrisons on the Asian border, and then Pompey attacks Rome's "borders maritime" in the Mediterranean. In both cases, the play makes it quite clear that Rome is thus besieged because Antony has been, in Caesar's words, "rioting in Alexandria." For one thing, Pompey readily agrees to a truce when he hears that Antony has returned to Rome. For another, we see that the Roman world can tolerate division; even competition between Antony and Caesar is not in itself a bad thing. As long as they can exchange women as Caesar and Antony do, these powerful men remain part of a common political body. Even when Caesar seizes Lepidus or breaks the treaty with Pompey, he does not really endanger the nation. In a word, all serious threats to Rome stem from Antony's alliance with Cleopatra.

To so locate the source of political disorder is to represent such disorder as pollution. Why else would Shakespeare dwell on the danger of the offspring of Antony and Cleopatra. As Caesar explains to his ·friends Maecenas and Agrippa, Antony's mismating with Egypt has engendered another illegitimate aristocracy whose blood will contend for legitimate authority over Rome:

> I' th' market-place, on a tribunal silver'd,
> Cleopatra and himself in chairs of gold
> Were publicly enthron'd. At the feet sat
> Caesarion, whom they call my father's son,
> And all the unlawful issue that their lust
> Since then hath made between them. Unto her
> He gave the stablishment of Egypt, made her
> Of lower Syria, Cyprus, Lydia,
> Absolute queen.

Maec.	This in the public eye?
Caes.	I' th' common show-place, where they exercise.
	His sons [he there] proclaim'd the [kings] of kings . . .
	(III.vi.3–13)

To his sister, Caesar more bluntly describes the danger Antony's alliance with Cleopatra poses: "He hath given his empire/ Up to a whore" (III.vi.66–7).

In destroying Antony and Cleopatra, Shakespeare accomplishes two things. First he relocates the sources of legitimate authority in Rome. Secondly, he establishes the figure of uncompromising male power over that of the autochthonous female. Shakespeare not only illegitimizes this figure of power by linking it to that of the grotesque body, he also subjects that body of the other to ritual purification. Shakespeare gives Cleopatra the entire last act to gather up the features associated with illegitimate authority. Having denied her the privilege of committing suicide in the Roman manner, he dresses her as Queen of Egypt, surrounds her with her eunuch and ladies in waiting, and then kills her off with an Egyptian viper. This elaborate scene of punishment purges the world of all that is not Roman. In this manner of delivering the world over to patriarchy, however, Shakespeare makes it very clear that a whole way of figuring out power has been rendered obsolete. One might call his play Shakespeare's elegy for the signs and symbols which legitimized Elizabethan power. Of these, the single most important figure was that of the desiring and desired woman, her body valued for its ornamental surface, her feet rooted deep in a kingdom.

4

FAMILY RITES
City comedy, romance, and the strategies of patriarchalism

With the crown, James inherited a well defined role. He inherited the ideology of patriarchy (with which he had been quite comfortable in Scotland), but he inherited this as it had been modified and revised by an Elizabethan iconography. The situation he inherited as the English monarch thus raised certain expectations for the display of his power. In his letter to Dudley Carleton on 12 April 1603, John Chamberlain gives us some indication of how James met and in meeting instantly modified the expectations of Elizabethan courtiers and hangers-on. So great was the rush north to bring the Scottish king news of the queen's death and by such means to seek patronage, place, or promotions, according to Chamberlain, a proclamation had to be issued to restrain the flow "of ydle and unecessarie posters into Scotland, the number wherof grew to be a great burthen to the countrie and brought all things out of order." Chamberlain goes on to report of men like John Davies and Edward Nevill who were among the first to succeed in courting favor with the new monarch:

> The King uses all very graciously and hath made Sir Rob: Carie of his bed chamber and groom of the stoole. John Davies is sworn his man and [Edward] Nevill is restored . . . to all his titles and fortunes. The tenth of this moneth the earle of Southampton and Sir Henry Nevill were delivered out of the Towre by a warrant from the Kinge. These bountiful beginnings raise all mens spirits and put them in great hopes, insomuch that not only protestants, but papists and puritanes, and the very poets with theyre ydle pamflets promise themselves great part in his favor; so that to satisfie or please all . . .would be more then a mans worke.[1]

His "bountiful beginnings" wrought a major change in Elizabeth's most characteristic policies and decisions. It brought release of the Essex co-conspirators, promoted a typically ambitious Inns of Court man like Davies to a knighthood, and quickly settled Nevill's long standing claim to be declared Lord Abergavenny. During the first year of his reign, James displayed the prerogatives of his position by granting – and lavishly so – what Elizabeth had formerly withheld – titles, honors, land, and lucrative patronage opportunities. Promoting the idea of the king as the source both of land and of noble lineage, James not only indulged in conspicuous gift giving, furthermore, he also tried his hand at matchmaking among the English nobility. Upon coming to England, he shrewdly decided to pursue a policy of arranging marriages he had developed in Scotland for purposes of making peace among the feuding clans. Aside from the disastrous marriage of the young Earl of Essex to Lady Francis Howard by which James had hoped to mend relations between their families, the new monarch's efforts at matchmaking helped somewhat to end the Elizabethan style of manipulating competition among rival court factions. Perhaps more important, his active supervision of the exchange of women among aristocratic families lent credibility to the belief that a new kind of patriarch had arrived.

Given the influx of Scottish nobility and the persistent desires of courtiers, however, neither this policy nor the king's generosity alone can explain the considerable easing of court factionalism. The pressure to forge the peculiarly Jacobean style of monarchy came by way of a new form of resistance requiring James to display the monarch's power in a new way. This resistance cannot be comprehended monolithically. It was not simply the opposition James met in parliament. Even to call it Puritan – a notoriously inaccurate term – is misleading. The fact is that during the last two decades of Elizabeth's reign certain political factions and religious sects, ranging from Catholics to Sabbatarians and from mining interests in Cornwall to cloth merchants in London, were growing dissatisfied with Crown policies. None of these dissident groups posed a serious challenge to Elizabeth's government, nor did she ever act in a way that caused this opposition to coalesce. When James came to the throne, however, the situation changed. In contrast with Elizabeth's regular practice, James did not pack his first parliament, and pent up complaints centering the abuse of royal prerogatives under Elizabeth suddenly found a voice.[2] Elizabethan policies with regard to wardship and monopolies were cited in speeches, while hope for a change in religious toleration was put forth in petitions from various corners. Moreover, compounding the problem of these more or less familiar complaints were challenges to the basic principles of patriarchy which arose from unofficial and politically suspect quarters. Though never a serious threat in themselves, the appearance of a coherent form of resistance in turn coalesced those – still in the majority – whose interests remained firmly bound to the king. In place of the Elizabethan situation where the threat to a centralized government appeared to come from competing patriarchs, then, the Jacobean court and its dependents understood the opposition as an assault on patriarchy itself. In response to this apparent threat, we find speeches, proclamations, plays, court entertainments, indeed the whole icono- graphy that grew up around James, cooperating to produce a more conservative royal authority by portraying a world without patriarchy as a world in grave danger. In the pages that follow I shall show how such dramatic forms as city comedy and absent monarch plays participated along with the dramatic romances in a struggle to rewrite the political body of the monarch. This was done not simply to revise Elizabethan patriarchy for a king, but also to meet the forms of resistance that kept rising against James's notion of patriarchy.

Whether he wanted to do so or no, James's manner of displaying authority changed the symbolic identity Elizabeth had forged. In his call for union with Scotland in 1604, for instance, James represented himself with a litany of biblical images for patriarchal power among which was the claim, "I am the Husband and all the whole Isle is my wife."[3] By identifying himself as husband to the state, James deliberately inverted Elizabeth's figure of the Virgin Queen wed to her people, but this was not his way of laying claim to power as a male. My discussion of Shakespeare's comedies argued that the Crown received certain advantages from reinstating patriarchal power in a female. The comic resolution itself suggests that, by calling forth competing suitors for her hand, the transfer of patriarchal power to the female seemed to create a society more inclusive and yet still as harmonious as before. In view of the historical pressures he confronted, we have to assume that more than adjusting the sex of this source of power to suit his own, James saw a political advantage in claiming the strategies of natural father in relation to the state. This figure invokes natural law as the basis for his claim to patriarchal power.[4] Such a representation of monarchy undermined the traditional argument of the contract which was being used to oppose patriarchy. Employing tropes which based political authority on the natural rights of husband and of father enabled James to link himself to earlier monarchs in a patrilineal system of descent. It also gave him the authority of the father over all families in the realm. To describe the whole island as his wife was further to remind parliament of an earlier age when England and Scotland were joined as Britain. The ideological center of this Jacobean theory of power can be isolated in James's treatise on *The Trew Law of Free*

Monarchies. There he conscientiously lays out the traditional assertion that the king was the natural father of his people: "And as the Father by his fatherly duty is bound to care for the nourishing, education and uertuous gouernment of his children; euen so is the king bound to care for all his subjects."[5] Where Elizabeth had represented power by withholding her affection, then, James employed the figure of the generous father who nourished his children and educated his subjects. And where Elizabeth's practice favored those suitors who would compete for the favor, James proposed to favor those children who would submit to his authority. His revision of Elizabethan strategies of state obviously required an entirely different way of staging power.

In the Christmas festivities of 1611, it was particularly appropriate for Jonson to present the monarch in the grandly hierarchical terms of his masque of *Oberon*. Throughout the previous year, the king had been locked in debate with parliament over just this issue of whether there were several bases for political power or indeed only one. When Jonson's *Oberon* was produced at court, then, the king had recently concluded negotiating with parliament on the matter of the Great Contract.[6] This proposal asked the Crown to give up certain traditional sources of income in exchange for a large subsidy and a yearly grant of money. After six weeks of debate, it was clear James's use of royal prerogatives, his notion of an absolute monarchy and his notorious liberality all contributed to parliament's unwillingness to accept Cecil's proposals on behalf of the king. Parliament's refusal to co-operate readily in relieving his debts infuriated James, making him less willing to compromise on crucial issues. In his speech to parliament on 21 March 1610, the king consequently tried to force parliament into relieving his financial dilemma. When he redefined their refusal to do so as a violation of divine law, he invoked the same conservative notion of patriarchy that also shaped *Oberon*, as I noted in the earlier discussion. His speech turned once again upon identifying royal power with that of God, and of the natural father as well:

> The State of MONARCHIE is the supremest vpon earth: For Kings are not only GODS Lieutenants vpon earth, and sit vpon GODS throne, but euen by GOD himselfe they are called GODS . . . In the Scriptures Kings are called GODS, and so their power after a certaine relation compared to the Diuine power. Kings are also compared to Fathers of families: for a King is trewly *Parens Patriae*. . . .[7]

The monolithic figure of state power does not simply represent the king as various authors and playwrights imagined the king would like to be represented; the king imagined political power in terms of this figure as well.[8] His logic ("but," "for") is overwhelmed by his use of repetition, which at first allegorically links secular power with divine but which ultimately represents "king," "God," and "father" as interchangeable concepts. James elaborated these points by drawing further analogies between the king's power and God's: like God and like the father (according to the law of nature), kings have the power to raise up, to reward, to make low, and to punish. According to this figure of speech, the king's authority is not only a metaphysical fact (he is called God) but a social fact (he is a father), as well as a fact of nature (he is the descendent of kings). Such a political figure allows for no legitimate form of authority other than his.

Establishing this view of the monarch's authority would certainly serve James's interests in dealing with parliament where the king's finances were the major point of contention. This is not to say that lavish spending opposed the responsible exercise of political authority. As Jacques Donzelot has pointed out, lavish forms of display continued despite the controversy they inspired throughout the seventeenth century because such displays helped to maintain aristocratic authority. Donzelot writes, "It was their sumptuary activity, the multiplication and refinement of the needs of the central authority, that was conducive to production. Hence wealth was in the manifest power that permitted levies by the state for the benefit of a minority."[9] On the matter of his liberality, James reminded parliament that they too viewed the ideal monarch as a generous one, ". . . I can looke very few of you this day in the face, that haue not made suits to mee . . . either of honour or profit."[10] To establish his need for supply, James similarly drew his logic from the historically regressive figure of monarchy that identified him as the original source of state power:

> the King that is Parens Patriae, telles you his wants. Nay, *patria ipsa* by him speakes vnto you. For if the King want, the State wants, and therefore the strengthening of the King is the preseruation and the standing of the State; And woe be to him that diuides the weale of the King from the weale of the Kingdome. (p. 318)

By insisting the king's wealth was one and the same as that of the kingdom, James also reminded the good members of parliament of the grounds for their right to sit.

Traditionally, the Crown was to supply its own needs from the fisc – those lands, revenues, and privileges the Crown possessed according to hereditary and inalienable right – and parliament was summoned to approve taxation only under the evident and urgent necessities of open war, the suppression of rebellion, or a coronation. In his first year and a half on the English throne, James heard numerous complaints about the inefficiency of his bureaucracy as well as charges that he misused fiscal sources of revenue. Throughout his first parliament there were serious disagreements over who constituted the law, James claiming for himself the power to be the *lex loquens*, while the Commons countered he could only be the law speaking with the aid of a sitting parliament.[11] To justify their rejection of the king's requests, ironically enough, parliament chose not to contest the hereditary prerogatives of the king. Indeed, they accepted those prerogatives as the basis of their own authority, claiming for parliament a separate history of rights and privileges which arose with – but often contested – those of the king. They granted James his status as the source of all authority, even their own, and thus his right to request funds of them. At the same time, however, parliament distinguished those of his needs which were needs of the political body from those which were illicit forms of display. Speaking for many in parliament, Sir Henry Neville informed the king, "Where your Majesty's expense groweth by Commonwealth, we are bound to maintain it, otherwise not."[12] To think of the monarch in this way was to drive a wedge in the figural logic of traditional monarchy, for this identified the display of wealth and title with the proper exercise of aristocratic authority.

If we sense the presence of a counterargument for a decentralized government, it is because this view kept surfacing during the early years of James's reign as a challenge to his insistence on absolute authority. James was the first monarch to claim sovereignty according to ancient rights and privileges that gave him complete authority over parliament. By the close of that first parliament, as we have seen, some men in the Commons insisted to the contrary, that the king's supreme authority belonged to him only in parliament, not when he acted alone.[13] A third perspective was offered by Sir Edward Coke who, speaking for the supreme authority of the common law, argued, ". . . when an act of Parliament is against common right and reason . . . the common law will control it, and adjudge it to be void."[14] Concerning these words of Coke, Alan G.R. Smith writes, "If taken at face value they would seem to make decisions of the king, Lords, and Commons, taken in Parliament . . . subject to the overriding authority of the common law as interpreted by judges."[15] These various institutions of the state operated with the common belief in a centralized political model. Yet each competed intensely for that power, each laid special claims to that power, and each therefore represented itself at the top of a different hierarchy. Taken together, these views yield a political model with three contending centers of power. They also demonstrate the degree to which, at that moment in history, power could not be imagined in any form other than a hierarchy.[16] Although this particular debate concerning the true nature of hierarchy took place several years after the rash of disguised monarch plays which appeared at the beginning of the reign of James, I shall argue that these plays laid out essentially the same set of options and confronted the same paradox that would later erupt in political debate. Governed by the same codes as the debates in parliament, the plays were involved in a single sense-making process, one manifestation of which therefore serving to illuminate the other.

I make this detour through extra-literary material mainly to insist upon the theater as part of a larger symbolic field. When James came to the throne, the stage mounted a defense of patriarchy to combat the gathering cultural forces which not only threatened that very notion of patriarchy but also assaulted the existence of the theater. The theater, always political, took up the materials of the drama, disassembled them, and out of the bits and pieces that had gone into Elizabethan displays of power, produced new dramatic forms. These made visible the king's particular version of patriarchy and justified the existence of the theater as well. The preceding chapter demonstrated how, for instance, the unruly woman of Elizabethan comedy was criminalized and the world of inversion and of the carnivalesque took on sinister features as they appeared on the Jacobean stage. We saw, too, how regularly Jacobean tragedy reenacted the scene on the scaffold as it reinscribed the criminal's body with her crimes against monarchy. Capitalizing on these very tendencies were the city comedies and absent monarch plays that so abruptly commanded the stage. These new dramatic forms reworked the materials of Elizabethan theater to make them demonstrate a need for a new kind of monarch. The desiring aristocratic woman of romantic comedy suddenly found herself out of place on the stage. She could no longer rectify the disorder there, for she had become one of its causes. City comedy thus stages the sinister side of comic desire, a city of night, an urban underworld run by greed and illicit desires, made by coneycatchers and whores, and peopled by gulls and wittols. These forces of disorder are unleashed upon the world when patriarchy is absent.

Rather like a mosaic, each form of Jacobean drama contributes a piece to a composite figure of authority. City comedy authorizes the positive representation of power displayed in dramatic romance much as the anti-masque heralds the masque. The forces of disorder on the tragic stage or in the city comedies coexist with the idealized representation of order as a bounteous feast table in a mutually constituting relationship of figure to ground. *Henry VIII* offers a perfect example of this phenomenon. In the face of the true monarch, the grotesque body in the person of Wolsey, aptly called a lump of suet, proves incapable of subverting royal power. As if by magic, Henry's appearance transforms the cardinal's parody of aristocratic display into a ceremonial feast that celebrates royal power. In such fashion, the patriarch who heaps rewards upon those who submit to his authority makes all the difference between a thoroughly corrupt social order and one denoting both purity and plenty. As they transformed the theater into a framework within which scenes of pollution, perversion, and violence could be staged – the features for which Jacobean drama is known – dramatists demonstrated repeatedly that the patriarch alone could bring order into a world given over to diseased forms of desire. Scenes of families dismembered by cruel monarchs, scenes that hinted at violence done to women and children by insanely jealous fathers, and scenes that represented a monarch whose heirs were either corrupt or lost to the world, directed desire toward a traditional patriarch, a closed community, and a secure line of power. Jacobean theater thus constructed an ideal resembling the politically disengaged monarch with which Sidney opened his *Arcadia*; the figure of the community as one restricted to the natural family appears to have offered the means of resolving the political dilemma where it had formerly been the means of generating conflict.

II

The plague made it necessary to close down the theaters during the year 1603. Their reopening in April 1604 saw a new form of comedy which revised the materials of Elizabethan romantic comedy so drastically as to render the earlier form all but obsolete. Loosely termed "disguised ruler plays," these include Middleton's *The Phoenix* (1604), Marston's *The Malcontent* (1604) and *The Fawn* (1604), Day's *Law Tricks* (1604), Dekker and Webster's *Westward Ho!* (1604), Dekker's *Honest Whore II* (1604–5), the anonymous *London Prodigal* (1604), and Sharpham's *The Fleire* (Stationer's Register: 1606, 13 May).[17] Shakespeare, too, participated in this remarkable show of theatrical solidarity with *Measure for Measure*. While it is not unreasonable to consider this play as *sui generis* within the Shakespeare canon, it is important, I believe, to remind ourselves how commonplace its dramatic strategies appear against the background of the first theatrical season of James's reign.[18] For although this kind of play enjoyed a notably sudden and brief reign upon the London stage, I will argue, it had an important part to play in a larger historical process both formed by and forming the way people saw themselves in relation to a political reality.

All of the absent monarch plays initially represent social relations in a manner which overturns the ideal configuration realized by romantic comedy; thus they create a situation where patriarchal prohibitions against the outbreak of desire have been either suspended or completely ignored. If in romantic comedy desire humanizes the law, then by creating a situation where desire runs out of control, the absent monarch plays conduct a different order of political argumant. What is true of *Measure for Measure* is true of the rest as well: each of these plays uses a shape changer or trickster, as romantic comedy does, but the trickster of later drama has the stature of monarch. Like the transvestite woman of Elizabethan comedy in his manner of taking on and then shedding a disguise, this kind of monarch brings order where desire had reigned. The disguised monarch's power derives from his ability, as Phoenix says, to "Look into the heart and bowels of this dukedom" (I.i.99).[19]

With the removal of the divinely anointed monarch or his heir from the court, the Jacobean audience saw a duke, king, or father situate himself at the margin of the court where he could view the governed thus left to their own devices. It is worth recalling that unlike the premise of disguised monarch plays, the Renaissance monarch understood himself or herself as deriving power from being the object of the public gaze. If not always in full view of his court, she or he was nonetheless visible in the institutions of state, in the church, at the courts of law, on the coin of the realm, or upon its stages and scaffolds. King James was easily as sensitive as Elizabeth to the power inherent in displays where his every word and deed were carefully noted by an audience both human and divine.[20] Represented as something separate from the monarch, the state rather than the monarch assumed the status of the object on which Jacobean comedy focused attention. It must have been a remarkable moment in Renaissance drama when all the major playwrights imagined the state in a manner resembling some bureaucratic mechanism overseen by deputies, imposters, or usurpers.

To imagine that the true and divinely anointed king would leave the state to such substitutes is not merely to shift the direction of the gaze but also to question the very relationship between the monarch and the state that supposedly materialized his power. To be sure, monarchs in Elizabethan plays and prose romances occasionally go into disguise, but in doing so none detaches the state from the presence of the monarch.[21] *Henry V* affords a case in point. Disguised as a common soldier, the king walks among his troops. As he does so, however, we are never asked to consider the state as a separate institution; the state walks with him. If Elizabethan drama had a single strategic intention, it was to forge the structural interdependence of monarch and state. That major playwrights should suddenly open a gap where the theater had symbolically closed it just a few years before suggests that these men were organizing the materials of the theater according to new strategies of display. This is not to suggest the theater in some way overturned the Elizabethan style of display. Given that the existence of the theater depended upon serving the interests of monarchy, it is far more likely that dramas were staged to remain constant to their purpose of authorizing the monarch in the face of a new political challenge. In suggesting the possibility of a monarch-free bureaucracy, I must hasten to add, absent monarch plays offer no alternative to a monarchy. Quite the contrary, their whole purpose is to demonstrate what happens with the loss of the monarch's presence; the ensuing disorder calls forth new and distinctively Jacobean strategies of representing the orderly state.

Either deposed or else willfully abandoning his rightful place, the monarch takes up an ignominious position as traveler, friar, malcontent, or fawning courtier. Upon his departure, the machinery of state overwhelms the deputies, substitutes and usurpers of power, inevitably catching them up in the heartless mechanism over which they wrongfully seek authority. In *The Malcontent*, the usurper Pietro is cuckolded by his wife and then overthrown by the calculating Mendoza. Pietro's fate repeats itself when Mendoza tries to seize power only to find himself a cuckold too. Shakespeare's Angelo affords another example of the mutability of power once it has passed into the hands of deputies. Appointed to serve in place of Duke Vincentio, Angelo uses his authority to force Isabella into bed, but this only makes him subject to the sentence of death he imposed upon her brother for illicit fornication. In allowing the legal apparatus of the state to work on its own, then, these plays repeatedly demonstrate how much more powerful it is than any deputy.

Like the debates over sovereignty which divided the king from the Commons and the bench, these plays introduce the idea of political decentralization as a crucial element in an argument for absolutism. It is important to remind ourselves that absolutism did not mean autocracy; the king was granted absolute power only in so far as he was absolutely subject to the law of God.[22] Accordingly, these plays prove the true monarch, and only the true monarch, not only masters the law but also devotes himself to it. He has no desire to overturn the law even when it has been perversely turned against him. Malevole, the deposed duke in *The Malcontent*, for instance, steadfastly refuses his friend's urgings to mutiny (I.i.25–7), and although he serves as an agent to the corrupt Mendoza, he scrupulously avoids committing a crime. For this reason, too, these plays never fail to demonstrate that it is the power of the law rather than some other form of magic which restores social order. Duke Vincentio relies on "craft" – the art of substitution, not that of transformation – to correct the abuses engineered by his deputies. In this respect, his authority has the power as well as the limitations inherent in the figure of the pun.

Having argued that Portia operates as such a figure of speech in

Elizabethan comedy, I would like to draw a comparison between the behavior of the absent monarchs and that of an Elizabethan counterpart. In taking on the disguise of judge, Portia suffers humiliation much as Vincentio does in being betrayed by Angelo and insulted by Lucio. The deposed Malevole is humiliated in similar fashion, and the Fawn is mocked for wanting to wed such a young bride. In this less exalted form, however, Portia can play the key substitute in a game of substitution which rescues Antonio and frees Bassanio to marry her. When she is revealed to be what she really is in relation to Bassanio, furthermore, she has redefined the power she embodied as her father's daughter. She is male and female, of Venice and of Belmont, both his patron and the betrothed of Bassanio. In other words, she embodies many facets of political power before bestowing that power upon Bassanio. Disguise enables an expansion and complication – a modernization – of the form of patriarchy Portia inherited from her father. Duke Vincentio resembles Portia as he works his craft by fulfilling the terms of the law even more precisely than Angelo. The whole point of his doing so, however, is to demonstrate how the presence of the monarch changes the institution of state. From one serving the meanest interests of his substitutes, the state becomes one which maintains tradition and therefore serves the interests of the entire community. (This could never be said of Portia, much less of Venetian law.) The bed trick is an even more obvious case of substitution which rigorously observes the law. Craftiness of this order resolves all these plays, allowing Phoenix to protect his father, for example, and Fawn to oversee the courtship of his son. In each case, the protagonist's ability first to conceal and then to reveal himself, allows him to play a game of substitution which brings the powers of inversion and disguise – usually within the domain of popular practices – exclusively under the monarch's control.

These powers of disguise, of substitution, of staging scenes which transfer authority or reveal a crime, characterize the Jacobean theater as surely as they do the monarch's statecraft. Lacking these administrative qualities, the usurpers and deputies who take over the state seem to produce a situation where the traditional differences between truth and falsehood, virtue and vice, justice and tyranny are threatened with collapse. Such arbitrariness characterizes Angelo's and Escalus's style of authority. Angelo is unable to distinguish between kinds of fornication and thus proves incapable of making legal distinctions. Having made all acts of fornication the same, he betrays his office by turning his own desires to the very end he had condemned in the name of the law. Nor, for all his good intentions does Escalus have much better access to the truth. Unable to penetrate the disguise of the friar, this deputy accuses the disguised duke of slandering Angelo. The implicit pluralism of these double deputies lends an air of sheer arbitrariness to the law. And if corruption and ignorance efface all difference between truth and falsehood and virtue and vice, this is to call the very notion of law into question. The dilemma obviously requires some overarching authority to administer the administrators. Thus we have arrived at a situation very much like the one portrayed in the anti-masque where unruliness and disorder allow the ideal monarch to step forward and display his power.

The city under deputies in *Measure for Measure* requires someone who can substitute true criminals for false ones, make distinctions among apparently equivalent crimes, and so reveal the operation of justice. Only Vincentio appears capable of deciding that Claudio's fornication is not equivalent to Angelo's, much less to Lucio's as he restores hierarchy among them. The arbitrariness of an interpretation acquires the certainty of a truth as the duke sets up a series of judgments, each giving way to a more precise evaluation of Angelo's crime. First, he lets Angelo off the hook for fornication on grounds he was betrothed to Mariana and must now marry her. Isabella's plea for justice must be discounted, but on the same ground that Angelo abused the law in executing Claudio. In Vincentio's words, "The very mercy of the law cries out . . ./ An Angelo for Claudio, death for death" (V.i.407–9). Isabella exculpates her brother's executioner on grounds Claudio "did the thing for which he died," only to have Vincentio identify yet another basis for legally condemning him: Angelo violated the official procedures for Claudio's execution. In that it was Vincentio in the guise of a friar who ordered a pirate's head be substituted for that of Claudio, only the duke can retrace the substitutions. These reveal the criminal rightfully punished by law and the prospective father, Claudio, preserved from Angelo's abusive use of power. In performing the substitutions which exculpate Angelo, Vincentio exculpates the law itself, and it reasserts mastery over the instruments of state, we should note, through the regulation of sexual behavior. In this way Angelo fulfills his legal obligation to Mariana, Claudio undoes his crime against Juliana, and Lucio receives punishment befitting one who has slandered the duke.

Unsettled from the beginning by Duke Vincentio's decision to test Angelo's mettle, more than one critic has felt Shakespeare loaded the dice against the dour deputy. Rather than a plot of entrapment, however, Shakespeare's point in delegating the prerogative to oversee marriage is to demonstrate that such a function inheres in the monarch alone. The outbreak of unseemly desire does not condemn Angelo so much as it calls for a form of authority to control the desires which can suddenly erupt in all other men. When political authority comes back into the world it does so in a scene of revelation which obviously aims at inspiring awe.

Confessing his crimes, for example, Angelo acknowledges Vincentio's authority as one of metaphysical proportions,

> O my dread lord,
> I should be guiltier than my guiltiness,
> To think I can be discernible,
> When I perceive your Grace, like pow'r divine,
> Hath looked upon my passes. (V.i.366–70)

Isabella similarly humbles herself before the duke's "unknown sovereignty." Such scenes of revelation tie the dramatic strategies of these plays directly to the myth King James was fond of citing as a way of authorizing the Scottish monarchy. When claiming his right to control the law, James reminded his Scottish audience that he was descended from Fergus, who not only introduced monarchy into Scotland but was also the source to its land, titles and laws.[23]

By removing the monarch, these plays demonstrate the power inherent in the patriarchal principle itself as they invoke a regressive and magical-mythic – notion of the monarchy. All of those features which modern literary folk find so disturbing about Vincentio actually aim at creating this single theatrical effect: the revelation of an earlier, rarified and magical form of patriarchy as the principle of political order. I am suggesting that we may attribute the disturbing elements of absent monarch plays, like the gruesome aspect of Jacobean tragedy, to the need for new strategies of authorizing monarchy. Desire – now reinscribed in the male – exerts a destructive force in these plays. Its power is such that only the most literal use of the patriarchal principle can save the situation, bringing unity where there was dissension, hierarchy where demonstrable inversions of power held sway, and purity where there had been obscenity and pollution.

III

His relationship to the theater makes particularly clear the contrast between Elizabethan strategies of display and those instituted by James. Where Elizabeth had prudently withheld her purse and her patronage, preferring to receive theatrical performances like so many tributes from members of her court, the new king quickly seized control of the theater. Margot Heinemann describes the measures James took to insure the theater served his interests:

> Control and censorship on behalf of the crown in Jacobean times was much tighter than it had been under Elizabeth. Within three or four years of his coronation James had virtually taken into royal hands the

control of players, plays, dramatists and theatres. Those few great nobles (barons and above) who had formerly been allowed to license players to travel were now deprived of that right, and all the companies that remained came under direct royal patronage. . . .[24]

The desire to bring the theater under royal patronage, however, was not merely motivated by a wish to censor its content and prohibit it from speaking against the interests of the Crown. Censorship could have been maintained without the monarch assuming such a burden.

Patronage of the theater was perfectly consistent with the other popular activities James thought necessary for good rule. In the *Basilikon Doron* James advises young Prince Henry to put plays in the category with those festival practices that may be useful for promoting good fellowship in the kingdom:

> In respect whereof, and therewith also the more to allure them to a common amitie among themselues, certaine days in the yeere would be appointed, for delighting the people with publicke spectacles of all honest games, and exercise of armes: as also for conueening of neighbors, for entertaining friendship and heartliness, by honest feasting and merriness: For I cannot see what greater superstition can be in making plays and lawful games in Maie, and good cheere at Christmas, then in eating fish in Lent, and vpon Fridayes, the Papists as well vsing the one as the other.[25]

Along with "honest feasting and merriness," then, dramatic performances served quite specific interests of the Crown. Having suggested in the preceding section how absent monarch plays reworked the materials of the theater, I would like to look briefly at Jacobean city comedy, that larger category of drama to which absent monarch plays are usually attached, and suggest its contribution to the new poetics of power.

Jacobean city comedy acquires its peculiar character by virtue of the fact it excludes the courtly figures found in romantic comedy and absent monarch plays, as well as the rural laboring poor of the pastorals. Jacobean comedy represents the city as a set of social features – neither aristocratic nor impoverished laborer – to be associated with life in the city and its suburbs. So represented, the city of city comedy is staged as a series of distinct character types whose speech indicates social affiliations and sources of income ranging from gentry to servants, from merchants to artisans, from procurers to cutpurses. And because of the satiric nature of this relationship, when thrown together in this way, the cacophony of voices does not indicate the region of one's origin but the possibility of a character's economic or social vulnerability. Drawn from coneycatching pamphlets, from prose accounts of cant speech, and from the caricatures developed in epigrams and satires so popular among Inns of Court men in the 1590s, these dramatic satires create something of a Dickensian sense that each individual is a particular tic of some massive disruptive force controlling London. City comedy individuates various forms of economic identity and brings each forward to be displayed in sexual or economic relations where inevitably one is either predator or prey. In *A Chaste Maid in Cheapside* – with the notable exception of the goldsmith's daughter of the title and her gallant – we encounter a sterile knight whose wife must be inseminated in order to claim an inheritance, a gentleman impoverished by his fertility, a whoring knight, who would prey on the socially ambitious goldsmith, a wittol who feeds off the whoring knight, a welsh whore kept by the whoring knight and the pedantic son of the goldsmith she marries, not to mention the avaricious artisan, the drunken puritan women, the greedy promoters who enforce lenten observance, and various minor characters who step forward to present their particular twists and turns of desire. City comedies often have those larcenous figures from the London underworld who may take center stage in such a play as *The Alchemist* or appear briefly as in *The Roaring Girl* to remind us we are witnessing life in the city. Visible for only a moment, these characters seem to be so displayed strictly for the purpose of populating the city. The sheer number of characters – over thirty in *Bartholomew Fair*, for instance – and the narrow range of differences which distinguish one from the other make the exposition of plot nearly impossible. It is difficult indeed, as L.C. Knights observed about Middleton's characters, to remember which of the many characters in city comedy belong to the same play, or for that matter, despite their wit, to distinguish one plot device from another.[26] We must assume the city is represented then not as a backdrop but as the object of display. The city is important, I am suggesting, precisely because it represents the city of early seventeenth-century England in a particular way. City comedy divulges its human content to create the cumulative impression that we have witnessed but a small fraction of a densely populated environment teeming with different types of activity, most of which is corrupt and all of which requires some grand new ordering principal.

Sharing affiliations with no comparable city in Shakespeare's romantic comedies, the city represented in Jacobean comedy undergoes the same transformation when put into writing as representations of the city in nondramatic kinds of writing. The prose pamphlets by the likes of Green, Nashe, and Dekker, for instance, not only served as source material but also as a model for that behavior of language which is supposed to represent the city. One can see this as well in something as different from the coneycatching pamphlets as that dense and richly textured city Stowe maps in *A Survey of London*. He recounts how aristocratic structures lost their hold on city architecture as the crush of people led to the division and then the subdivision of buildings into meaner accommodations. Here he recounts the fate of "one large messuage builded of stone and timber" which belonged to the Earl of Oxford during the reign of Henry V:

> in processe of time the landes of the Earle fell to females, amongest the which one being married to *Wingfielde* of Suffolke this house with the appurtenances fell to his lot, and was by his heire Sir *Robert Wingfield* sold to M. *Edward Cooke*, at this time the Queenes Atturney Generall. This house being greatly ruinated of late time, for the most part hath beene letten out to Poulters, for stabling of hourse and stowage of Poultrie, but now lately new builded into a number of small tenements, letten out to strangers, and other meane people.[27]

Even more than erecting buildings, the practice of dividing the space within established buildings to create tenements for "strangers, and other meane people," is the most common way of representing the new city, its buildings and its inhabitants. The same view that depicts the city in Stowe's description gives rise as well to the reductively individuated characters of city comedy. This representation reveals the creation of progressively meaner living accommodations the distinctive features of older and grander structures are divided and individuated. Such a view of the city appears in Elizabethan and Jacobean royal proclamations, in Privy Council orders, and in the writings of London officials. On 22 June 1602, for example, a royal proclamation was issued "Prohibiting further Building or Subdividing of Houses in London." Among the reasons for prohibiting the subdivisions of houses in London was a belief that it increased the size of the population. Overcrowding in turn promoted concern that "such multitudes could hardly be governed by ordinary justice," much less employed or fed. In such a proclamation the fear is writ large that the plague would spread rapidly where people were so "heaped up together and in a sort smothered with many families of children and servants in one small house or tenement."[28] This great mixture of people thus constituted a source of political unease as one historian notes:

> in 1607 the recorder of London described four large buildings which housed eight thousand inhabitants, of whom eight hundred had died in the last plague visitation: ". . . if it be not reformed," he stated, "the people cannot have food nor can they be governed."[29]

In addition to familiar literary materials drawn from Elizabethan drama, as well as the caricatures from satire and epigram, the London of the city comedies was composed out of and thus refers back to these surveys, prose pamphlets, proclamations and chroniclers' reports. This London calls to mind the city under plague in Foucault's account.

I have found his discussion of the city useful in trying to understand what is at stake in the representation of the Jacobean city of night. *Discipline and Punish* argues, among other things, that those in charge of the plague-infested city of the late seventeenth century applied the same disciplinary techniques middle-class culture would eventually use in creating a modern institutional culture. The figure of the city under plague materializes the operations of the plague's destructive power and mobilizes in turn the strategies which finally make the plague a thing of past history. The power of the plague, according to Foucault, lay in its ability to cause confusion. As a contagion, it was transmitted when bodies mingled. It was for this reason associated with other forms of illicit combinations such as rebellions, riots, and vagabondage. "Against the plague, which is mixture," he writes, "discipline brings into play its power, which is analysis."[30] The plague ultimately serves the state as it calls forth the disciplinary practices that turn the city into "a segmented, immobile, frozen space. Each individual is fixed in his place. And, if he moves, he does so at the risk of his life, contagion or punishment" (p.195). Although the city under plague may appear to an historically later eye like the strategies of a nascent middle-class culture, its differences from that culture are crucial for our understanding of city comedy. In my view, neither the positive nor the negative features of middle-class culture are on display there. To the contrary, a very different political formation can be observed which the emergence of the middle class almost two hundred years later tends to prevent us from seeing.

In his account of the formation of modern society, Harold Perkin reminds us that what we mean by the middle class simply did not exist before the latter part of the eighteenth century. The old society – that of the sixteenth, seventeenth, and early eighteenth century – was largely composed of a group called "the middle ranks" whose social organization was quite different from that of the middle classes of a modern industrialized society. The older social organization he describes as "a finely graded hierarchy of great subtlety and discrimination in which men were acutely aware of their exact relation to those immediately above and below them, but only vaguely conscious except at the very top of their connections with those of their own level."[31] "Between the landowners and the labouring poor," Perkin writes, "stretched the long, diverse, but unbroken chains of the 'middle ranks'" (p. 22). These chains determined that socioeconomic differences which bound each individual to those above and below him in a relation of dependency and domination should determine one's identity. We should note, further, that history offers Perkin no positive form for representing this social body. The middle ranks, in his view,

> were distinguished at the top from the gentry and nobility not so much by lower incomes as by the necessity of earning their livings, and at the bottom not so much by higher incomes as by the property, however small, represented by stock in trade, livestock, tool, or the educational investment of skill or expertise. (p. 23)

Perkin's description stresses the heterogeneous quality of the middle ranks, and because it is bound within a vertical system of relations, this group can only be defined as neither nobility nor laboring poor. One of the reasons for the absence of a positive ethos for this group clearly has to do with the fact that, in the historically earlier city, power can only be thought of in terms of patronage relations. Any bond other than relations of generosity and service was by definition a distortion of patronage, which made the city appear – even to Perkin – as a Hobbesian universe of greedy people who preyed upon one another. In this respect, he provides a useful corrective to our tendency to read city comedy as if it were about the middle class or the proto-middle class. At the same time, I will insist, Perkin's account is not any less a representation than the relatively homogeneous class which displaced the older notion of the middle rank. What I am suggesting is that this negative representation of the middle rank is itself a product of seventeenth and early eighteenth-century writing.

We might return to the figure of the plague to see how this bit of cultural history was written under the pressure of a particular ideology of representation. Because the plague is viewed as something produced by and reproducing illicit forms, mixtures, boundary violations of all sorts, it must then be met with regulation, documentation, and analysis. To say this, however, is to accede to the belief that the bureaucracy so mobilized threatens the state itself in such a way that only institutional structures provide a remedy. Such thinking would come into its own by the end of the seventeenth century. As my discussion of absent monarch plays suggests, however, Renaissance England had not yet made such a semiotic move. For one thing, *Measure for Measure* clearly demonstrates that the bureaucracy itself, rather than providing a cure for disease, actually encouraged its spread. This is to say, the city represents disorder in terms that call forth the patriarch whose power alone can regulate the state. A royal proclamation of 22 June 1602 prohibited the building or subdivision of buildings in London. This proclamation affords a glimpse of the ultimate nature of the danger posed by the plague. Having invaded the city and from there dispersed throughout the realm, "great mortality should ensue to the manifest danger of the whole body thereof, out of which neither her majesty's own person (except by God's special providence) or any other whatsoever could be exempted."[32] In a word, this passage understands the plague as an assault on the queen's body. To prevent its outbreak, then, the queen must act to protect herself and her subjects. By virtue of the same logic, Jacobean city comedies create a framework sorely in need of patriarchal authority. Indeed, the very constructs which govern the way social historians and literary scholars understand the social alignments composing the middle rank during the seventeenth century no doubt arise in part from Jacobean representations of the city. We might go so far as to think of these comedies as the first instance of the modern use of "representation," in the modern sense of the term. Taken together they determine the way an entire field of economic and social relations will come to be understood and evaluated.

Evidently there was good reason to see London as a place organized according to an inverse principle of patronage and a site where patriarchy would be opposed. Once James came to the throne, the city was placed in a particularly difficult relationship to the Crown. Like other important urban centers, its governance was based on charter, which ideally spelled out something akin to a contractual relationship between the city and the Crown. This notion of power would not have been particularly appealing to such an imperious king as James. The city – as opposed to the outparishes and the liberties which were administered neither by guilds nor by the municipal government – was ruled by an oligarchy whose membership was based on money rather than blood. To qualify as one of the twenty-six aldermen of London required a minimum of ten thousand pounds in property, and once chosen, an alderman sat for life. Although the common council of two hundred and fifty supposedly constituted a more inclusive form of political representation, then, it in fact drew its members from among a small number of wealthy citizens, the selection of which was in the hands of the few. Perez Zagorin describes the process in this manner,

> In theory the choice of councilmen belonged to the freemen – citizens – i.e. to all persons free of any of the city companies and hence possessed of the right to trade – who constituted the wardmote for this purpose. Practice, however, had come to limit the election of councilmen to a minority of well-to-do residents who had usurped the wardmote's power.[33]

At odds with national interests, resistant to Crown demands for loans and entertainments, a haven for dissident religious views, and governed by a principle which substitutes money for the metaphysics of blood, London surely provided one way of representing the opposition to patriarchal authority.

To control this opposition, the Crown sought to establish its model of the state as the only possible form of political order. In 1613, the Privy Council again issued a proclamation to limit building in greater London. Then two years later, in 1615, James officially ordered gentry and aristocracy to return to their country estates where they were expected to maintain centers of hospitality. His speech to the Star Chamber in 1616 returns to the matter of his proclamation of the year before. Leah S. Marcus has demonstrated the importance of this speech to James's policies, as well as to the topography of court entertainments that ensued.[34] After dwelling on problems of the judiciary, he not only encouraged members of the gentry and nobility to display themselves in the countryside, he launched an attack on London as well. The published version of that speech represents the city as a place attracting so many people that "all the countrey is gotten into *London*; so as with time, England will onely be *London*, and the whole countrey be left waste."[35] Women, attracted by foreign fashions, force their husbands and fathers to abandon the country for London only to spend money and tarnish their virtue. To correct these "forreine toys," he says, "let vs . . . keepe the old fashion of *England*: For it was wont to be the honour and reputation of the English Nobilitie and Gentry, to liue in the countrey, and keepe hospitalitie. . . ."[36] Twenty years before, on 2 November 1596, Elizabeth had issued a proclamation similarly ordering hospitality to reign in the countryside, but hers was intended to combat poor harvests as well as to marshal defenses against the threat of an invasion by Spain. Worried about civil disturbances, James saw both the problem and its resolution differently. In response to a hungry populace and the threat of a Spanish invasion, Elizabeth saw the presence of the aristocracy as a strategic distribution of her force throughout the kingdom. By the time James voiced his concern over the possibility of civil disorder, however, the whole notion of popular power had changed. One might compare the change to that of the figure of festival one can observe in shifting from an Elizabethan history play like *Henry V* to the Jacobean *Henry VIII*. No longer do the materials of festival dramatize forms of resistance. With James, these materials have already been appropriated as an instrument of state authority. Festival is now conceived as a framework for the containment rather than for the release of forces inherently opposed to the patriarchal principle.

My point is to consider aristocratic hospitality as the king's preferred solution to the political problem posed by London and by the isolated political groups who resisted his authority. In his speech of 1616, James expresses the fear, among other things, of a popular rebellion: "if insurrections should fall out (as was lately seene by the *Leuellers* gathering together) what order can bee taken with it, when the country is vnfurnished of Gentlemen to take order with it?"[37] It is not the people he fears, but a specific political faction, the Levellers, and this fear does not arise because they represent a threat to his power in and of themselves. The fear is they will gain popular support and turn it against the monarch. To oppose the Levellers, James declared the aristocracy must put on a positive show of power through displays of generosity. The attractions of the city appeared to stand in the way of his policy. Thus he describes the problem in terms of sexual corruption and economic loss, the features of city comedies. Of the effects of the city on women he says, "if they bee wiues, then their husbands; and if they be maydes, then their fathers must bring them vp to *London*: and here, if they be vnmarried they marre their marriages, and if they be married, they loose their reputations, and rob their husbands purses" (p. 343). Every city comedy accordingly demonstrates how the city inverts patronage relations. Rather than plots that turn on generosity or display economic plenitude, these plays dramatize a profound economic hunger.

In the terms of modern culture, we should note, this economic desire appears to be greed where the city comedies call it "covetousness." It is important to stress the difference between Jacobean desire and that said to motivate capitalism. Unlike the acquisitive desire which provides a basis in nature for modern political economy, "covetousness" was neither represented as man's natural legacy nor understood as the agency for his success. The Renaissance understood it to mean a purely destructive hunger that led to rapaciousness. It is highly significant, then, that covetousness takes over social relations in city comedies when patronage relations have been cut loose of their aristocratic base. Inverting the principle of generosity, which insures the harmony of an aristocratic community or court, patronage – no longer tied to blood – defines a situation where one individual preys upon another. Such a situation demands a higher form of authority – a patron of patrons so to speak – who restores the proper relations of patron to client. Yet city comedy feels no compulsion to bring a monarch on stage for purposes of a resolution, nor for that matter does James ever suggest that the king might intervene and impose order on life in the city. No courtly ceremonies materialize within the framework of city comedy. All the same, I will argue, the plays represent the city in a manner that authorizes patriarchy. Consequently, the whole strategy James proposed for dealing with the issue of a corrupt London can be viewed as an adaptation of the dramatic strategies enacted in the theater over the preceding ten to twelve years.

City comedy deliberately turns upon the relationship between patriarchy and paternalism. Indeed, the plays make clear that these exist as separate notions and represent opposing forms of political organization. They mark this difference by demonstrating the general incompetence of natural fathers, uncles, and grandfathers who almost always try to prevent the marriage of a virtuous maid to a reformed gallant. In *A Chaste Maid in Cheapside*, Yellowhammer would marry his daughter to Sir Walter Whorehound and his son to Whorehound's mistress. All this, out of a desire to improve himself by having his children marry up! In *The Roaring Girl*, covetousness also makes Sir Alexander Wengrave prevent his son from marrying. With notable regularity, plays by Marston, Middleton, Jonson and Dekker find paternal characters unable to fill the role of patriarch when they act as the head of household. This principle is underscored by their abuse of the principle of inheritance. Surveying the plots of city comedies from 1603 to 1613, Michael Shapiro writes,

> In the typical satiric city comedy, a prodigal gallant endeavors to regain his land or his money or both from a usurious, miserly father figure . . . In all cases, the young man has a moral if not a legal claim to the land or money. . . .[38]

It is in telling the difference between paternalism and patriarchy, furthermore, that inheritance becomes the issue at hand in all of these plays. In *Epicoene*, an attempt to disinherit the nephew presents a challenge to the principle of patrilineal descent. Jonson could not be clearer on this point. To the news Morose would disinherit Sir Dauphine Eugenie, Jonson gives Truewit the following lines:

> I'll tell thee what I would do. I would make a false almanack get it printed; and then have him drawn out on a coronation day to the Tower-wharf, and kill with the noise of the ordinance. Disinherit thee! he cannot, man. Art thou next of blood, and his sister's son? (I.i.215–20)[39]

The figures of festival seem to side with the interests of "the next of blood" when Morose is subjected to the noises of coronation-day celebrations and wed to a woman who is a man.[40] By the same token, *A Mad World, My Masters* turns on a benevolent grandfather who is the figure of hospitality itself. He can neither be gulled nor robbed by a grandson who wants to steal his inheritance before it has legally passed down to him. For this attempt to violate the principle of genealogy, the playwright marries off the disrespectful grandson to his grandfather's courtesan – still with the assurance he will inherit in due time.

In keeping with the threat that paternalism poses to patriarchy is the strategy of splitting the female characters. No women in city comedy are allowed to harbor the desires which made the Elizabethan romantic heroine politically important. Features that could have combined to make a Hermia, Portia, Rosalind, or Viola, can only provide the stuff of separate and oppositional characters. *Measure for Measure* demonstrates as well as any play this tendency to cut categories where Elizabethan comedy was wont to dissolve boundaries. Comparing this play to its Elizabethan source in Whetstone's *The Historie of Promos and Cassandra* (1578), one finds that Shakespeare has divided the materials comprising Cassandra to form Isabella and Mariana. Similarly, *The Malcontent* sets the chaste wife of Malevole against Pietro's promiscuous wife to create a conflict between chastity and desire. In every case, this conflict nullifies the fantasy of marriage based on desire. Isabella may enter a convent or marry Duke Vincentio, but in contrast with the heroines of romantic comedy, she may never pursue her own desires. The woman of desire is automatically sullied, it appears, while the woman who lacks all desire steps forth as the female component of comic resolution. A woman of no desire, like Isabella in *Measure for Measure*, demonstrates the Jacobean relation of submission to patriarchy. Through acts of obeisance, she elicits a display of generosity on Vincentio's part, which is the most positive face of political authority.

So long as kinship remains the language of politics, disruption of its rules is tantamount to political chaos.[41] Thus inversion of patronage relations organizing the city invariably makes itself felt in sexual transgressions, all of which may be read as assaults against the Jacobean notion of monarchy. In *The Malcontent*, accordingly, the ambitious courtier Mendoza knows that he must seduce Altofront's wife to wrest hold of political power. Just as chastity assumes idealized forms in Altofront's wife, so we find eroticism debased. A few lines from *Measure for Measure* are sufficient to show how desire has been transformed from a farce promoting social health to one that proves destructive. As Claudio explains, "Our natures do pursue, / Like rats that ravin down their proper bane, / A thirsty evil, and when we drink we die" (I.ii.128–30). The city world generally contains but one virtuous female, as the exception to the rule, who exists in danger controlled by the forces ruling the city. Although this female appears to be a throwback to the earlier comic heroine who aggressively arranged her own marriage, they differ in a basic respect: the women in city comedy who take on this patriarchal prerogative are never aristocratic women. This is crucial – more crucial than their gender – to their use of such authority. Because these women are not aristocratic, they, unlike the women of romantic comedy and Jacobean tragedy, are not in fact usurping the prerogative of the aristocratic male. When Moll Yellowhammer marries Touchwood Junior, then, or when the young Wengrave marries Mary Fitzallard, these women do not present a direct challenge to patriarchal power. To the contrary, they countermand some paternal figure – usually a father – who lacks the ability to properly oversee the exchange of women in his family.

In this light, the comic resolutions that so clearly disturb any attempt to arrive at some moral interpretation of these plays make perfect sense. There is nothing wrong, for example, with Sir Bounteous Passage marrying off his whore to his grandson. Sir Bounteous privileges the principle of genealogy over that of competition as he punishes the grandson for trying to rob his generous grandfather. Satire is aimed at certain corrupt practices, as Margot Heinemann explains, and the city corrupts knights and gallants as readily as merchants. For all the city's power to disrupt and overturn it, however, the aristocratic principle of patriarchy invariably triumphs over paternalism. *A Chaste Maid* is a case in point. It concludes by having the impotent Sir Oliver Kix reward Touchwood Senior for administering the "magic waters" to Lady Kix which have made his lady pregnant. More than that, this knight offers the impoverished and too-fertile Touchwood Senior the most generous form of patronage:

> I am so endeared to thee for my wife's fruitfulness
> That I charge you both, your wife and thee,
> To live no more asunder for the world's frowns;
> I have purse and bed and board for you;
> Be not afraid to go to your business roundly;
> Get children, and I'll keep them. (V.iv.79–84)[42]

However uncomfortable the modern reader might feel with this arrangement, as a conclusion to a play riddled with sexual disease and greed, it nevertheless fulfills the Jacobean conditions for comic resolution. Sir Oliver declares the child his, and the child assumes its position within a genealogical system of descent. Through this child, the patrimony remains in the family, and Whorehound is disinherited. The generous Sir Oliver takes a politically appropriate measure, then, when he shares his wealth with the man who cuckolds him. Yet another example can be seen in *A Trick to Catch an Old One*. Wit-Good the gallant may have been a profligate and foolishly pawned his estates to his uncle, but it is the uncle, Lucre, who refuses to observe the rules of kinship. For this Lucre is gulled and Wit-Good recovers his patrimony. As the principle of blood once again wins out over the intolerable principle of economic competition, we seem to have a consistent rule guiding the construction of many if not all of these plays: so long as the principles of genealogy are observed, other social and economic violations can go unnoticed in restoring a society to order.

These plays, then, are part of a much larger argument in which the dominant class confronted various practices which authorized a different basis for political authority. I would argue that a middle class as we now understand it does not supply the counterargument of these plays. At the same time, critics who feel those in the middle classes – more properly, the middle rank – were receiving shabby treatment at the hands of Jacobean playwrights are correct. An assortment of groups, sects, and factions – neither aristocracy nor laboring poor – were being represented in decidedly negative terms. For another hundred years after the passing of citizen comedy, this group would continue to be so represented. Long after patriarchy gave way to paternalism as the dominant way of thinking political power, the figures of feast table and festival continued to bind the populace to the aristocracy in what E.P. Thompson has termed a "moral economy."[43]

IV

City comedies ask us to tolerate all manner of questionable sexual practices in the name of genealogy. There are no other grounds for playwrights to withhold their condemnation of forms of social behavior which must strike us today as cruel, immoral, or at the very least distasteful. Aside from the seeming excesses and follies usually cited, the satirist aims his attack in these plays at fathers, uncles, nephews, or grandsons who attempt either to divert a patrimony or to seize it prematurely. This ideological matrix informs all the Jacobean dramatic genres. It unites city comedy and absent monarch plays with dramatic romance in a common strategic intention: to authorize patriarchalism over and against paternalism. Unlike city comedy, however, the romances represent the aristocratic body on the stage, and, in contrast with absent monarch plays, the romances debate the politics of the family. In turning to Shakespeare's dramatic romances, then, I will focus on their use of the family to dramatize the need for a patriarchal figure who can reform corrupt social practices, supervise the exchange of women and insure the proper distribution of power. If they are about nothing else, romances deliberate the relationship between family and government.

To introduce this discussion of the romances, let me first sketch another representation of the family we have seen mocked and scorned in city comedy. It is worth recalling that the family was the site of intense political conflict from the late sixteenth to the middle of the seventeenth century. Sermons, handbooks, pamphlets, treatises, royal speeches, along with other kinds of writing, took up contending sides in the representation of the family, its structure and governance. Although various factions within the Jacobean political world called for somewhat different models of the family, it was understood by one and all that to discuss family organization was to speak a political language. Nowhere is the inherently political nature of the family more evident than in Puritan handbooks and sermons on marriage and household organization. I have decided to use the term "Puritan" for lack of a better one, I should add, even though the term lacks much historical accuracy. As Patrick Collinson advises, "Puritanism was not a distinct and coherent philosophy but a tendency and puritans were not a sect of their own but a presence within the Church. . . ."[44] The sermons and treatises produced by this rather amorphous group of people indeed indicate quite different local and religious interests. Nor do they agree on many of the fine points of doctrine. Taken as a whole, however, it is fair to consider them as a form of political opposition, particularly in their view of marriage, its celebration, its goals, and the relationship therefore between household and state.

Puritan writing represented the family as a fiefdom within the state over which the monarch had little or no authority. It offered a place, in other words, which could be governed as a theocracy. The title of Robert Cleaver's *A Godly Form of Household Government* indicates the bold outline of this political strategy. His manual begins by insisting that the smallest domestic unit of the family – parents and children – is a separate and wholly self-enclosed political unit, "A household is as it were a little commonwealth, by the good gouernment whereof, God's gloree may bee aduanced. . . ." "The commonwealth," he continues, ". . . standeth of seueral families."[45] Twenty years later, in *Of Domesticall Duties*, William Gouge reiterates the claim that, "a familie is a little Church, and a little commonwealth."[46] And again, William Perkins's *Christian Oeconmy* (1609) speaks of the family as a "simple society" that is "under the government of one."[47]

Though Puritan writing represents the family in terms which may superficially resemble those of a modern, companionate marriage, there is no mistaking the historical difference between the earlier version of the self-enclosed family and our own. Far from understanding the family as something other than a political unit, these sermons and tracts closed the family off from the state in order to define a separate political domain placed under the authority of the husband/father. This is not to say these authors saw the family as an alternative model of social relations. To understand the household as independent from the state, they in fact recapitulate the dominant, hierarchal model of social relations even as they enclose that structure within the family. Cleaver is typical in using "governor" as the preferred term for the father, the husband, the master, and when she is overseeing servants and children, then, also the wife.

"There are two sorts in euery perfet familie," he writes, "the Gouernour" and "Those that must be ruled" (p. 4). Although these authors could not imagine a form of political organization that was not a monarchy, they did represent the household as a political hierarchy capable of contesting the state.

While family historians have debated whether or not this minority view of the family was more or less authoritarian than the one it was challenging, no one doubts the Puritan sermons and treatises were calling for a self-governing domestic unit. That is to say, the family requires rigid government according to Puritan authors, but the governor is not answerable to the monarch on matters of family governance. Nor, by the same token, should the monarch be allowed to interfere in the management of the smaller commonwealth. Richard Grenham's "Treatise of a Contract before Marriage" insists there is only one authority to whom the household governor is answerable: "Now, brother, you must so gouerne as you must giue an account vnto God himselfe."[48] This minority view of state power granted the king his authority on other matters, but established comparable if separate grounds for the father's power over "those that must be ruled" in his household. In *A Bride Bush or Wedding Sermon*, William Whately equates the responsibility of the household governor with that of the state. The end of household government, in his view, ". . . as all other gouernment of Nations, Kingdomes, Countries, Cities and Townes, is . . . the good and benefit of the party gouerned for the glory of God the chiefe Lord and Gouernor of all."[49] Whately claims further that "God hath ordained Gouvernors priuate and publique vnder him" (p. 21). This is just one of many statements which distinguish the domestic domain from one under the monarch's control in order to establish an allegorical relation between the two.

The subversive potential of such allegorizing is clear. Perkins, for instance, defines the family in a way that makes all families structurally identical as they differ only in the number of members per domestic unit. A family could be as small as "three, because two cannot make a society," he writes, "and above three under the same head," to as much as a thousand "in one family, as it is in the households of princes and men of state in the world" (p. 416). Applying the same rules to the royal household as to the common domestic unit, Cleaver arrives at the bold conclusion, "it is impossible for a man to understand to gouerne the common-wealth, that doth not knowe to rule his owne house . . . so that hee that knoweth not to gouerne, deserueth not to raigne" (p. 5). In a sermon to his parish in Blackfriars, Gouge extended this argument to undermine Church Government: ". . . a Bishop that cannot rule his own house, is not fit to gouerne a Church" (p. 18). No doubt it disturbed many in the government and Church to read such statements as Cleaver's or to hear talk of this sort in Blackfriars. This writing proposed an alternative to blood as the basis for political authority as it proclaimed the goal of childrearing and household government was to produce "heirs of the covenant." Worse yet, to claim that any domestic unit is essentially the same as any other domestic unit was to equate the royal family with any other family. By implication, such an equation predicated the monarch's authority on his ability to behave as a good parent.

It was a simple matter to argue on the basis of this paternalistic principle, as some did, that the father's authority over his family could not be overruled by the monarch. In opening this possibility, Puritan representations of the household seized hold of the language of power and turned it to representing an independent political domain. Evidently this did not pose much of a threat to aristocratic power during Elizabeth's reign. We find, for example, that *The Taming of the Shrew* concludes with Kate's declaration to the effect that her husband is "lord," "head," "sovereign," and "prince" over the household. By such acknowledgement of his power, her resistance comes to an end, and the eldest daughter is the first to authorize patriarchy. The play, in other words, entertains no distinction between the formation of the domestic unit and adherence to the dominant rules of kinship. As they create this distinction, the romances thus identify themselves with the politics of a later age. As they subordinate domestic relations to the laws of genealogy, furthermore, they reinscribe the self-enclosed family within the kind of argument James himself made on behalf of his particular style of patriarchal rule.

Thus we encounter one of those moments in history when an otherwise innocuous statement acquires far-reaching political implications. As members of a later culture, this distinction may be largely lost on us now, yet nothing could stand more sharply in contrast to the language of Cleaver's governor of the household than King James's figure of the *parens patriae*. Quoted earlier, the passage from James's address is worth recalling here:

> In the scriptures Kings are called Gods, and so their power after a certaine relation compared to the Diuine power. Kings are also compared to Fathers of families: for a King is trewly *Parens patriae*, the politique father of his people. And lastly, Kings are compared to the head of this Microcosme of the body of man.[50]

Thus James situates all families within a single hierarchy over which he has the sole authority of father. The handbooks tried to bar that authority at the door of the household in granting the *pater familias* paternalistic rule. The distinction between the two positions is as sharp as it is basic.

Given this, the Jacobean theater was never more political than when it staged a king as a father and a court as a household, for to do so was to consider whether the king was properly bound to the rules of the father or the father bound by the metaphysics of blood.

Consider, for example, the opening of the second act to *The Winter's Tale*. Mamillius, the son and heir to King Leontes, begins to tell a tale to his pregnant mother at her invitation. "Come on, and do your best/ To fright me with your sprites; you're pow'rful at it," (II.i.27–8) she teases him. The occasion to tell a story just for her – to whisper in her ear, no less – calls for a kind of self-display, but Mamillius's narrative never progresses beyond its formulaic opening, "There was a man . . . Dwellt by a churchyard" (II.i.29–30). At the very moment when the boy is to become the sole object of his mother's attention, his angry father violently intrudes upon them to charge the mother with adultery. The boy's attempt to frighten her with a tale of the supernatural becomes mere child's play in the face of the father's ferocity. In the third act, we learn the young prince has died out of anxiety for his mother's wellbeing. This brief episode can be used, I believe, as a paradigm for all the dilemmas of dramatic romance. A scene which calls attention to itself in this instance as a spectacle is a scene of terror precisely because it dismantles patriarchy. In a brief moment, the king is transformed into a jealous husband, the queen becomes an abused wife, and the legitimate heir to the throne perishes.

At stake in Mamillius's death is not the inversion of a family relationship but the disruption of political order – the survival of the state itself. That this is the boy's sole reason for being becomes clear in the first scene of *The Winter's Tale* where Archidamus and Camillo describe him as an "unspeakable comfort," "a gentleman of the greatest promise" who provides a "physic" for the health of the country. "They that went on crutches ere he was born," Camillo says, "desire yet their life to see him a man." To this Archidamus responds, "If the King had no son, they would desire to live on crutches till he had one" (I.i.39–46). Mamillius provides a restorative to his country's health, then, because he guarantees the continuation of the king's line. He stands as the living symbol of the genealogical principle, and like the fate of Perdita, the disappearance of Hermione and the aberrant behavior of Leontes, the loss of Mamillius provides the means by which the play engages a larger political argument. Such catastrophic events threaten to destroy a kingdom not simply because they mean patriarchal authority has gone awry, but because they make clear patriarchy has gone awry in a way which threatens the monarch's body; together these events eliminate the possibility of a legitimate heir to the throne.[51] In Jacobean terms, then, they are a direct assault on the body politic, not the natural body, significantly, but that of the crown in perpetuity.

The other romances similarly stage a shocking scene in which domestic violence overturns the politics of blood. *Pericles* begins with a tale of incest. One would be hard put to find a clearer violation of the patriarchal principle even though only a patriarch can commit such a violation. To frustrate any possibility of exchanging his daughter and only heir in marriage, Antiochus "made a law / To keep her still and men in awe" (lines 35–6). The episode with Antiochus is brief but violent. Skulls of unsuccessful suitors testify to the fate awaiting whoever fails to answer the riddle correctly. Lest we should think, however, that the riddle offers a way out of this radical form of self-enclosure for the royal family, a suitor is also marked for assassination if he successfully interprets the riddle. This dilemma serves the rather simple and direct function of dispatching Pericles on the various journeys which comprise the plot of this romance. Yet most if not all of the misfortunes he subsequently suffers originate in the desire of Antiochus to seek sole and permanent use of his daughter's body in violation of the principle of genealogy.

The dramatic action of *Cymbeline* also proceeds from a crisis created when paternalism overrides patriarchal responsibilities. At stake early in this play, too, is the father's right to determine the mate for his daughter. Acting as if his family were simply another domestic unit, Cymbeline generates tremendous violence: the banishment of Posthumus, the flight of Imogen and the war with Rome. To make it clear that he does not hold her culpable for choosing a husband over and against her father's wishes, Shakespeare shows that Imogen's marriage observes the rules of her caste. The opening lines of the play define Imogen as the "kingdom's heir" and Posthumus as "a poor but worthy gentleman." Beyond compare in virtue, the young nobleman has a distinguished bloodline and a titled father; what is more, he has been reared at court by Cymbeline himself. But Shakespeare does not leave it at that. He invests Posthumus Leonatus with all the trappings of someone fit to continue the royal line. He summons up the young man's ghostly family and then arranges the descent of Jupiter to show the match meets with approval of a higher and more exalted kind. He declares, in other words, that Imogen has observed a higher law in overturning the rule of her natural father.

Shakespeare underscores this point as he lays out Cymbeline's reasons for prohibiting her marriage to Posthumus. Cymbeline allowed domestic interests to overrule the obligation of a king to continue the royal line. He was distracted from this obligation when his second wife cloaked her plot to overthrow the traditional pattern of inheritance in shows of domestic love:

> she purpos'd,
> By watching, weeping, tendance, kissing, to
> O'ercome you with her show, and in time
> (When she had fitted you with her craft) to work
> Her son into th'adoption of the crown. . . . (V.v.52–6)

Under such insidious sway, the king was not only led to betray his blood by proposing to mate Imogen to the loutish Cloten, he also allowed himself to be talked into betraying his fealty to Caesar. In this way, Shakespeare insists that for a monarch to adhere to such a domestic ideal is as unnatural an act as the incest which destroys the royal household of Antiochus in *Pericles*.

Prospero is another monarch betrayed by family affiliations. His negligence in the service of the state allowed his brother both to seize the throne and to order the murder of the duke and Miranda. These, then, are the terms in which Shakespeare has Prospero represent his own part in the political treachery:

> . . . my trust
> Like a good parent, did beget of him
> A falsehood in its contrary, as great
> As my trust was, which had indeed no limit,
> . . . He being thus lorded,
> Not only with what my revenue yielded,
> But what my power might else exact . . .
> . . . he did believe
> He was indeed the Duke, out o' th' substitution,
> And executing th' outward face of royalty
> With all prerogative. (I.ii.93–105)

Prospero himself entrusted Sebastian with the only power capable of overturning the legitimate power of state, the power of the monarch. This initial decentering of power sets in motion a series of inversions. Sebastian put his state in fealty to Alonzo's Naples. By profiting from Prospero's overthrow, Alonzo subsequently then betrays the tradition of patriarchy and subjects himself to the treachery of his own brother. As a result of this succession of plots the legitimate heirs to both kingdoms – Miranda and Ferdinand – stand to be disinherited. In this fashion, Shakespeare splits the assault on patriarchy between Prospero and Alonzo; Prospero loses his throne through the assertion of paternal principles, while Alonzo loses his son for complicity in Prospero's overthrow. But it is not the difference between the two dukes that matters for purposes of my argument so much as the fate they share. In acting out a common fate, the two dukes underscore the principle at stake in the play. That is, both betray patriarchal obligations – Prospero's to administer and Alonzo's to maintain – and as a result place their own lives in jeopardy.

To assault the natural family, Shakespeare lends it some of the more negative features of the grotesque body. These suggest that if empowered to rule itself, the natural family does not observe a natural principle. Quite the contrary, it disrupts nature. Among the spectacular elements of the dramatic romances must be listed those monstrous and disfigured characters who are the unlovely products of the natural family. Most monstrous when they act to replicate the inverted power relations which have spawned them, they always mount a direct attack on royal genealogy. Caliban and Cloten are obvious cases in point. They display oral as well as genital forms of aggression. Cloten, we are told, is even more brutish than usual when, intent on raping Imogen, he "foamed at the mouth," and rushed after the princess "With unchaste purpose, and with oath to violate/ My lady's honor" (V.v.276–85). Under the influence of drink, Caliban becomes "an abominable monster," "A howling monster, a drunken monster" (II.ii.179–80). Along with other grotesque features Shakespeare also allowed him this well-known retort to his creator, "You taught me language, and my profit on't/ Is, I know how to curse" (I.ii.363–4). Such spilling over characterizes his sexual behavior as well. Caliban almost succeeded in raping Miranda. Had he not been stopped, it is said, he would have "peopled else/ This isle with Calibans" (I.ii.350–1). In *Pericles* Shakespeare makes Cleon's wife into a monstrous figure when he has Gower describe Dionyza as the embodiment of "That monster Envy" (IV.ind.12). In plotting to murder Marina, she upholds the interests of the natural family so "that her daughter/ Might stand peerless by the slaughter" (IV.ind. 39–40). This queen's name alone identifies her with riotous excess, but Shakespeare further underscores her disruptive nature by telling us that Dionyza and her husband presided over a city so profligate that it devolved into a state of insatiable hunger to be rescued from starvation by the generosity of Pericles. And not to be overlooked among these monstrous products of the natural family is the monstrous father in *The Winter's Tale*, perhaps the most monstrous of all the inversions of patriarchy one encounters in the romances. Driven by jealousy, Leontes not only plots to poison his boyhood friend and orders the death of his newborn daughter, but he also turns his son into a bastard and brands his faithful wife a whore.

Although the monstrous never takes the same form from one play to another, it always displays the same rhetorical behavior. No matter how these characters assault the royal family, they prove incapable of damaging it. Though they possess all the potential for the violence inherent in the grotesque body, the monsters of romance lack the vitality associated with Elizabethan versions of the figure. With the regularity of an obsession, Shakespeare unfolds the monstrous potential within the natural family only to reveal that the self-enclosed family is in fact incapable of subverting the state. Whether it is in Caliban or Leontes, all that is dangerous is already contained within a figure which insures its own subordination to monarchy. Thus these monsters display the debased nature of the natural family in a way that ultimately authorizes the power of the state. The father who is not ruled by a law higher than his paternity becomes a tyrant, and the family that seeks to reproduce itself against the laws of genealogy does so by violent mismatings and rape. In this way, dramatic romance unfolds a logic which seems rather deliberately to refute the one organizing Puritan representations of the household.

But these scenes of violence – the scattering of royal families, the momentary triumphs of paternalism and the brief sovereignty of domestic love – are ultimately all for show. In contrast with the Elizabethan chronicle histories, there is no indication here that the monarch can be challenged by any legitimate power rising from below. The playwright even goes to some lengths to make it clear that no one but a king can give away the power of the king. Thus when the natural father suddenly appears to be empowered, that power invariably comes from the monarch. This is true whether the functions of father and patriarch are contained within a single body as in the case of Leontes and Cymbeline, or represented by a pair of brothers as is true of Prospero and Sebastian, or displayed in two competing kings such as Antiochus and Pericles. Disbanding the royal family thus allows Shakespeare to stage miraculous scenes of its recovery. By the same token, he has each self-contained domestic unit triumph momentarily only so that its behavior can be appropriated as testimony to an authority that is outside of and superior to the natural family. In other words, the paternally organized family provides the occasion not for resistance but for spectacular displays of patriarchal authority.

Shakespeare's whole purpose in working with the materials of romance is to produce a paradox which allows him to revise certain aspects of aristocratic power. This strategy clearly governs the monstrous elements which arise in the natural family. In these figures, nature is no longer nature; Caliban is a "salvage" man. Housed in such a creature, desire will never bring the right lovers together as it does in the romantic comedies, nor will ambition acquire the legitimacy it achieves in the chronicle histories. Where both disease and ambition behave according to the laws of nature under Elizabeth, they oppose the metaphysics of blood on the

Jacobean stage, a revision necessary where a natural family opposes the family of state. From this basic revision of earlier materials, a number of others necessarily ensue. Nature is not nature in Jacobean romances, because nature has become contaminated in portraying a family not bound to genealogy. What becomes identified as nature is in fact a higher nature, then, nature ruled by the metaphysics of blood.

The royal family embodies this higher nature to which the common family is rightfully subordinated. When governed by desire or ambition, as the domestic unit generally is, elements of city comedy infiltrate representations of the family, and desire assumes debased forms. The need to elevate the blood above the natural body of the monarch calls forth the intrusive machinery for which romance is noted along with its scenes of domestic violence. Diana directs Pericles to her temple at Ephesus where he finds his wife, just as earlier in the play Thaisa's body became the instrument through which the gods display their power by returning her body to life. Prospero's magic not only allows the duke to recover his kingdom, it also gives him the control over nature he requires to insure the permanence of his line. Finally, Shakespeare stages a series of scenes in *Cymbeline* which represent political power in supernatural terms. I have already mentioned the appearance of Posthumus's family ghosts as well as the spectacular descent of Jupiter, both of which sanctify Imogen's marriage by affirming her husband's blood. Shakespeare stages yet another display of the mysterious power which preserves Cymbeline's family despite the father's efforts to dismantle it. Note the terms in which Belarius speaks of the principle of nature at work within two princes who have no idea of their noble identity:

> O thou goddess,
> Thou divine Nature, thou thyself thou blazon'st
> In these two princely boys! . . .
> 'Tis wonder
> That an invisible instinct should frame them
> To royalty unlearn'd, honor untaught
> Civility not seen from other, valor
> That wildly grows in them but yields a crop
> As if it had been sow'd. (IV.ii.169–81)

The play unfolds the force which mysteriously compels the boys to rescue a king who, unbeknownst to them, is their father. The revelation of such a supernatural force distinguishes the monarch from earlier heads of noble families who succeeded in competing for the throne.

By so shifting emphasis from the natural to the metaphysical body of the monarch, however, Shakespeare was not contradicting his earlier dramatic strategies. He remained perfectly in touch with the cultural work that Renaissance theater had always performed. It must be remembered that when James came to the throne, dramatic representations of the monarch's body had been used for forty years to represent the English state embodied by Elizabeth. Although it was in James's interest to make certain distinctions between his rule and that of the late queen, this was not the sole imperative according to which Shakespeare revised his dramatic strategies. No matter which line one pursued in the argument concerning the queen's two bodies, her power was incontestable. Since Elizabeth inherited the crown both by right of blood and by right of her father's will, her body could bond the blood to the territory of England. James made no such claim. According to the laws governing property at that time, his foreign birth prevented him from inheriting English territory. James's power rested on blood alone. As each monarch sought to represent herself or himself in a manner that enhanced the power of the Crown, each in turn had to pursue this single objective by strategies of representation tailored not only to the individual monarch in question, but also — and perhaps more importantly — to the specific political opposition they confronted as a matter of political policy. Elizabeth had to deal with competing families within the kingdom who either sought the throne for themselves or else sought means to control the body of the queen. In Puritan claims made on behalf of a form of sovereignty unmediated by the body of the king, James confronted a very different threat to his authority. This was no competition among members of the nobility for the throne, but a form of opposition that sought to restrict the monarch's power over his subjects. Against representations which granted the household autonomy and reduced the royal family to the status of another household within the state, there were those which exalted the body of the head of state as ontologically different from the head of household.

Carrying the same hypothesis further, I would like to suggest that the artist's own self-display in these highly self-reflexive dramas was shaped by the opposition the monarch confronted. I have described romance in terms of two forms of dramatic display. One presents scenes of domestic violence in which the natural family disrupts the royal line; the second announces the reappearance of patriarchy as a supernatural force. These forms display the power of the playwright, I have argued, because this is how he displays the power of the state. By scattering the natural family and then inscribing it within a metaphysical body, Shakespeare made earlier dramatic materials speak for the state against a form of resistance which opposed not only James's regressive notion of patriarchy but also displays of this authority upon the stage. Few would disagree that the last two acts of *The Winter's Tale* include some of the most self-conscious efforts at artistic self-display in the Shakespearean canon. The scene of the sheep-shearing festival in Act Four is, among other things, a remarkable set piece in which we are entertained by songs and ballads, pastoral poetry and literary debate, country dances and a masque of seven satyrs. Indeed, the entire fourth act reads as if Shakespeare were running through a repertoire of literary forms and tropes – unbidden – for our view. The scene in fact calls to mind the encyclopedic quality of Sidney's *Arcadia* by which the poet announced the availability of his artistic skills to the Crown.

One might say that tropes of theatricality that make the self-reflexive component so prominent in romance all call attention to the higher order of this power in calling attention to the artificial nature of its representation. As the scattered family reunites to conclude the romances, for one thing, onlookers bear witness to the miraculous nature of these events. In *The Winter's Tale*, an anonymous gentleman testifies to the "wonder" of Perdita's return in terms that instantly mythologize this fortunate turn of events in the history of the state:

> The oracle is fulfill'd; the King's daughter is found. Such a deal of wonder is broken out with this hour that ballad makers cannot be able to express it. (V.ii.22–5)

By the same token, Prospero promises he will "bring forth a wonder" by revealing Alonzo's lost son, and Sebastian indeed declares Ferdinand's return "A most high miracle." Scenes of wonder announce the triumphant recovery of his lost sons to Cymbeline, as well as Pericles' reunion with his daughter and the astonishing return of his wife from the dead. Critics generally agree that Shakespeare meant these to be received as miraculous events, but that these constitute his strategy for rewriting the king's body is never factored into their aesthetic considerations.

Yet Shakespeare is hardly subtle in making the reunited family demonstrably stronger and more pervasive than the royal family prior to its disruption. He never fails to include among the attributes of the figure of the reunited family some increase in its territory. Thus Pericles rejoins Thaisa to discover her father is dead. No gratuitous gesture on Shakespeare's part, this death extends Pericles' domain to his father-in-law's kingdom as he places Tyre under the titular rule of his daughter and son-in-law: "[We] will in that kingdom spend our following days./ Our son and daughter shall in Tyrus reign" (V.iii.80–3). In uniting contending kingdoms within the blood, Shakespeare's dramatic strategy bears striking resemblance to the argument that James himself regularly mounted in calling for union with Scotland. Just as the marriage of Perdita

and Florizel unites the kingdoms of Polixenes and Leontes, so Prospero's
blood will govern both Naples and Milan as Miranda takes Ferdinand as
her husband:

> Was Milan thrust from Milan, that his issue
> Should become kings of Naples? O rejoice
> Beyond a common joy . . .'' (V.i.205–7).

Such a statement at once identifies the objective of the play itself and also
points to the political logic underlying James's own use of the blood as a
unifying principle.

As the spectacle of Jacobean power unfolds, the extension of the
monarch's domain also concentrates his power within a single line. The
epilogue to *Henry V* offers a useful contrast to this phenomenon. That
epilogue anticipates the disintegration of the kingdom into contending
factions and the loss of the foreign territory Henry V had won. Such a
political scenario was possible because the power of England was thought
to be bonded to the body of a specific monarch. When we witness the
monarch's power centralizing in the romances with the extension of his
kingdom, we have to consider how the very nature of the monarch has
changed to make this strategy possible. By concluding with scenes which
display the power patriarchy contained within the royal family, romances
declare the metaphysical basis for state power. When a strange girl is
brought before the mourning Pericles, then, Shakespeare does not have
her identify herself as the lost daughter, Marina. Instead he makes her say,
"My derivation was from ancestors / Who stood equivalent with mighty
kings . . ." (V.i.90–1). What is important is less the meeting of father and
daughter than the continuity of political power. Similarly, Shakespeare has
Pericles identify his lost daughter as "The heir of kingdoms and another
[life]/ To Pericles thy father" (V.i.207–8). And when Leontes' counselors
urge the king to marry, Paulina advises, "Care not for issue, / The crown
will find an heir" (V.i.46–7). In other words, Shakespeare prevents
Perdita's return from being understood simply as a daughter's reunion
with her natural father when, in the most explicit terms possible, he
represents Perdita and Leontes in terms of the crown and its heir.

It should be clear at this point in my argument how the unfolding of
disorder within the domestic unit operates to reinscribe this unit within a
hierarchy governed by the metaphysics of blood. Figures of domestic
violence, among which the monsters of romance are simply the most
memorable, appropriate resistance of the kind one finds in Puritan
treatises on marriage. Contained within these figures, resistance can
assume no positive form. But as it determines the shape which disorder
and violence assume, this alternative ideal of the family calls forth a

specific form of order. Paradoxically, then, it is with the emergence of a static and timeless family portrait that romance reveals its topicality. For it is in devising tropes of resurrection that Shakespeare not only produces the most spectacular moments in these plays but also throws the full force of his dramatic materials on the side of the king and the majority interests of his audience in the struggle over the representation of the family.

First of all, the return of the dead to life provides the means of uniting the family. Thus we have all plots which scatter the family resolve themselves as they reveal the true identity of the lost line under the same cloak of accident and temporality. But the trope of resurrection operates, at the same time, to shift the object of representation from the natural to the metaphysical body of power. Thus we encounter certain moments when plot crystalizes into figures whose blatant artificiality declares a metaphysical logic at work through that of the play. So Ferdinand declares:

> I have
> Receiv'd a second life; and second father
> This lady makes him to me. (V.i.194–6)

The descent of Jupiter in *Cymbeline* demonstrates Imogen's adherence to a higher law of patriarchy, as I have argued, but it also transforms her, together with her father and brothers, into a composite figure of genealogy:

> The lofty cedar, royal Cymbeline,
> Personates thee; and thy lopp'd branches point
> Thy two sons forth; who, by Belarius stol'n,
> For many years thought dead, are now reviv'd,
> To the majestic cedar join'd, whose issue
> Promises Britain peace and plenty. (V.v. 453–8)

Of all the scenes that use the trope of resurrection to materialize the metaphysical body of the monarch, none can compare with that in which the statue of Hermione comes to life. In staging this scene, Shakespeare transforms the theater into Paulina's chapel. In ritual fashion the aristocratic body then comes back to life part by part, each part receiving due reverence. Leontes approaches to kiss the statue only to be restrained that he may "awake" his "faith." After these rites are observed, Hermione steps forth as the words of Paulina invoke her presence:

> Music! awake her! strike!
> 'Tis time; descend; be stone no more; approach;
> Strike all that look upon with marvel. Come;

I'll fill your grave up. Stir; nay, come away;
Bequeath to death your numbness; for from him
Dear life redeems you. You perceive she stirs.
Start not; her actions shall be holy, as
You hear my spell is lawful. (V.iii.98–105)

Borrowing many of the trappings for dramatizing the resurrection of
Christ, in this passage, Shakespeare materializes a form of power in the
natural body that is not of the natural world. This play works a variation
on the concluding scene of *Cymbeline* where Jupiter's message attests that
a higher law works through the royal family of Britain. With the
apotheosis of Hermione performed upon the stage, the aristocratic body
becomes a *deus ex machina* in its own right. We might regard this as the
ultimate revelation of the strategy at work in all the romances – a perfect
collaboration of art and ideology. For this reason and no other,
Shakespeare can proclaim Paulina's "spell" as "lawful" as Hermione's
"actions" are "holy."

It is fair to say that all the dramatic strategies which distinguish
romance aim at mythologizing the royal family. Nowhere is the cultural
intention of the drama more apparent than in the family portraits whose
formation resolves the conflict between patriarchy and paternalism. All
dramatic materials have been organized to produce this configuration
which elevates the blood above the natural body and detaches the state
from the vicissitudes of political conflict. It is useful to note how the same
imperative to represent the power inhering in the metaphysical body
distinguishes *Henry VIII* from other chronicle history plays. The play
comes to a close as it portrays Henry VIII, the infant Elizabeth, her two
godmothers and assorted nobles and church officials in the configuration
of a holy family. Cranmer's oracular speech proclaims the continuity of
the line from Henry to James much as the soothsayer interprets Jupiter's
message in *Cymbeline*: this child shall "leave her blessedness to one . . . as
great in fame as she was" (V.iii.43–6). Her dying is in turn compared to
that of the phoenix come back to life. The "blessedness" which passes
from Henry to Elizabeth and on to her successors represents political
power in a highly mystified form, one that achieves its authority on the
stage through continuity and remoteness, not on the basis of trial through
competition. The dramatic romances remind us that while history resides
in the transition from one generation to the other, state authority
ultimately depends on a force which transcends history.

In conclusion, we might see how this family compares with the one
Sidney portrayed in opening his *Arcadia*, for in their difference lies the
distinction between the prose romance of an earlier age and the dramatic

romances which graced the Jacobean stage. Sidney began with the dilemma of a king who played the *rex abscondus*, removing the crown from the world of political conflict and withholding his eligible daughters from the world of desirous men. Sidney obviously threw his creative energy into solving the problem of how to return the family to the political world without creating lethal competitors, as prophesied, upon marrying off the king's daughters. There was no question that Basilius had to return; a king was not a king unless he was an active political leader. Thus it is a curious reversal of Elizabethan rhetorical imperatives we encounter with Shakespeare's dramatic romances. For in this later form of romance all the playwright's ingenuity has turned to staging scenes which transform the monarch's body into an artificial and self-enclosed figure remote from the theater of action.

The period which saw the production of this figure of power was also the period when opposition to the theater gained intensity. The opposition came from the same factions who coalesced around the notion that the family was a private domain separate from that of the king. While the stage was being attacked as a place of monstrosity, as a space where men could dress as women, and where Sabbath laws were regularly broken, James defended the theater along with the practices of festival. Evidently he felt these practices enhanced his power in the face of rising opposition. This is to arrive at the obvious truth that the Jacobean theater, like its Elizabethan counterpart, staged displays which created political literacy among the people who mattered. Like the scaffold or the feast table, in other words, the stage was a place for disseminating an iconography of state. It is not difficult to imagine, then, why there were voices that wanted to rid England of this place. Renaissance drama always assumed the pure community was one and the same as a political body. The aristocracy's power was never really in question on the stage, and any time the theater debated the matter of how one gained access to that power, the desirability of the pure community was only confirmed. Indeed, when the argument concerning the access to aristocratic power concluded, Renaissance theater came to an end.

NOTES

INTRODUCTION

1 This tendency for criticism of the history plays to divide along such predictable lines was first noted by Harold Jenkins, "Shakespeare's history plays: 1900–1951," *Shakespeare Survey*, 6 (1953), 1–25. His categories still obtain, as recent criticism of the history play shows.

2 For Joanna Baillie's theory of the passions, see her "Introductory discourse" in *The Dramatic and Poetical Works of Joanna Baillie* (London, 1851), pp. 1–18. Hazlitt in "On the living poets," writes of Miss Baillie, "Her tragedies and comedies, one of each to illustrate each of the passions, separately from the rest, are heresies in the dramatic art. She is a Unitarian in poetry. With her the passions are, like the French republic, one and indivisible: they are not so in nature, or in Shakespeare." *English Romantic Writing*, ed. David Perkins (New York; Harcourt Brace, 1967), p. 635.

3 For a study of Shakespeare and his contemporaries from such a perspective, see Jonathan Dollimore, *Radical Tragedy: Religion, Ideology and Power in the Drama of Shakespeare and his Contemporaries* (Chicago, Univ. Chicago Press, 1984). For another example, see Stephen Greenblatt, "Invisible bullets: renaissance authority and its subversion, *Henry IV* and *Henry V*" in *Political Shakespeare: New Essays in Cultural Materialism*, eds. Jonathan Dollimore and Alan Sinfield (Ithaca and Manchester, Cornell Univ. Press & Manchester Univ. Press, 1985), pp. 18–47.

4 Charlotte Brontë, *Shirley* (Harmondsworth, Penguin, 1974), p. 114. Citations of the text are to this edition.

5 My use of the term "political unconscious" derives from Fredric Jameson, *The Political Unconscious: Narrative as a Socially Symbolic Act* (Ithaca, Cornell Univ. Press, 1981).

6 George Devereux, *From Anxiety to Method in the Social Sciences* (The Hague, Mouton, 1967).

7 Devereux defines countertransference as "the sum total of those distortions in the psychoanalyst's perception of, and reaction to his patient which causes him to respond to his patient as though he were an early imago and to act in the analytic situation in terms of his own — usually infantile — unconscious needs, wishes and fantasies" (p. 42). See also, Harold F. Searles, *Countertransference and Related Subjects* (New York, International Univ. Press, 1979).

8 Michel Foucault, *Discipline and Punish: The Birth of the Prison*, trans. Alan Sheridan (New York, Vintage, 1979), p. 51.

9 I must mention at this point the importance of Stephen Orgel's concept of the illusion of power in Renaissance culture and Stephen Greenblatt's notion of Renaissance self-fashioning in helping me to recognize the applicability of Foucault's scene on the scaffold to Renaissance literature. Greenblatt's figure, developed in *Renaissance Self-Fashioning: From More to Shakespeare* (Chicago, Univ. Chicago Press, 1980), was important to my thinking because of the link it forged between the symbolic practices of Tudor courtiers and churchmen and the behavior of writing. Orgel made the same connection for me in regard to the Stuart court as Greenblatt did for Tudor practices and further, in his analysis of the politics of the masque in *The Illusion of Power: Political Theater in the English Renaissance* (Berkeley, Univ. of California Press, 1975). Stephen Orgel was the first to argue that spectacle was a form of power.

CHAPTER 1 STAGING CARNIVAL

1 Two important social historical studies which discuss the politics of Elizabethan sonnets and pastorals are Arthur Marotti, "'Love is not love': Elizabethan sonnet sequences and the social order," *ELH*, 49 (1982), 396–428 and Louis Adrian Montrose, "Of gentlemen and shepherds: the politics of Elizabethan pastoral forms," *ELH*, 50 (1983), 415–59.

2 Although Gascoigne, Lyly, Greene and Lodge certainly preceded him, Sidney's accomplishment was far and away the most important and influential for the 1590s and later. It is also clear that both Greene and Lodge were familiar with his *Old Arcadia* which he began between 1577 and 1578. Walter R. Davis, *A Map of Arcadia* (New Haven, Yale Univ. Press, 1965), chs 3–6 and his *Idea and Act in Elizabethan Fiction* (Princeton, Princeton Univ. Press, 1969), pp. 55–93; G.K. Hunter, *John*

Lyly: The Humanist as Courtier (London, Routledge & Kegan Paul, 1962), pp. 286–8.

3 Critics differ on exactly how we are to understand his preoccupation with desire and turn to searching its philosophical antecedants. Most agree that his preoccupation with desire is almost unique among romance writers. Two different positions with regard to love in Sidney are Mark Rose, *Heroic Love: Studies in Sidney and Spenser* (Cambridge, Harvard Univ. Press, 1968), pp. 37–72 and Dorothy Connell, *Sir Philip Sidney: The Maker's Hand* (Oxford, Clarendon Press, 1977), pp. 9–33.

4 Sir Philip Sidney, *The Countess of Pembroke's Arcadia*, ed. Maurice Evans (Harmondsworth, Penguin, 1977), p. 395. Citations of the text are to this edition.

5 Lawrence Stone and Jeanne C. Fawtier Stone, *An Open Elite? England 1540–1880* (New York, Oxford University Press, 1984), pp. 108–47. They observe, "The English elite never fully made up its mind whether to follow the patrilineal or the cognitive principle in organizing the transmission of title and property" (p. 108). J.P. Cooper, "Inheritance and settlement by great landowners from the fifteenth to the eighteenth centuries," in *Family and Inheritance: Rural Society in Western Europe 1200–1800*, eds. Jack Goody, Joan Thirsk and E.P. Thompson (Cambridge, Cambridge Univ. Press, 1976), pp. 198–233, esp. 209–13.

6 Sir Thomas Smith, *De Republica Anglorum: A Discourse on the Commonwealth of England*, ed. L. Alston (Shannon, Irish Univ. Press, 1972; rpt. 1906), p. 30.

7 Wallace T. MacCaffrey, "The Anjou match and the making of Elizabethan foreign policy," in *The English Commonwealth: 1547–1640*, eds. Peter Clark, Alan G.R. Smith and Nicholas Tyacke (New York, Barnes and Noble, 1979), pp. 59–75.

8 William Camden, *The History of the Most Renouwned and Victorious Princess Elizabeth, Late Queen of England*, ed. Wallace T. MacCaffrey (Chicago, Univ. of Chicago Press, 1970), p. 139.

9 *John Stubbs' Gaping Gulf with Letters and the Relevant Documents*, ed. L.E. Berry (Charlottesville, Univ. Virginia Press, 1968), p. 34.

10 Sir John Harrington, *Nugae Antiquae* (Hildesheim, Georg Olms, 1968), III, 180–1.

11 This story is disputed by Katherine Duncan-Jones and Jan Van Dorsten (eds.), *Miscellaneous Prose of Sir Philip Sidney* (Oxford, Clarendon Press, 1973), pp. 34–5.

12 Sir Philip Sidney, *Miscellaneous Prose*, p. 50.

13 *The History of . . . Princess Elizabeth*, pp. 136–7.

14 *The History of . . . Princess Elizabeth*, p.132.

15 *The History of . . . Princess Elizabeth*, p. 133.

16 Lawrence Stone, *The Crisis of the Aristocracy, 1558–1641* (Oxford, Clarendon Press, 1965), p. 55. Though a power elite, its power on the one hand was declining from what it had enjoyed under the first Tudors, but on the other hand, this power was not necessarily *perceived* to be on the decline. Penry Williams, *The Tudor Regime* (Oxford, Oxford Univ. Press, 1979), pp. 428–52 and Keith Wrightson, *English Society, 1580–1680* (New Brunswick, Rutgers Univ. Press, 1982), pp. 18–38.

17 *The Crisis of the Aristocracy*, p. 97.

18 Roy Strong, *The Cult of Elizabeth* (London, Thames & Hudson, 1977), p. 23.

19 For the account of the Court of Wards, I have drawn on Joel Hurstfield, *The Queen's Wards: Wardship and Marriage under Elizabeth* (London, Frank Cass, 1973).

20 *The Crisis of the Aristocracy*, p. 660; Don E. Wayne, *Penshurst: The Semiotics of Place and the Poetics of History* (Madison, The Univ. of Wisconsin Press, 1984), pp. 69–71.

21 Millicent Hay, *The Life of Robert Sidney, Earl of Leicester (1563–1626)* (Washington, The Folger Shakespeare Library, 1984), p. 171.

22 *Nugae Antiquae*, II, 137–9. On this episode, see Louis Adrian Montrose, "'Shaping fantasies': figurations of gender and power in Elizabethan culture," *Representations*, 1 (1983), 79.

23 *The Letters of Queen Elizabeth*, ed. G.B. Harrison (New York, Funk and Wagnalls, 1935), p. 238.

24 Thomas Birch, *Memoirs of the Reign of Queen Elizabeth* (New York, AMS, 1970; rpt. 1754), p. 75.

25 For these details I am drawing on James Osborn, *Young Philip Sidney, 1572–1577* (New Haven, Yale Univ. Press, 1972).

26 "Place and patronage in Elizabethan politics," in *Elizabethan Government and Society*, eds. S.T. Bindoff, J. Hurstfield and C.H. Williams (London, Athlone, 1961), pp. 95–126. See also *The Crisis of the Aristocracy*, pp. 257–68, 445–99; Alan G.R. Smith, *Servant of the Cecils: The Life of Sir Michael Hickes* (Totowa, NJ, Rowman & Littlefield, 1977), pp. 51–80; *Patronage in the Renaissance*, eds. Guy Fitch Lytle and Stephen Orgel (Princeton, Princeton Univ. Press, 1981).

27 Neville Williams, *All the Queen's Men: Elizabeth I and Her Courtiers* (New York, Macmillan, 1972), pp. 250–1.

28 *Letters and Memorials of State*, ed. Arthur Collins (New York, AMS, 1973; rpt. 1746), II, 122.

29 *Letters and Memorials of State*, II, 122.

30 Leonard Tennenhouse, "Sir Walter Ralegh and the literature of clientage," in *Patronage in the Renaissance*, pp. 235–58 and in the same volume Arthur Marotti, "John Donne and the rewards of patronage," pp. 207–34.

31 Edward Edwards, *The Life of Sir Walter Ralegh . . . Together with his Letters* (London, 1868), II, 51–2.

32 *The Life . . . Together with his Letters*, II, 52.

33 Louis Adrian Montrose has discussed some aspects of Elizabethan prestation in "Gifts and reasons: the contexts of Peele's *Araygnment of Paris*," in *ELH*, 47 (1980), 433–61.

34 F.J. Levy, "Philip Sidney reconsidered," in *English Literary Renaissance*, 2 (1972), 17.

35 *Young Philip Sidney*, p. 509.

36 *Young Philip Sidney*, p. 510.

37 *De Republica Anglorum*, p. 38.

38 *De Republica Anglorum*, pp. 39–40.

39 Leo Salingar, *Shakespeare and the Traditions of Comedy* (Cambridge, Cambridge Univ. Press, 1974), p. 261.

40 E.K. Chambers, *The Elizabethan Stage* (Oxford, Clarendon, 1951), I, 350.

41 *The Elizabethan Stage*, IV, 325.

42 *Shakespeare and the Traditions of Comedy*, p. 264.

43 Mikhail Bakhtin, *Rabelais and His World*, trans. Helene Iswolsky (Cambridge, Massachusetts Institute of Technology Press, 1968), p. 255. My discussion of Bakhtin is indebted to the work of Peter Stallybrass and Allon White in their *The Politics and Poetics of Transgression* (Ithaca, Cornell Univ. Press, 1986). The authors kindly allowed me to consult portions of their book in manuscript.

44 Alan Sinfield, "Power and ideology: an outline theory and Sidney's *Arcadia*," in *ELH*, 52 (1985), 273.

45 George Puttenham, *The Arte of English Poesie* (Menston, The Scolar Press, 1968), p. 159.

46 *The Arte of English Poesie*, p. 155.

47 Natalie Zemon Davis has discussed this figure with regard to Renaissance French culture, "Women on Top," *Society and Culture in Early Modern France* (Stanford, Stanford Univ. Press, 1975), pp. 124–51.

CHAPTER 2   RITUALS OF STATE

1 As C.L. Barber notes, "In making Oberon, prince of faeries, into the May king, Shakespeare . . . presents the common May game presided

over by an aristocratic garden god," *Shakespeare's Festive Comedy: A Study of Dramatic Form and its Relation to Social Custom* (Princeton, Princeton Univ. Press, 1959), p. 159.

2 The problems with Henry VIII's will have been detailed by Mortimer Levine in *The Early Elizabethan Succession Question: 1558–1568* (Stanford, Stanford Univ. Press, 1966), see especially pp. 99–162.

3 This summary draws upon Marie Axton's fine study, *The Queen's Two Bodies: Drama and the Elizabethan Succession* (London, Royal Historical Society, 1977). Ernst H. Kantorowicz, *The King's Two Bodies: A Study in Medieval Political Theology* (Princeton, Princeton Univ. Press, 1957).

4 E.P. Thompson, "The moral economy of the English crowd in the eighteenth century," in *Past and Present*, 50 (1971), 76–136.

5 While a number of critics have held to some version of the thesis that Richard was more a poet than a king, the most extreme is Mark Van Doren, *Shakespeare* (New York, Henry Holt, 1939), p. 89.

6 Joseph A. Porter, *The Drama of Speech Acts: Shakespeare's Lancastrian Tetralogy* (Berkeley, Univ. California Press, 1979), argues Bullingbroke is the figure for the drama itself as opposed to Richard whose theatricality is always contained by Henry, pp. 175–7.

7 See, for example, Sherman H. Hawkins, "Virtue and kingship in Shakespeare's *Henry IV*," in *English Literary Renaissance*, 5 (1975), 313–43.

8 Henry Angsar Kelly, *Divine Providence in the England of Shakespeare's Histories* (Cambridge, Harvard Univ. Press, 1970). Kelly shows that the workings of providence in the two tetralogies is neither consistent nor continuous.

9 I am indebted to Peter Stallybrass for calling these lines to my attention.

10 Norman Rabkin summarizes the critical discomforts many have with this play, *Shakespeare and the Problem of Meaning* (Chicago, Univ. of Chicago Press, 1981), pp. 33–62.

11 *The Letters of John Chamberlain*, ed. Norman McClure (Philadelphia, The American Philosophical Society, 1939), I, p. 115.

12 Elizabeth Jenkins, *Elizabeth the Great* (New York, Harcourt Brace, 1958), p. 321.

13 Sir John Harrington, *Nugae Antiquae* (Hildesheim, Georg Olms, 1968; rpt. 1779), I, 64–5.

14 Geoffrey Bullough, *Narrative and Dramatic Sources of Shakespeare* (New York, Columbia Univ. Press, 1973), VII, 185.

15 *Correspondence of King James I with Sir Robert Cecil and Others in England*, ed. John Bruce (London, Camden Society, 1861).

16 Quoted in Joel Hurstfield, "The succession struggle in late Elizabethan England," in *Freedom, Corruption and Government in Elizabethan England* (Cambridge, Harvard Univ. Press, 1973), p. 108.

17 I am following Harold Jenkins in the Arden *Hamlet* (London, Methuen, 1982), p. 1.

18 *Letters and Memorials of State*, ed. Arthur Collins (New York, AMS, 1973; rpt. 1746), I, 83.

19 Thomas Birch, *Memoirs of the Reign of Queen Elizabeth* (New York, AMS, 1970; rpt. 1754), II, 463.

20 G.P.V. Akrigg, *Shakespeare and the Earl of Southampton* (Cambridge, Harvard Univ. Press, 1968), pp. 120–1.

21 *Shakespeare and the Earl of Southampton*, p. 127.

22 Michel Foucault, *Discipline and Punish: The Birth of the Prison*, trans. Alan Sheridan (New York, Vintage, 1979), p. 35.

23 *Narrative and Dramatic Sources*, VII, 30, 172–6.

24 Nashe writes, "Yet English Seneca read by candlelight yields many good sentences, as 'blood is a beggar,' and so forth; and if you entreat him fair in a frosty morning, he will afford you whole Hamlets . . . of tragical speeches," *The Unfortunate Traveler and other Works*, ed. J.B. Steane (Harmondsworth, Penguin, 1972), p. 474.

25 Peter Stallybrass, "Carnival contained: patrician festivity and nationalism in early modern England," (forthcoming).

26 Christopher Hill, *Society and Puritanism in Pre-Revolutionary England*, 2nd edition (New York, Schocken, 1972), pp. 145–218.

27 Margot Heinemann, *Puritanism and the Theater: Thomas Middleton and Opposition Drama under the Early Stuarts* (Cambridge, Cambridge Univ. Press, 1980), p. 32.

28 *Puritanism and the Theater*, p. 31.

29 Leah S. Marcus, "Herrick's *Hesperides* and the 'Proclamation made for May,'" *Studies in Philology*, 76 (1979), 52.

30 *Ben Jonson: The Complete Masques*, ed. Stephen Orgel (New Haven, Yale Univ. Press, 1969), 1. 105, Citations of the text are to this edition.

31 Stephen Orgel, *The Illusion of Power: Political Theater in the Renaissance* (Berkeley, Univ. California Press, 1975), pp. 66–70.

32 Jonathan Goldberg has pointed to the many ironies in Jonson's representation of this homage, *James I and the Politics of Literature: Jonson, Shakespeare, Donne, and Their Contemporaries* (Baltimore, Johns Hopkins Univ. Press, 1983), pp. 123–6.

33 For discussions of the features of masque and romance *Henry VIII* exhibits, see Ronald Berman, "*Henry VIII*: history and romance," in *English Studies*, 47 (1967), 112–27; H.M. Richmond, "Shakespeare's *Henry VIII*: romance redeemed by history," in *Shakespeare Studies*, 4

(1968), 334–49; Lee Bliss, "The wheel of fortune and the maiden phoenix of Shakespeare's *King Henry the Eighth*," *ELH* 42 (1975), 1–25; Edward I. Berry, "*Henry VIII* and the dynamics of spectacle," *Shakespeare Studies*, 12 (1979), 229–46.

CHAPTER 3 THE THEATER OF PUNISHMENT

1 Marie Axton, *The Queen's Two Bodies: Drama and the Elizabethan Succession* (London, Royal Historical Society, 1977), p. 12.
2 *The Queen's Two Bodies*, p. 12.
3 I am employing Foucault's notion of sexuality in *The History of Sexuality*, trans. Robert Hurley (New York, Pantheon, 1978). Thus the queen's sexuality is not only historically different from the forms it takes in our culture but hers is also different from other forms in her own culture.
4 Claire Cross, "Churchmen and royal supremacy," in *Church and Society in England: Henry VIII to James I*, eds. Felicity Heal and Rosemary O'Day (London, Macmillan, 1977), p. 27.
5 Patrick Collinson, "The downfall of Archbishop Grindal and its place in Elizabethan political and ecclesiastical history," in *The English Commonwealth 1547–1640: Essays in Politics and Society* (New York, Barnes and Noble, 1979), p. 53.
6 John Phillips, *The Reformation of Images: Destruction of Art in England 1535–1660* (Berkeley, Univ. California Press, 1973), p. 119.
7 Quoted in Francis Yates, *Queen Elizabeth as Astrea: The Imperial Theme in the Sixteenth Century* (London, Routledge & Kegan Paul, 1975), p. 78.
8 She of course could also be treated as the Amazon queen when the occasion permitted as Winifred Schleiner has shown, "Divina virago: Queen Elizabeth as an Amazon," in *Studies in Philology*, 75 (1978), 163–80. See also Louis Adrian Montrose, "'Shaping fantasies': figurations of gender and power in Elizabethan culture," in *Representations*, 1 (1983), 76–8.
9 Roy C. Strong, *Portraits of Queen Elizabeth I* (Oxford, Clarendon, 1963), p. 39.
10 Peter Stallybrass, "Carnival contained: patrician festivity and nationalism in early modern England," ms.
11 *Tudor Royal Proclamations: The Later Tudors 1553–1587*, eds. Paul L. Hughes and James F. Larkin (New Haven, Yale Univ. Press, 1969), II, 240.
12 *Portraits of Queen Elizabeth I*, p. 5.
13 *Portraits of Queen Elizabeth I*, p. 40.

14 David M. Bergeron, "Elizabeth's coronation entry (1559): new manuscript evidence," in *English Literary Renaissance*, 8 (1978), 3–8 and his *English Civic Pageantry, 1558–1642* (Columbia, Univ. South Carolina Press, 1971), pp. 12–23.

15 For accounts of the pageants for Edward and Mary, see Sydney Anglo, *Spectacle Pageantry and Early Tudor Policy* (Oxford, Clarendon, 1969), pp. 280–343. Mary had allowed foreign companies to underwrite many of the costs of her pageant, and Edward, Reformation prince though he may have been, had the papal representative in his train.

16 (Anon.) *The Quenes Maiesties Passage through the Citie of London to Westminster the Day before her Coronation* (New Haven, Yale Univ. Press, 1960), pp. 28–9.

17 On the politics of such aesthetic display in addition to Bergeron's discussion, see Jonathan Goldberg, *James I and the Politics of Literature: Jonson, Shakespeare, Donne and Their Contemporaries* (Baltimore, Johns Hopkins Univ. Press, 1983), pp. 28–30 and Mark Breitenberg, " 'The Hole matter opened': iconic representation and interpretation in *The Queen's Majesty's Passage*," in *Criticism*, 28 (1986).

18 Glynne Wickham, *Early English Stages 1300–1600* (London, Routledge & Kegan Paul, 1963), II.i.75–90.

19 For the documents, see E.K. Chambers, *The Elizabethan Stage* (Oxford, Clarendon, 1951), IV, 269–71, 324.

20 Ann Jennalie Cook, *The Privileged Playgoers of Shakespeare's London 1576–1642* (Princeton, Princeton Univ. Press, 1981), p. 100. See, for example, Privy Council Minutes 25 February 1592 and 19 February 1598 in *The Elizabethan Stage*, IV, 307–8 and 325.

21 Martin Butler, in *Theatre and Crisis 1632–1642* (Cambridge, Cambridge Univ. Press, 1984), pp. 293–306, takes issue with Cook's representation of the audience. Hers, he notes, while offering a useful corrective to Harbage's idealization of the lower classes, makes the audience too homogeneous a group of privileged playgoers. For my purposes the important point is less the exact socio-economic makeup of the audience and more the representations of the signs and symbols of state authority the stage mounted.

22 T.S. Eliot, for example, called *Titus* "One of the stupidest and most uninspired plays ever written." "Seneca in Elizabethan translation," *Selected Essays* (New York, Harcourt Brace, 1932), p. 67. For a brief summary of other examples of the low esteem in which *Titus* has been held, see Nicholas Brooke, *Shakespeare's Early Tragedies* (London, Methuen, 1968), pp. 13–15.

23 Stephanie Jed, "Salutati's *Declamatio Lucretiae*," paper presented to the Renaissance Society of America, 1985.

24 *The Riverside Shakespeare*, ed. G. Blakemore Evans (Boston, Houghton Mifflin, 1972), p. 1049, note to V.iii.36.

25 Page duBois, "A disturbance of syntax at the gates of Rome," in *Stanford Literature Review* (1985).

26 *Tudor Interludes*, ed. Peter Happe (Harmondsworth, Penguin, 1972). Citations of the text are to this edition.

27 This summary is based on the death of the duke in *The Revenger's Tragedy*.

28 John Webster, *The Duchess of Malfi*, ed. John Russell Brown (Cambridge, Harvard Univ. Press, 1964).

29 John Webster, *The White Devil, Selected Plays of John Webster*, eds. Jonathan Dollimore and Alan Sinfield (Cambridge, Cambridge Univ. Press, 1983).

30 George Chapman, *Bussy D'Ambois, Drama of the English Renaissance*, eds. Russell Fraser and Norman Rabkin, II (New York, Macmillan, 1976).

31 Mary Douglas, *Purity and Danger: An Analysis of the Concepts of Pollution and Taboo* (London, Routledge & Kegan Paul, 1978), p. 113.

32 Ambroise Pare, *On Monsters and Marvels,* trans. Janis L. Pallister (Chicago, Univ. of Chicago Press, 1982), p. 27. Stephen Greenblatt has discussed the Renaissance phenomenon of monsters and sexuality in "Fiction and friction in *Twelfth Night*." I wish to thank him for allowing me to consult his manuscript.

33 Michel Foucault, *Discipline and Punish: The Birth of the Prison*, trans. Alan Sheridan (New York, Vintage, 1979), p. 55.

34 John Webster, *Appius and Virginia, The Complete Works of John Webster*, ed. F.L. Lucas, III (London, Chatto and Windus, 1927).

35 Stephen Greenblatt, *Renaissance Self-Fashioning: From More to Shakespeare* (Chicago, Univ. of Chicago Press, 1980), p. 234.

36 *The True Chronicle Historie of King Leir, Narrative and Dramatic Sources of Shakespeare*, ed. Geoffrey Bullough, VII (New York, Columbia Univ. Press, 1973).

37 *The Queen's Two Bodies*, p. 131.

38 *James I and the Politics of Literature*, p. 40.

39 *James I and the Politics of Literature*, p. 46.

40 *English Civic Pageantry*, p. 144.

41 *Narrative and Dramatic Sources of Shakespeare*, ed. Geoffrey Bullough (New York, Columbia Univ. Press, 1966), V, 358.

CHAPTER 4   FAMILY RITES

1 *The Letters of John Chamberlain*, ed. Norman Egbert McClure (Philadelphia, The American Philosophical Society, 1939), I, 192.

2 R.C. Munden, "James I and the 'Growth of Mutual Distrust': king, Commons and reform, 1603–1604," in *Faction and Parliament*, ed. Kevin Sharpe (Oxford, Clarendon Press, 1978), pp. 43–72.

3 *The Political Works of James I*, ed. Charles H. McIlwain (Cambridge, Harvard Univ. Press, 1918), p. 272.

4 For a discussion of patriarchy and politics, see Gordon H. Schochet, *Patriarchalism in Political Thought: the Authoritarian Family and Political Speculation and Attitudes Especially in Seventeenth Century England* (Oxford, Basil Blackwell, 1975).

5 *Works of James I*, p. 55.

6 Alan G.R. Smith has analyzed the contending positions during the debate on the Great Contract in "Crown, parliament and finance: the Great Contract of 1610," in *The English Commonwealth 1547–1640: Essays on Politics and Society*, eds. Peter Clark, Alan G.R. Smith and Nicholas Tyacke (New York, Barnes and Noble, 1979), pp. 111–27. See also Wallace Notestein, *The House of Commons, 1604–1610* (New Haven, Yale Univ. Press, 1971), pp. 225–434.

7 *Works of James I*, p. 305.

8 See, for example, Jonathan Goldberg, *James I and the Politics of Literature: Jonson, Shakespeare, Donne, and Their Contemporaries* (Baltimore, Johns Hopkins Univ. Press, 1983), pp. 85–112.

9 Jacques Donzelot, *The Policing of Families*, trans. Robert Hurley (New York, Pantheon, 1979), p. 13.

10 *Works of James I*, p. 320.

11 *The House of Commons*, pp. 278–327.

12 *The House of Commons*, p. 421.

13 Alan G.R. Smith, "Constitutional ideas and parliamentary developments in England," in *The Reign of James VI and I*, ed. Alan G.R. Smith (New York, St. Martin's Press, 1973), pp. 161–3.

14 "Constitutional Ideas," p. 162.

15 "Constitutional Ideas," p. 162.

16 For a discussion of this apparent paradox, see Michel Foucault, *Power/Knowledge: Selected Interviews and Other Writings*, trans. Colin Gordon *et al.* (New York, Pantheon, 1980), pp. 14–65.

17 The matter of dating several of these plays is a complicated one. R.C. Bald, for example, argued *The Phoenix* was written in 1602, "The chronology of Thomas Middleton's Plays," *Modern Language Review*, 32 (1937), 33–43, but his dating is based exclusively on internal evidence and his argument is highly conjectural. For the dates of the Marston plays, see *Parasiter or The Fawne*, ed. David A. Blostein (Baltimore, Johns Hopkins Univ. Press, 1978), pp. 32–6. For the Webster plays I have followed Cyrus Hoy, *Introduction, Notes and Commentaries in the Dramatic Works of Thomas Dekker* (Cambridge,

Cambridge Univ. Press, 1979), II. For dating the remainder of the plays I have adhered to E.K. Chambers, *The Elizabethan Stage* (Oxford, Clarendon, 1951), III.

18 The tendency to emphasize the unique features of the play is reflected by the persistance of the very category of "problem play" in which *Measure for Measure* has been placed. Richard P. Wheeler has reviewed the history of the category in *Shakespeare's Development and the Problem Comedies: Turn and Counter-Turn* (Berkeley, Univ. California Press, 1981), pp. 2–3, n.1. See also Michael Jamieson, "The problem plays, 1920–1970," in *Shakespeare Survey*, 25 (1972), 1–10.

19 Citation to the text is to *The Works of Thomas Middleton*, ed. A.H. Bullen (London, 1895), I.

20 In the introductory "To the reader" of the *Basilikon Doron*, King James writes, ". . . Kings being publike persons, by reason of thier office and authority, are as it were set (as it was said of old) upon a publike stage, in the sight of all people where all the beholders are attentiuely bent to looke and pry in the least circumstance of their secretest drifts . . ." (*Works of James I*, p. 5). See also Stephen Orgel, *The Illusion of Power: Political Theater in the English Renaissance* (Berkeley, Univ. California Press, 1975), pp. 42–3, and Jonathan Goldberg, "James I and the Theater of Conscience," *ELH*, 46 (1979), 379–98.

21 For an account of the plays that employ this device, see Josephine Miles, *The Problem of Measure for Measure* (New York, Barnes and Noble, 1976), 125–96.

22 "Constitutional Ideas," pp. 160–4.

23 The account of Fergus is to be found in *Works of James I*, pp. 61–2. Following the account James writes, "The kings therefore in *Scotland* were before any estates or rankes of men within the same, before any Parliaments were holden, or lawes made: and by them was the land distributed (which at first was whole theirs) states erected and descerned and formes of gouernement deuised and established," p. 62.

24 Margot Heinemann, *Puritanism and Theatre: Thomas Middleton and Opposition Drama Under the Early Stuarts* (Cambridge, Cambridge Univ. Press, 1980), p. 36.

25 *Works of James I*, p. 27.

26 L.C. Knights, *Drama and Society in the Age of Jonson* (London, Chatto & Windus, 1962), p. 258, n. 4.

27 John Stowe, *A Survey of London*, ed. Charles Lethbridge Kingsford (Oxford, Clarendon, 1908), I, 163.

28 *Tudor Royal Proclamations, The Later Tudors 1588–1603*, eds. Paul L. Hughes and James F. Larkin (New Haven, Yale Univ. Press, 1969), III, 244–5.

29 Perez Zagorin, *The Court and the Country* (New York, Atheneum, 1970), p. 136.
30 Michel Foucault, *Discipline and Punish: The Birth of the Prison*, trans. Alan Sheridan (New York, Vintage, 1979), p. 197.
31 Harold Perkin, *The Making of Modern English Society 1780–1880* (London, Routledge & Kegan Paul, 1969), p. 24.
32 *Tudor Royal Proclamations*, III, 246.
33 *The Court and the Country*, p. 127.
34 "'Present Occasions' and the shaping of Ben Jonson's masques," *ELH* 45 (1978), 201–25.
35 *Works of James I*, p. 343.
36 *Works of James I*, p. 343.
37 *Works of James I*, p. 344. These Levellers are no relation to the later group of the same name.
38 Michael Shapiro, *Children of the Revels: The Boy Companies of Shakespeare's Time and their Plays* (New York, Columbia Univ. Press, 1977), pp. 56–7.
39 Ben Jonson, *Epicoene or The Silent Woman*, ed. L.A. Beaurline (Lincoln, Univ. of Nebraska Press, 1966).
40 Ian Donaldson has discussed these features of the charivari in *The World Upside Down: Comedy from Jonson to Fielding* (Oxford, Oxford Univ. Press, 1970), pp. 37–45.
41 For a discussion of kinship as a language of politics, see Maurice Godelier, "The ideal in the real," *Culture, Ideology and Politics*, eds. Raphael Samuel and Gareth Stedman Jones (London, Routledge & Kegan Paul, 1982), pp. 12–38.
42 Thomas Middleton, *A Chaste Maid in Cheapside*, ed. R.B. Parker (London, Methuen, 1969).
43 E.P. Thompson, "The moral economy of the English crowd in the eighteenth century," in *Past and Present*, 71 (50), 76–136.
44 Patrick Collinson, "The Jacobean religious settlement: The Hampton Court conference," in *Before the English Civil War: Essays in Early Stuart Politics and Government* (New York, St. Martin's Press, 1984), pp. 28–9.
45 Robert Cleaver, *A Godly Form of Household Government* (London, 1598), p. 1.
46 William Gouge, *Of Domesticall Duties: Eight Treatises* (London, 1622). Gouge dedicates his book to his parishioners in Blackfriars who have already heard these treatises some time ago.
47 *The Works of William Perkins*, ed. Ian Breward (Appleford, The Sutton Courtenay Press, 1970), III, 416. This treatise was originally published in 1609.

48 Richard Grenham, "A Treatise of a Contract before Marriage," in *Godly Treatises of Diverse Arguments* (London, 1599), p. 292.

49 William Whately, *A Bride Bush or Wedding Sermon* (London, 1617), p. 16. This was originally published in 1608.

50 *Works of James I*, p. 307.

51 David Bergeron rightly criticizes the popular and ahistorical use of the concept of patriarchy when he asserts "patriarchy is not under attack in this play, however much the men may be found wanting," *Shakespeare's Romances and the Royal Family* (Lawrence, The Univ. of Kansas Press, 1985), p. 159.

INDEX